BODIES

IN

REVOLT

BODIES in

HOLT, RINEHART AND WINSTON

NEW YORK   CHICAGO   SAN FRANCISCO

REVOLT

A Primer
in Somatic
Thinking

THOMAS HANNA

Published simultaneously in Canada by Holt, Rinehart and
Winston of Canada, Limited.

Library of Congress Catalog Card Number: 77-122249

First Edition

Designer: Carl Weiss
SBN: 03-085321-4
Printed in the United States of America

DEDICATION

*I wish to dedicate this book to
one half of the American population:
those who are
twenty-five years of age or younger.*

CONTENTS

Motto for the twenty-first century:
"Anything is possible"

BODIES

IN

REVOLT

A WORD OF INTRODUCTION

During the eight weeks stretching from the dry, hot end of May and winter to the wet, cool days of early July and summertime in Guadalajara, I have been sitting on a rooftop. My house out on the western edge of Guadalajara has a little, squarish maid's quarters built on top. It is painted dead white.

Inside this rooftop house is a small room with some boxes stacked against one wall. Against the west wall is a long brown typing desk that I bought for fifty pesos at a used furniture store. Along the north wall there is a window, a door and an old straightbacked chair which holds a hotplate, a small coffeepot and a dirty green cup and saucer. In the east wall, there is a door leading to the bathroom with one cold water shower and a john without a seat—the bathroom floor is so arranged that, if you take a shower, the water drains down into the main room rather than down its own drain. Consequently, I have only taken one shower up here: my initial shower of discovery and of mopping up.

During these weeks I have had a fine vantage point to watch eucalyptus and royal poinciana trees blaze out their flowers and then lose them. The Mexican pine seems not to have changed its dusty turquoise color. At this moment a thunderstorm is marching up from the east, and I can already smell the moisture and the fine musty odor I have always liked. Within a few minutes, big dun-colored drops, two inches wide, will splatter and spread over the roof that lies just outside my door.

I have just finished this book. I wish to apologize for its imperfections. If in its general tenor it lacks clarity, it is because I should have written it in eight days rather than eight weeks. And if there are any disturbing scholarly blunders, chalk it up to the fact that I didn't bring any books with me to this western corner of Mexico, but only some notes. The chapters themselves are deliberately uneven, sometimes saying much, sometimes saying only a little, but in all cases saying enough to introduce the uninitiated into the world of somatic thinking.

Each of the three sections of the book is different and is doing a different thing and, accordingly, the style changes each time. In the first section I am trying in whatever ways I can devise to help the traditional-minded break away from the deadening weight of deeply entrenched ways of thinking about the human race and its world, and catch the scent of the somatic way of thinking. In the second section basic information is laid out, as simply and pointedly as I know how, concerning the research and theory of the somatic scientists and philosophers. There are, of course, a number of other somatic researchers and thinkers who could not be discussed; but those with whom I have dealt in Section Two happen to have been central in the development of my own somatic thinking. The third section shifts gears once again and focuses the somatic attitude and the data behind it on the present evolution of our culture and on what appears to me to be the emerging shape of the twenty-first century.

Whether *Bodies in Revolt* is either a finished book or a scholarly book is indifferent to me. What is not a matter of indifference is that someone had to write a book of this kind and that it had to be written soon. There have been few times in history when a nation was so in need of a *Guide for the Perplexed.* No one else seemed to be ready to write it, so I was compelled to.

I want to thank the American Council of Learned Societies for taking a chance on such a piece of writing by paying for my time. They are exemplary, in that if foundations as well as governments do not begin subsidizing experimental and revolutionary projects, the next few generations will have to map out the future despite their aid rather than with it.

This is not a book of science, philosophy, or literature. It is a free essay. By tradition, literary persons write both lovely and extraordinary things, but they are not supposed to mean what they say; that's what makes them literary persons. And by tradition, philosophers write rather cautious and restricted things because, by the rules of their game, they're not to make the mistake of saying what they mean.

What I have tried to do in this book is to say what I mean, and to mean what I say.

T.H.

Guadalajara, Mexico
July, 1969

SECTION ONE

THE
EVOLUTION-
REVOLUTION
OF
SOMAS

1

GETTING THE BOOK STARTED

At present, and for the remaining third of the twentieth century, human bodies are in a state of cultural rebellion. In the technological societies—all of Europe and particularly the United States—there is now emerging a novel kind of human being: a mutant, who will come increasingly to dominate our society and who will at the same time create a novel culture for our society. What has happened is rather simple: men have, through an enormous expenditure of aggressive energy, succeeded at last in creating a new environment, a technological environment which has engineered and transformed the earth into an environment which no longer ignores man's existence and needs but which positively supports them. In return, the enormous quantities of energy released by this environment are creating a new kind of man, a cultural mutant.

For a century or more we have sensed this change: men have prophesied it, feared it, hoped for it and dreaded it like a formless fatality which was so portentous and so radically different that to judge it supremely good or supremely evil amounted to the same thing: namely, that a period in human history was approaching which was so explosively novel that it could not be judged with any clarity at all beforehand. The period of the past century or more has been a period of anxiety, of unheralded dislocation and human suffering. It has been demonstrably a time of "What is the meaning of it?" and "Where are we going?" It has been a time when human power and human aggression have finally expanded to an all-encompassing terrestrial dimension, with a consequent destructiveness and pride and terror never, in its extent, equalled in human history. So much so that even the best of our prophets have often been doom prophets, seeing the Apocalypse just ahead. And, accordingly, some of the best of our hopes have been the marginal hopes for survival, so that we might at least start all over again after the deluge had subsided. How strange that at the summit of human power, aggressivity and pride, men should be prepared to retire to mythical caves, fearful and cowed, and ready to settle for the least—marginal life—rather than the most— abundant and transformed life.

However, the explosions of the past century and more have not been for naught; indeed, one of the dawning revelations of the present moment is that nothing done by human beings is for naught. What has been taking place has now reached its term, and the long anxiety and foreboding no longer needs to wait for its spectre to loom up over the horizon. The spectre has appeared and, like all spectres, it looks startlingly different and less awesome than the ghost of our fretful imaginings within the cave. The spectre is now embodied; we can see it, and in seeing it, come to understand it, and in understanding it, acquiesce to and welcome its inevitability.

This spectre now becoming embodied is not a monster. It is a human being—an emerging mutant human being: as fragile, young, as groping and tentatively proud as the earliest proto-men finally come down from the haven of trees onto the fearsome and promising earth. The father of this emerging, proto-mutant human has been all of the seminal theoretical minds of two millennia who made our societal structure possible. The mother was all the technological, engineering bodies which labored to bring forth a technological society, a coherent post-industrial society which is now at the mature stage of using its technological abilities to correct the ecological imbalance and pollution created by its industrial foundations. The midwife was all the scientific and philosophical minds who struggled to guide, interpret and aid in what was to be a difficult and painful birth. And it is these latter—the prescient scientific and philosophical brains of the past century or more—to whom we must now look if we are to understand and interpret and, finally, participate in the birth of a new and far more resplendent human being.

The men I am speaking of are the "revolutionary" scientific and philosophical thinkers, those who *have* been and still *remain* difficult for the bulk of Western society to understand and think along with. With their several concerns and various directions of approach, it has been these revolutionary thinkers who have foreseen, interpreted and urged us to accept the coming of the cultural mutant, and who have, in diverse ways, tried to give us to understand the somatic and environmental reasons for this coming. It is a matter of putting together the thinking of the revolutionaries and of showing the kind of consistent pattern that emerges from their common voice. And that is the concern of this book: it concerns the cultural mutant and how we already have a way of understanding this new human being if we learn to hear the common voice of these revolutionary thinkers.

Like a renascent John the Baptist, Immanuel Kant gave the first shout to reverberate through the two-dimensional wilderness of Western intellectuality; but it remained for Darwin—one of the greatest of all observers—to see the path and make it straight for what was to come. Marx saw the path, and he saw it to be so broad as to allow not one man but all of humanity eventually to move through. Kierkegaard, in compensation, saw not the broadness of the path nor the quantity that would pass through but, rather, what it would finally require to be a single one of those who would walk this path. And the other existential thinkers further enriched this vision, as did the related explorations of those who called themselves phenomenologists. These varied thinkers who came after Kierkegaard explored the path and the requirements either with great carefulness or with great sensitivity: certainly Husserl, Heidegger and Jaspers, who have led the whole cortege of existentialists and phenomenologists. Even the overweening Sartre, who has sought to be all things to all men and has ended with a magnificent half-a-loaf. Even the muddled and courageous Christian existentialists who, in laboring to drag a moribund religious tradition into a wholesome and beckoning future, have succeeded doubly in nailing down the lid on a dead God by their very homage to the new man.

But certainly Merleau-Ponty, whose thoughts, cut short so soon in their course, might have succeeded in just those places where Sartre could not, simply because those thoughts centered relentlessly upon our bodies and our perceptions. And, unquestionably, Camus, the thinker who never claimed to be anything but an artist, who merely "did his job," reflecting his times to his fellow men. And artist he was, inasmuch as he refracted through his being all of the horrors and confusions of our century; and yet, because of this refraction, the works of contemporary man somehow emerged from this prismatic passage colored with hope and with a singing lyricism and sensuality.

But, preeminent among the scientific thinkers who made our thoughts veer radically from the past was Freud, the remorseless, ever exploring, ever wandering Jew, who took Kant's Copernican Revolution and drove it home with a combined insight and honesty rarely achieved among human intellects. But not only Freud but also the remarkable Piaget—patiently, ingeniously and lovingly puttering among young human beings in the schools of Geneva, trying to ferret out the somatically organized and environmentally evoked secrets of human intelligence in the same way that Freud spaded among the somatic structures of human emotions.

In other scientific areas there was the related task of confirming and reconfirming the presence of structured somatic processes within both past and present living bodies, not just our own but those of all living bodies, just as Darwin had indicated. This was the work of the ethologists, the "biologists of behavior," who first began their research in the United States and now have seen it flourish in Europe. Especially Lorenz—as patient with animals as is Piaget with children. Lorenz: who has shown us that not only are all men our brothers but all animals are our uncles and cousins, deserving of our understanding and love because we are all of the same wondrous family, sharing the same kind of past and the same somatic ways of meeting and dealing with the present.

And the philosophical complement to ethologists such as Lorenz and to developmental psychologists such as Piaget was, of course, Cassirer—the marvelous, almost horizonless intellect whose profoundly idealistic Teutonic bones could not withstand the pull of a monumental scholarship that led him to describe human consciousness and its groping intelligence all along the course of its protracted evolution: from the first groping pictures and words of primitive men to the purely abstract equations and formulae of contemporary scientific men.

And then there was Wilhelm Reich, perhaps the only authentic disciple of Freud, half mad with an ambition to see through the structures of men into the structures of all living organisms and then to see through those structures into the structure of physical matter and then to see through the nature of matter into the final nature of the cosmos. Reich was proof that the possibility of the Renaissance Man is not dead. He was also proof that such men risk dying within the federal penitentiaries of the United States.

And, finally, the true madman of the past century or more, the "clown" who knew that he was unborn while living and would become born only posthumously: Nietzsche, who was reconciled to not being understood in his own time, reconciled to wait so that his books would eventually prepare the way for a "new consciousness" and a new mutation in man at a later time. Nietzsche, who saw and predicted the agony and nihilism that we would blunder through and who, at the same time, sensed the *Tauwind*, the warm, moist spring breeze that was blowing from the Overmen of the future. Nietzsche who, in the absence of a God that had metamorphosed into oblivion, was not only able to forgive the world and men for what they were but was able to accept them, love them and sing about them with a kind of joy which we shall only come to understand when we all become madmen and clowns and mutants.

These are the men that will be spoken of, some directly, some only indirectly, some at length and some in passing; but within the thought of all these men there is a common pattern and a common voice. It is this common pattern that must be brought out; it may help us to understand, accept and aid in what is taking place within ourselves: the human race.

2

THE WATERSHED:
A SECOND TRY AT
GETTING THE BOOK STARTED

Perhaps this should be put in a different way. At best, this will be a difficult book for some humans to stomach, and the task is to get a difficult book off to at least a fair start. The problem appears to be that, for many persons, the word revolutionary is a fright word. As our young proto-mutants recognize, myriad are the people who become uptight when they see or hear words like revolution and radical.

And this is true. It is the same with words like fuck or prick or cunt: they are fright words; they immediately bring a certain somatic reaction. Did you notice a peculiar tremor, a feathery kind of constriction when you first saw them on the page? Or, better still, did you notice that when you first turned the page those particular words leaped out independently and captured your eye. You perhaps "saw" them before you got around to the business of "looking at" anything on the page. If this happened, then you have already learned something about the body—*your* body and its extraordinarily acute reactions to anything of interest in its environment. Also you have perhaps learned something about perception and how it is that one "sees," "hears" and generally senses much more and much more quickly than the so-called "mind" or "consciousness" perceives.

Indeed, to see "fuck" written on a page is, for many, their first lesson in what Sigmund Freud so assiduously pointed out: that our whole corporeal being immediately perceives and picks out features in our environment which are, in this case, frighteningly alluring, and quickly organizes our conscious attention so that we can defensively focus upon the threat and cope with it in some practical manner. This quick, double reaction of unconscious perception-and-defense is what Freud first called "resistance" and, later, "repression"; it is quite common among Westerners, from the Urals to California, and is one of the many somatic mechanisms that will be mentioned in the pages which follow.

That peculiar tremor or constriction which you may have felt in some degree when spotting the fright word is specifically an activity of what Wilhelm Reich speaks of as your "muscular armor," that is, the autonomic muscular constrictions which might be felt in the pelvis, diaphragm, chest, shoulders or even in some portion of the neck or face when certain words are heard or certain images are seen. This resistance reaction means that what you see is something to which your entire body may be attracted but *against* which your cultural training has, during previous years, so habituated you to protecting yourself from as being dangerous, that you now, by autonomic reaction, "see" it and armor yourself against it even before your cultured consciousness has to handle the direct force of it.

So then, rather than speak of *revolution*, it would perhaps be not only more advisable but would be far more accurate to speak of *evolution*, inasmuch as this is precisely what is entailed.

At the present time we are within the period of a watershed in human evolution, and it is in terms of evolutionary process that we may best speak of this event: this is to say, in terms of living, organic bodies—such as ourselves—and the changing environment in which we are situated and with which we are adapting and changing.

Although the general message of this book must await the somatic and environmental data that will be reviewed in Section Two, the initial message can be stated as follows: As we close out the last third of the twentieth century, we are witnessing the closing out of an immensely long period in human culture and, simultaneously, we are experiencing an abrupt and sharply accelerated mutation into a radically different human culture. The key to understanding this evolutionary event is that we have successfully constructed a technological society. The key to understanding the accelerated pace of this mutation is, equally, our technological society. We did not know it before, nor did we dream of it, but now that it is upon us it is clear to see that when cultural mutations take place in something as startlingly new in human history as a technological society, they take place rapidly: the evolutionary change, rather than being slow and imperceptible, becomes a revolutionary change. In brief, in a technological environment that is radically new, a radically accelerated environmental adaptation is taking place, so that at present "evolution" and "revolution" have become synonymous. And, for good or for ill—depending on one's cultural and somatic stance—this identification of evolution and revolution will henceforth be the future situation of a technological human society. This message concerning what is happening may—and *will* to most persons—appear frightening, repulsive and, most certainly, incredible: nonetheless, the import of the message is that, from this point in history onward, we are off to the races. And this is one of the reasons for what is written in the Frontispiece: Motto for the twenty-first century: "Anything is possible."

It is not merely production figures in relation to population which are the absolute index of our having crested into technological maturity, but rather there is a far more crucial index which tells us what we have achieved: namely, that we have become *self-conscious* of being a technological society. We are now critically self-conscious, for the first time, of the misuse and abuse of technology and are taking sides *against* it in favor of the earthly environment which for so long we have fought to control and conquer. Only a technologically mature nation can become conscious of the totally needless imbalance and pollution which careless use of technology can cause. To become nationally concerned about such an extraordinarily delicate and abstruse problem as ecology is the absolute index of our moving now into a post-technological society where cleaning up pollution and balancing the delicate forces of nature are, themselves, problems which technology can solve.

Now if men for the first time in their history have succeeded in creating a technological society—with all the hyper-energy communicational, transportational and social engineering this entails—then it is clear that some equally novel and radical human reaction will take place: namely, that the successive generations living in this transformed environment will themselves—in the most practical, healthy and inevitable manner—adapt to this new environment; which is to say, they will mutate. These mutants will, by and large, *look* the same, but they will not *feel* the same (because their bodies are responding to a new environment), nor will they *perceive* the same (because they have, from birth, been experiencing this novel environment) and, most obviously, these mutants will not *behave* the same (because their behavior must be practicably adapted to what they feel and perceive their environment to be).

And this has been the initial impact of the evolutionary-revolutionary adaptation: the proto-mutants are, to the sensibilities of the cultural traditionalists, *misbehaving*. The proto-mutants cannot be understood: what they feel about the world is, for the traditionalist, simply mysterious; the way in which they look at their world is unaccountable; the way in which they think about their world is outrageous. And, of course, the way they behave in this world is senseless, evil and destructive.

And so, there we are: *le conflit des générations,* the "generation gap," is upon us; except that the conflict is not between generations but between traditional and mutant cultures. And it is not only in the United States (where, for technological reasons, it is the most acute), nor only in Western Europe (where the proto-mutants are profoundly frightening the established protectors of the social past), but it is equally the case in the communist world: the ferment among the young in the Middle European nations and the open revolt in Czechoslovakia have not been merely passing nuisances to the Soviet Union and to the political establishments in its associated communist sphere; this ferment and revolt is only beginning. And it is beginning for precisely the same reasons that it has begun in the capitalistic nations: because the communist nations are also succeeding in their goal of creating a technological society, namely, a society in which men are able to control and engineer the earthly environment in such a way that it now works *for* the survival of man and not as an impassive, heedless and alien threat that works against man's fragile, needful existence.

They, the communists, however, are now becoming frightened at the inevitable results of their achievement: their newly minted technological society is transforming its people into a new type of people. And so, the communist "establishment" is in the same appalling situation as the capitalist "establishment"; its newer generations are happily and inevitably mutating with their new environment; and their fresh feelings, perceptions and behavior are destructively at odds with the cultural past. This is ironical, inasmuch as Marx, in his early writings, largely predicted such an outcome in his notion of *praxis*. By the same token, this is obviously why the establishment theoreticians tend to disparage Marx's early writings, while the younger neo-Marxists devour them.

The initial message of these pages is that our creation of a new kind of environment is, by consequent adaptation, creating a new kind of human being whose behavior is groping to adapt to that environment. Thus, this behavior will be new and different: it will be "misbehavior." It will be "immoral," "destructive," "senseless" and all the many other unhappy things which the cultural traditionalists see taking place.

The cultural mutants will, as the traditionalists suspect, see to the destruction of much of two or three millennia of Western culture. As long as the technological society exists, more such mutants will appear with each generation, and eventually—no matter how savagely the traditionalists fight against it—eventually and inevitably the cultural mutants will come to dominate. They will be of a sufficient number that they will begin to control the political, economic and educational institutions.

Already they are at work. They are beginning the creation of a new human culture comprised of new forms of behavior and founded upon new feelings and perceptions of their novel environment. They will, at some period in the future, achieve dominance—perhaps as early as the beginning of the twenty-first century. There is no way, short of the self-destruction of all technological societies (which, I do not question, might be the desperately repressed last resort of the millennia-old establishment), that this evolutionary-revolutionary mutation can be halted. Instead, as I have said, one may attempt to understand it and, by virtue of this, accept it with humane gracefulness, perhaps even aiding it. After all, it would seem only fitting that the cultural tradition should display some positive paternal interest in the mutant child it has fathered.

3

THE PRACTICALITY
OF IMMORALITY

Up until now, we have been speaking of "behaving and misbehaving within an evolving environmental situation" —with such a choice of words this description of our present circumstance may not seem at all offensive to many cultural traditionalists. If so, it will be appropriate to inch forward another step and use the more traditional words: morality and immorality.

Scratch the cultural traditionalist deeply enough—even the most sophisticated or blasé—and you will discover that he feels and knows that there are some actions which are bad or wrong and that there are others which are definitely good or right. Probed deeply enough, he will reveal to you that certain kinds of behavior are not simply bad or wrong for *him* to perform but they are wrong for you, for me and for anyone else (possibly he would make an exception for aborigines or certain races and nationalities; however, this is not tolerance but, rather, covert racism, i.e., "They, not being humans like you and me, are exempt").

The cultural traditionalist definitely *knows* that there are certain human actions which are clearly right or wrong; he knows this simply and automatically, in the same way that he knows strawberries are delicious or that the bottom of an iron is hot and painful. When he sees or hears of certain "immoral" actions, it is not that he checks a list of do's and don'ts and "decides" or "thinks" or "believes" it is wrong; rather, his entire somatic being immediately feels and knows that this action is bad and immoral—his body amply expresses the wrongness he experiences in response to that action. He abruptly feels a hurt, a sadness, a sting or an anger. His traditionally cultured body lifts its shoulders a little, turns its head up and a bit sideways, or his diaphragm drops slightly and then slowly forces a sighing breath through his mouth. Or he might respond less pathetically: his back stiffens and straightens, his shoulders rise half an inch, his diaphragm becomes somewhat taut, imperceptibly drawing in a preparatory breath through dilated nostrils, while the muscles in his neck and lower jaw tense, teeth almost or slightly touching, and his corrugator and orbicular muscles pull his eyes and brow into a slight frown. He feels like and looks like he is ready for action, ready to attack: standing there with his elbows squared, chest protruded and hands beginning to clinch into fists. He does not need to think about and "decide" that the action is immoral, nor does he need to express in words that it is immoral: prior to either decision or words, he has already somatically experienced and incarnated the immorality of what he has just seen or heard about. He feels this immorality in his very bones—or, to be more inclusive, within his musculature and central nervous system.

What, then, *is* immorality or morality? Most evidently it is an expressive somatic response *to* something within the individual's environment. To say that another man's behavior "is immoral" is to say, rather, that *you* experience a particular complex of neuromuscular events in response to his behavior. *What,* then, and *where* is the "immorality" itself? Without question, the "where" is the body and the "what" is an autonomic neuromuscular activity of the body.

The immorality itself is not, therefore, "in" the other man's action, inasmuch as any number of persons may have very different responses to the very same action. In the final, somatic sense, this is what Nietzsche meant when he suggested that men's moral judgments about the world or anything in the world do not tell us anything at all about the world but *do* tell us a great deal about the men who make the moral judgments.

Also, Nietzsche was quite correct in observing that nothing in our world is either good or bad—in itself, our environment is innocent, and it contains nothing that corresponds to what men term moral and immoral. In this respect, the lyrics of Oscar Hammerstein are sagacious in proclaiming that "you gotta be taught to hate": surely when an entire company of soldiers notes the fact that all of them hate the same things, then it appears evident that a uniform cultural training has been at work.

But how is it that men can have these fundamental somatic responses to events in their environment when, at the same time, we know how different these responses can be from individual to individual and from culture to culture?

If Mr. Hammerstein was kind enough to offer us one

clue, still it is obvious we cannot conclude that all such moral feelings are taught to us by someone else, for then we would slip into the infinite regress of asking, Who taught the teacher that this was immoral? and Who, before that time, taught the teacher's teacher? etc. Infinite regress always indicates that we have lost our purchase on reality, and in this instance it means that we are neglecting to hold fast to our awareness of the original and primitive manner in which all of us experience somatic responses to events in our environment. What we are neglecting—and what we have consistently forgotten and ignored for millennia— is our bodies.

In general, there are only two ways in which our somatic selves can obtain information about our environment. One way is for this information to be imprinted within us ("taught" to us) *after* our birth, during the course of the individual development of our lives; this is *ontogenetic* information. The other way is for this information to have *already* been imprinted within us *as of* the moment of our birth; this is *phylogenetic* information.

This is to say that our information concerning the appropriate way of responding to events in our environment may have been acquired partly during the contemporary period of our bodily existence and partly during the infinitely long period of bodily existence which, genetically, has preceded and led up to the moment of our individual births. The ignored importance of this latter, phylogenetically acquired behavioral information is in large measure the central concern of this book, and it will be dealt with rather thoroughly in Section Two.

For those who have not yet learned to think somatically and phylogenetically, it may suffice for the moment simply to indicate that a frog does not have to be taught, or even must he wait for a second chance, to know that the fly moving across his visual scan is a "good" thing which he wants; instead, his opto-motor responses automatically dispose him to leap forward and whip out his tongue with accuracy a fencing master would envy. The mother goose does not need to teach the young graylag gosling—nor does he need to undergo the experience a first time in order to learn—that a slowly, gently gliding silhouette against the sky, of a certain dimension and with slow wing beats, is a "bad" thing that is automatically feared and sought escape from. The newborn gosling "knows" the white-tailed eagle phylogenetically.

Nor does this same gosling, now grown older, need to be told when he swims by another graylag, who is lying low in the water, stretched out along the surface, that this low-lying conspecific is a "good" thing and a highly sexy thing. Even if he is reared so that he has never before seen this low-lying behavior, the male goose will nonetheless be turned on by what he sees and will automatically launch into the typical treading, copulatory movement.

The neonate human baby needs no teaching in order to know that of all the objects he may touch and smell, the "best" object is a round, soft object which he *already* knows how to position in his mouth and suck upon, while coordinating his breathing with his swallowing so as not to choke.

These are examples of behavioral information acquired phylogenetically; many other examples will be mentioned later. What is important for the moment is to understand that what we call "moral" responses (that is, affective somatic responses to certain happenings in our environment) are acquired phylogenetically as well as ontogenetically: that is, some of these responses we bring with us into birth and others we acquire or elaborate after birth. As I shall make clear, in a fundamental sense it is the latter imposi-

tion of ontogenetic responses over the primordial phylogenetic responses which is at the heart of Freud's discovery.

Morality, then, is not only something *within* men which
can be equated with certain somatic responses, but this
moral response is acquired in two ways: some moral
baggage we bring with us and other baggage we acquire
during the course of our individual development. But the
baggage acquired later on is not (as both Freud and Piaget
have shown) acquired only by verbal learning—which
comes much later—but is first acquired through *non-verbal*
learning and adaptation to all the many objects and persons with which we are living and interacting from birth
onward. This is to say that it is one thing to pronounce,
"No!" to a child and scold him, but it is a far more dramatic and impressive event for a human infant to have a
desired object wrenched away from him while he is
slapped and while he sees the face of his profoundly beloved mother contorted with anger. Even on this ontogenetic level, the moral training which the child is receiving has nothing to do with the verbal formulae which we
once thought so essential to morality and moral education.

What is obvious is that when we speak of morality and
immorality, we are dealing with a human situation which
is far more interesting and complex than we have, heretofore, thought it to be. Heretofore, we had believed that
morality had to do with commandments, laws and dicta
(all verbal and highly social phenomena), but now it has
turned out that morality centers in rather primitive bodily
experiences and activities, the patterns of which have been
with us from birth or have been acquired later, first
through non-verbal interaction with our world and, later,
through verbal interaction.

In sum, it would seem that what philosophers and theologians have had to say about morality has, with few ex-

ceptions, had only the scantiest relation to what human beings *experience* as morality. Theologians, in beatific obliviousness of their own or anyone's bodies, have written and preached for centuries about "laws" and "commandments" which come from "out there" and are somehow given or revealed to us by something or someone that just happens to be without a body. Philosophers, for their part, have taken equal delight in analyzing and in arguing over ethical "principles" and "formulae"—as to whether they are "true" or "logically consistent" or "operationally definable." Doubtless, if we go to our traditional theologians and philosophers to learn about morality we shall discover well nigh nothing, inasmuch as the *verbal* "laws" and "principles" over which they fret have only the slightest *ex post facto* relevance to the actual human phenomenon of morality. Such discussions are irrelevant because the discussants have been trained to exist in sublime disassociation from their own or anyone else's immediate somatic experience. One might, as profitably, listen to eunuchs poetize over the bliss of sexuality. But notwithstanding this crushing somatic irrelevance, our senescent cultural tradition has in the past, and still in the present, continued vigorously to support, defend and finance just such pointless discourse.

Whitehead termed it "misplaced concreteness." Nietzsche termed it "putting the last first." Both men were speaking of the same egregious error of Western intellectuals—treating the final, most abstract verbal residue of a given reality as if this abstract verbal residue *was* this given, substantial reality, as if it was so purely the expression of this given reality that it was far *more* real than the given concrete reality from which it was distilled. Symptomatic examples would be something like the following. One says, "The eternal, spiritual God originated moral laws and gave them to mortal, fleshly men with whom He has no direct contact," rather than saying, "Mortal, fleshly men originated moral laws and attributed them to an eternal, spiritual God with whom they have no direct contact." Or one says, "Principles of human behavior are ethically true if they conform to the principles of logical self-evidence or empirical verification," rather than, "Principles of logical self-evidence or empirical verification are ethically true if they conform to the principles of human behavior." Within the alternatives of these inverted statements we see a fairly adequate illustration of the radical difference between the cultural traditionalists and the cultural mutants.

I am not suggesting that traditional theology and philosophy are "untrue," but, instead, I am making the factual assertion that, for an ineluctably growing proportion of persons in a technological society, they are tediously irrelevant; for these persons, what theologians and philosophers have to say is simply not meaningful or applicable to their own lives and to their daily problems of adjusting their behavior to the world which they perceive.

Despite the pathetic efforts of theologians to make their doctrines relevant by becoming non-Christian Christians and atheistic theists, traditional Christianity is vanishing from technological societies within an accelerating twilight of indifference. Throughout the Western technological nations, Christianity and Judaism have finally become the protective concerns of the elderly and, particularly, of women.

It is particularly pathetic that the cultural-mutant viewpoint is not widely heard in philosophy; but philosophy, even though adamantly free from the religious tradition, is itself deeply enmeshed in the more subtle and infectious cultural tradition of the West. Even young existential and phenomenological philosophers quickly lose the gleam that originally attracted them and begin to mouth the words of a new tradition while patiently attempting to knit it to the past. The philosophical establishment, particularly in the Anglo-American world, is quite effective in discouraging and preventing such apostasy: the mutants are simply ostracized from the community—which is to say that the establishmentarians decide not to consider the mutant to be a philosopher. A simple verbal maneuver of redefinition and reclassification.

This is unfortunate inasmuch as philosophy therewith excludes itself systematically from any relevance and growth with the contemporary environmental scene. And this irrelevance is demonstrable in that it is certain that no one cares a fig about establishment philosophy except establishment philosophers. A national convention of philosophers is, typically, a cause for profound apathy to break out among the populace, particularly the young. One might think that an annual convening of the most highly trained human "thinkers" in the nation would be an occasion for explosive revelations and for enormous interest on the part of the American public. Instead, the press releases will recount that the philosophers met, talked and departed: a totally accurate reportage.

There is little hope for this situation. It is likely that during the next few generations, those who seek the goal of philosophical relevance will realize that they must become known as "non-philosophers" in order to gain an audience. In the meanwhile, those establishmentarians who thrill to the tea-time chit chat of the Oxford analysts or to the pseudovirility of positivism will, like the priests and pastors, find their conversations accompanied by a deepening twilight—a twilight where philosophers speak only to philosophers and theologians speak only to God.

If, then, we are to come at last to some understanding of morality and immorality, behavior and misbehavior, in a period of rapid cultural mutation, we shall do so only by responding to new sources of information, new patterns of thinking and, most importantly, to new criteria through which we can view our world, our fellow men and the experiences which we gather from them. We shall come to realize that the proto-mutants springing up throughout the technological world are neither "misbehaving" nor are they, in any relevant sense, "immoral": rather, they are behaving in a groping but positive manner in response to the fantastically productive and organically interrelated society which we have engineered. In the strictest sense, it is they, alone, who are "responsible," and the degrees of experimental success in their *responsive* adaptation to this technological environment can be gauged according to an equation such as this: balance the degree of their present adaptation to our technological environment against the degree of their early cultural education in a family and community environment which was culturally traditional.

What is certain is that the children of these proto-mutants will have a weaker restraining influence upon their responses and adaptations to their technological world. It appears obvious that each successive generation will be more openly and uninhibitedly responsive to this new environment and, accordingly, increasingly more consistent in their behavior and much clearer about their motivations and goals than are the present proto-mutants. These latter have been liberated from the traditional culture into the anxiety and confusion of a non-culture which cannot as yet exist, inasmuch as it will be their children and grandchildren who will eventually create and establish this culture.

All behavior is, by intent, practical. All moral codes are,

by intent, practical. A "right" code of behavior has the intention of aiding the individual to adapt his somatic being to the environment as he sees it. The more effective the adaptation, the more functional and healthy will be his life.

Traditional codes of behavior were also highly practical and effective within the kind of terrestrial environment in which men have, for millennia, lived. But the aggressive and very practical virtues of the long-lived traditional code of behavior have been effective in gearing human beings to the vigorous transformation of their terrestrial environment and to the incredibly successful creation of a technological environment—an environment never before experienced by the kingdoms of men on this earth, an environment where the old fears and the old terrors no longer exist because the drive toward technology was precisely a drive to eliminate these ageless fears and terrors, an environment—finally—which no longer controls men but which men, themselves, control.

The human race is a fantastic race: it has created a new earthly environment. And now it has begun the process of adapting to this new environment of which it had for so long dreamed and struggled. We have, at long last, freed ourselves from the old earth and will now, through the coming generations, learn to profit from what we have created. For the first time in human history we have the chance to discover what it actually means to live fully and openly as human beings.

The mutation is now in our midst. The evolutionary-revolutionary period of human history is now taking place. And it is not the Apocalypse, not the end of man. It is the twilight and end of the first magnificent and necessary culture of humankind; and it is the dawn and beginning of the second.

4

THIS BUSINESS OF
MINDS AND BODIES

Martin Heidegger has felt that the prime question to be raised by the twentieth century was the question of being. It is his understanding that we are oblivious to this, the most immediate and intimate aspect of our reality. Friedrich Nietzsche understood that the prime question of the twentieth century was the attainment of a new consciousness; he felt that men were not yet fully conscious, fully aware, fully perceptive. Both men were raising the same question. I wish also to raise this question, although in terms somewhat less psychological than Nietzsche and somewhat less metaphysical than Heidegger. I wish to raise the question of body.

Nietzsche and Heidegger are of a pair. Both felt that men were oblivious to—or had not yet attained to—a full awareness of who they were and what their world was. Also, both felt that this lucid, uninhibited perception of oneself and one's world was in the near future of mankind, that it was inevitable or, as Nietzsche was fond of saying, a "fatal" event, and that this event would be a major juncture in the history of man. They understood that men have not yet become awake, and that this future event would be exactly like an awakening. Both felt that mankind was still in its childhood and, like children, humans would not even realize that they were children until the seed of growth propelled them into the full consciousness which adulthood brings.

Moreover, both Nietzsche and Heidegger understood that this new consciousness of being was not an intellectual attainment: it could neither be taught nor learned; it would simply happen, it would be grown into. Like the enlightened consciousness sought by the yogins of Hinduism and Buddhism, this was not a new intellectual understanding but a new view, a new attitude, a new *Gestalt*. This inevitable event was the moment when men finally settled into themselves and their world openly, lucidly, honestly and without fear or anger. They felt that during the immensely long period of mankind's childhood, men were not able to be open or lucid or honest or unafraid of themselves and their world, but that forces were now clearly at work which would soon enable men to attain this radically new awareness.

Nothing appears more certain than that both of these men were somatic thinkers who sensed an evolutionary trend in the history of mankind which, at its climax, would be an evolutionary-revolutionary event in human history. Heidegger refers to this event as "crossing over the line." Neitzsche refers to it as the coming of the "Overman." This event is a new consciousness of our bodily being and

our environing world, and the time of this epochal mutation in human awareness is now upon us.

With the inevitable discovery of a new awareness of
ourselves, there will come an inevitable loss of a central
feature of our old awareness: the ancient and tenacious
notion that man is a composite of mind and body, of spirit
and flesh. Men, in their concern to distinguish themselves
from other animals, have been willing to recognize that
they, like all animals, are of body and flesh, but that the
authentic distinction of men is that they alone are minds
and spirits. Thus, the distinctive feature of man was this
mind or spirit, and it is on this presumably unique characteristic that the traditional philosophy and theology of
man has been weighted, i.e., man is body and MIND, man is
flesh and SPIRIT.

This fragmented, schizoid description of man is both absurd and pernicious; but it is often difficult to circumvent
once we begin to speak and use the words and figures of
speech that are intimately a part of our traditional culture.
Surely, the simplest and most exact way for a man to describe himself as man would be to thump his index finger
against his chest and loudly affirm to the world, "I am
man!" In a certain sense, this is what Nietzsche did: his
strategy was to bring our attention back to the central reality of ourselves as men by saying over and again, "Man,"
"the Whole Man," "the Healthy Man," "the Noble Man,"
"the Overman," until we would become fully conscious of
the full reality of being fully human. His other strategy
was to smash his rhetorical hammer against words such as
spirit, will, mind, ego and soul until all meaning and all reality was driven from them. The strategy of Heidegger was
to invent a new word for man: *Dasein,* the creature whose
"being is *here.*" This ingenious coinage is reaching for the
somatic reality of man: man is not simply a creature who

exists, but, rather, he exists *here,* he is located, situated and embodied *here* where he stands. I am not a free spirit: I am an embodied spirit who is always situated in a place, and this place—no matter where I may be—is always *here.*

The difficult task of all existential and phenomenological thinkers has been just this business of avoiding or overcoming a mind-body distinction which they knew to be false. Psychologists have been of little help, inasmuch as during their history they quickly disposed of the psyche, ruling it out of existence; then, believing that if they dealt only with the soma they would simply be physiologists, they avoided the entire issue by ignoring both and becoming behaviorists, which is to say, engineers.

During the course of this book I will use the word *soma,* because it has a certain freshness and because it is easier to recognize new wine when it is put into new bottles. "Soma" does not mean "body"; it means "Me, the bodily being." "Body" has, for me, the connotation of a piece of meat—a slab of flesh laid out on the butcher's block or the physiologist's work table, drained of life and ready to be worked upon and used. Soma is living; it is expanding and contracting, accommodating and assimilating, drawing in energy and expelling energy. Soma is pulsing, flowing, squeezing and relaxing—flowing and alternating with fear and anger, hunger and sensuality. Human somas are unique things which are belching, farting, hiccuping, fucking, blinking, pulsing, throbbing, digesting. Somas are unique things which are yearning, hoping, suffering, tensing, paling, cringing, doubting, despairing. Human somas are convulsive things: they convulse with laughter, with weeping, with orgasms. Somas are the kind of living, organic being which you are at *this* moment, in *this* place where you are. Soma is everything that is you, pulsing within your fragile, changing, growing and dying membrane that has been chopped off from the umbilical cord which linked you—until the moment of that severance—with millions of years of organic genetic history within this cosmos. The umbilical cord has been severed, and now you stand separated from the umbilical chain, a unique membranous bag of living bone and muscle and nervous tissue and blood—a collection of structured, breathing offal that is somehow you. Somas are you and I, separated without asking from the warm, protective, ever beloved bodies of our mothers, feeling a little alone and a little confused, wondering what it is all about, this sixty or seventy years of pulsing physiological autonomy that was given without asking and will be taken away without asking. Somas are the consistently stupid and incomparably intelligent automatons which bear either your name or my name. Some somas are males who sense that the fullness of humanity includes also being female but who cannot be female and so are driven to immerse themselves, merge and flow into the most beautiful of all things in this world: a loving, enveloping female soma. Some somas are females who sense that the fullness of humanity includes being also male but who cannot be male and so are driven to open themselves, merge and allow to flow into them the most beautiful of all things in this world: a loving, explosive male soma. Somas are males and females who know they belong together, because fitted together they make a whole and experience wholeness. Somas are the pathetic and splendid refugees from the egg and the womb that are at this moment writing this book and at this moment reading this book. Somas are you and I, always wanting life and wanting it more abundantly. Somas are you and I, brothers of a common membranous enclosure, a common mortality, a common environment, a common confusion and of a common opportunity, right now, to discover far more than we have ever known about ourselves. The only somas are those who are here and now; somas of the past will never write this book, nor read this book, nor think these thoughts; nor do somas of the future exist—they are still within the egg, and they will write and read better books, think other and more trenchant thoughts. Somas are you and I, at this moment and at this place we are in, beings whose evolutionary history has brought us to the revolutionary stage of realizing that the brave new world to be discovered is no longer "out there" but is the here and now of our immediate organic being. The brave new world to be explored by the twenty-first century is the immense labyrinth of the soma, of the living, bodily experience of human individuals. And we of the latter third of the twentieth century have been appointed discoverers and early cartographers of this somatic continent.

During the coming generations, human individuals will cease thinking of themselves as minds or spirits precisely to the degree that they begin discovering themselves in the immediacy of their somaticity. It is not my point that we *should* not consider the immediacy of our selfhood as mental or spiritual, but rather that we *shall* not do so: it is no less than a matter of mutational change. For millennia it has been of practical advantage for individuals of the human race to emphasize and place value upon that aspect of their behavior which they have called mental or spiritual; but what has now come to be discovered is that the so-termed mental and spiritual aspects of our bodily being are only one aspect of our human possibilities—and an aspect which has, moreover, constrained men to remain in an unbalanced and peculiar stance toward their environing world.

Let it be clear that I am not suggesting that there is no specific reality to what is called "mind" and "spirit"; what

I am suggesting is that the reality to which this refers is not a "thing" or "category" but is a human *function* whose predominance during a pre-technological epoch is being now mutated out in favor of a more balanced display of human functions in interaction with the present technological environment. A good part of what I am suggesting was indicated by Nietzsche when he maintained that those who champion "mind" and especially "spirit" are, thereby, displaying a hostility toward the natural world which environs them; their conception both of man and his way of behaving is, said Nietzsche, "anti-natural": it shows a preference for the nothingness of a world of gods and spirits to the somethingness of this environing world of nature and man.

I will state more precisely what Nietzsche at that period was unable to articulate, although what I am about to say will, perhaps, not carry as full a meaning as it later will, once we proceed in Section Three to draw together some of the ideas of the somatic scientists and philosophers.

Putting this in terms familiar to ethologists, I would say that "mind" or "intellect" or "spirit" or "consciousness" are indeed—as Nietzsche claimed—antipathetic to this environing world in precisely the sense that they involve an aggressive, defensive, protective function against a world that is seen as fearsome. This is to say that the various functions performed by human "mentality" have been practical necessities for the survival of mankind in the face of the uncertainties and dangers of a pre-technological environment. By the same token, to the degree that men have, by dint of the successful application of their intellectual functions, dissipated the uncertainties and dangers of an untamed, hostile environment and have successfully created a technological environment, this very need for and over-emphasis upon the aggressive functions of intellect will diminish.

Hence, the process of evolution does not indicate that the intellectual functions which made a technological environment possible will disappear but, rather, that they will now be of far less environmental usefulness than heretofore. Human mental functions—particularly the arithmetical/logical/rational schemas—were evolved specifically for the aggressive activity of conquest, control and manipulation of an untamed earthly environment, which was feared because of its obvious dangers and uncertainties. Mental functions were, therefore, practical human adaptations to a world which, otherwise, threatened our survival.

What many persons do not seem in the least to understand is that the somatic scientists and philosophers, by playing down the traditional and rightly honored functions of rationality and scientific technology, are not denying the significance and incalculable practical value of these functions, nor are they prophesying the death of these human achievements; rather, they are prophesying in their various ways that these intellectual functions are, by dint of their own potent achievements, becoming less environmentally important and that other somatic functions are becoming more environmentally important. Behind the vague and often confusing terms, "man's whole being," "man's real self," "the authentic," "complete," "fulfilled," "balanced" man, used by the somatic philosophers, is just this prediction that certain traditional functions of men will diminish while other mutational functions will finally come into play.

It has taken such a miserably long time for us finally to see that there is, after all, some avenue out of this tedious and protracted battle between the "two cultures" of the scientists and the humanists. The current evolutionary-revolutionary period will resolve the issue with the surprising judgment that *both* are right; it is only that both factions are so bound up in the present and so pigheadedly blind to the evolving future that they have thus far been unable to see that the future has cunning ways of providing comfortable accommodations for *both* parties of enemy camps—especially camps who shout at one another that "the world is not big enough for both of us." Not only is it big enough for both enemy camps, but evolution is our perennial reassurance that it is, ultimately, far bigger than that.

In the same manner that an over-emphasized "mind" will adapt to its proper balance, so also an over-emphasized "self-consciousness" will shrug itself down to more modest dimensions. Many thinkers might willingly give up seeing the essence of man in his mind or spirit or rationality, but they will eventually jump to a last-ditch holding position by proclaiming, "Man, alone, is self-conscious." Here again, alas, is that haughty-fearful effort to distinguish ourselves from those terrible things called animals, thereby ruling ourselves out of the animal kingdom. For my own part, I don't in the least mind associating myself with my uncles and cousins of the animal kingdom. For one thing, once you come to know an animal, you know where you stand with him, and this is not something I can allege about most of my friends and colleagues—and certainly not about university administrators. For another thing, the social behavior of animals among themselves is far more civilized than any human community I have come to know—even that of the Mexicans, whose absorption of Spanish culture into the stoic world-acceptance of Indian culture has produced one of the earth's most balanced common people, even though this balance is quickly disappearing as they are awakened by the lash of technology.

The problem of humans as over against animals is that they relate to each other and to their world primarily through words. Man is not the "rational" animal—Aristotle lacked ethological data. Freud and Cassirer are much more exact when they describe man as essentially an auditory and verbal animal. Freud was overwhelmed with this as early as his first visits to the demonstrations of hypnosis given by old Charcot. With a few words, Charcot could bring on somatic paralysis in a patient's arm; or, with a few words, the venerable Frenchman could cause the paralysis to disappear: the condition of the "body" was magically transformed by preternatural phonemes which went through the "mind." That was enough of a tip to lead Freud away from Helmholtzian physiology toward a new understanding of the somatic being of man.

And central to Freud's somatic conceptions (certainly by about 1917) was his recognition of the importance of auditory mnemonic traces, not only for a general understanding of human memory but also for understanding the manner in which "consciousness" adapts the needs of the soma to the restrictions of its environing world. These remarks intend to suggest two things: one, that what all human beings experience as *self*-consciousness is, indeed, an actual experience, but rather than being somehow mystical and imponderable, it is a perception made possible by the duplicating effect which words (and all "icons" or symbols) make possible in the perception of our outer environment or of our own somatic immediacy; two, that self-consciousness is far less significant than we believe—in fact, we function more frequently, more efficiently and more happily without it. I know, of course, that both of these suggestions are offensively vague. For the vagueness of the first, I apologize, for I shall not go farther in clarifying it; it is an intricate subject which must be developed separately in the context of a new psychology. But of the second suggestion, something more can be said.

If self-consciousness seems to you to be your prize human possession, tell me how often it has been in evidence during the reading of these last few pages. Ah, *now* you are suddenly self-conscious, by the fact that the previous *words* caused you to reflect upon and replicate your function of reading. Suddenly, you're *not* experiencing the efficient, flowing experience of reading; it has been halted and, instead, you are eddying about in the effort of *remembering* this flowing experience of reading. These are two obviously different functions, and there is no question but that, if you are ever to get through this book and understand it, it will be by virtue of the first process—the flowing, *un*self-conscious process—and not this game of replication which brings everything to a dead halt, in the effort of trying to "remember" (i.e., formulate in words and, perhaps, certain images) the autonomic somatic process that has been interrupted.

It is this *un*self-conscious, autonomic function that is responsible for getting us through life—or through books or movies or traffic or through conversations. Observe someone in conversation. Is he "thinking" about what he is going to say and then saying it? Is there this self-conscious hiatus between the "remembered word" and the word that is just now being pronounced?

And you, yourself: while engaged in conversation, your friend has heard your voice rise and fall, emphasize and stretch out; he has seen your forehead wrinkle, your eyes contract, the edges of your mouth rise in a smile, sink with a grimace; he has seen your shoulders shrug, your hands move and point, your torso gently bob on its spinal support. You've been doing all of these things: were you *aware* of them? Did you *intend* to do them? Did you deliberately say to yourself, "For the best effect, I'm going to say *these* words and use *these* gestures," and then proceed to do so? Of course not; if you had attempted this, nothing would have worked, and you would have been moving in halting, mechanical segments like a poorly operated marionette. Instead, you simply spoke and gestured, *un*conscious of the precise words and gestures.

This is to say that it was a soma which was speaking and gesturing, and that soma is *you* speaking and gesturing. But that halting, inefficient, mechanical self-reflector who is part of a sudden paralysis, this is not *you;* it is one of the minor functions *of* yourself as soma. You need not be worried over the fact that this traditional and quite phony "you" (i.e., this verbal repository) is not "conscious" of all the things you, the soma, are doing. It is our ancient cultural tradition, with its complex fear of the soma's flesh and the world's flesh, which motivates such worries. It is obviously and experientially the case that it is the *un*self-conscious you, the soma, who has been speaking; just as it is equally obvious that your friend has listened to these words and seen these gestures without saying to himself, "Ah, he said *this* word and now he's saying *that* word, and he's lifting his right elbow and—yes—he's raising his shoulders and putting out his upturned palms in a typical shrug." Your friend, the living soma before you, did not think or reflect on these things, inasmuch as if he did, he would neither have heard what you said nor understood your movements.

All that one need do is to reflect upon these matters in order suddenly to realize that only occasionally does one self-consciously reflect on anything at all. It does not take much reflection, moreover, to realize that you can't "think" unless you forget about the self-conscious task of thinking through a problem and simply *let* yourself think. The phony "you" of self-conscious experience cannot help you to think; it can, instead, only prevent you from doing so. The "mind" doesn't think: *you* think. And the only way of thinking is *not* to inhibit this somatic process of problem-solving by constricting oneself into the paralysis of self-conscious replication. Thinking, like perception, either flows through the soma with the selfless ease of moving through traffic or else it *constricts,* somatically, cutting off this flow and reducing the functional human individual to a minute fraction of his somatic being.

Despite their cursory nature, these few observations should suffice to make it strikingly clear how obvious it was for Freud to have noticed that most of what we do is controlled by "unconscious" functions. Nothing could be less mysterious than this "unconscious," and nothing so obvious as the fact that it is the unconscious functions of our soma that are the continuing means for our thinking, our seeing and perceiving, our speaking, our movements, even the way we scratch when we itch.

Depending upon your own somatic stance, you may or may not have seen, at the beginning of Chapter 2, how you as soma quickly perceive more than your "conscious mind" and how you deftly engage in lightninglike reactions when the word fuck appears on a printed page. Perhaps it happened once again. How curious it is that before "you" have actually read any of the words on the page, you have selectively picked out one of the words. But it is not in the least curious from an evolutionary ethological standpoint or a psychoanalytic standpoint: your soma has been conditioned to be on the alert for this terribly important word, and your soma saw it, picked it out and read it before the phony, clod-footed "you" of your educated "mind" could notice it. Quite clearly, if we have thus discovered that our soma is—presumably without benefit of formal education—more effective in reading and visual discrimination than our "mind" and "self-consciousness," then we shall be forced to conclude that these latter functions are but a fractional part of the perceptual and intelligent functions of ourselves. *We,* it appears certain, are far more than either "mind" or "self-consciousness"; and not only that, but we somas are far more potent and efficient, as well as intelligent and perceptive, than these fractional aspects of our total functional being.

This is why I have suggested that the question for the latter third of the twentieth century is the question of the body: the living body which is the soma. And this is why I have suggested that we shall be happily blessed if we experience a diminution of our concern for seeing ourselves as essentially "minds" or bearers of "self-consciousness." These must diminish so that the soma, so that *we* may become magnified.

When young Isaac McCaslin wanted to see Old Ben, the great and mythic bear which roamed within the primeval forest of William Faulkner's great short story, *The Bear,* he had to give up something before the bear would grant him the vision of his presence. In the story, Isaac—when he went out alone into the forest to search for Old Ben—sensed that he would never see him if he carried his gun. So he laid it aside. Later, he realized that this was not enough, and he laid down his compass and also his watch. Then, shorn of the corruptions of civilization, bereft of the instruments of fear which artificially protect men from the fear of hurt and the fear of lostness, then Isaac was pure enough for the marvelous bear to appear. And appear he did: naked of artifice like Isaac, unprotected like Isaac and confident in the self-sufficiency of his own ancient bear-ness even as Isaac was confident of his own ancient human-ness and of the pride and pity, the honor and love and all the other ancient somatic verities which Faulkner knew so well.

And Hermann Hesse also knew them well. Despite the many prisms of sophistication through which Hesse grappled to see the world clearly, he too knew what it meant to become uncorrupted and to attain human purity. And so, Harry Haller—the twentieth-century Faust, who had attained all things of the mind only to discover that they had no function for living but only for dying—Harry could cease to be *der Steppenwolf* and come to understand his full humanity only when a young, empty-headed trollop taught him the full sensuality which his body was capable of feeling. Harry did the fox trot and Harry made love; and the voice of his muted soma gradually began to flood through him, informing him of the fuller being within him of which he had been oblivious. And, eventually, he learned of the immensity of himself as soma: that he and all men were magnificent somas—moving, changing and constantly adapting to the game of this worldly environment. It was no longer a matter of "figuring out" the reason for life's chess game of forever changing, adapting and beginning anew—"ultimate reasons" for life are the delusions of fractional men who believe in the ultimacy of mental, rational functions—rather, Harry learned that it was a question of loving to play the game, of loving the adaptations, of learning to laugh over the sheer exuberance and joy of being allowed the chance to play.

And not only Faulkner and Hesse. There are many, many other such novelists and poets: indeed, every work of modern literature that smells of health and growth, that ends, without having cheated, in an unqualified human affirmation—these are the gifts to us of the somatic writers who, like the scientists and philosophers we shall now look at, have allowed us to see that man is not only infinitely more magnificent than he thinks he is, but he is actually becoming so.

BEHAVIOR
AND MUTATION
IN MAN
AND OTHER
FINE ANIMALS

PART I

SOMATIC SCIENTISTS

1

THE BIOLOGY OF
THE PAST: DARWIN

Charles Darwin went to Cambridge University with the intention of becoming an Anglican priest. He was, however, incapable of holding his gaze steadfastly fixed upward at spiritual matters; things that lived and moved distracted his attention, and he began to look at the world round and about him and became, instead, a naturalist. And a very good one. He so well mastered the art of naturalistic observation that he became not only one of the greatest of all observers but was also the greatest seminal force in the history of biology.

Darwin was not merely a peerless naturalist whose gaze took in his environment both sweepingly and in detail; he was also a theorizer whose audacious synthetic abilities accounted for biological history in such a way that, from his time onward, the extraordinary nature of somatic beings could no longer be ignored.

His delightfully canny abilities as an observer are amply displayed in his chronicles of *The Voyage of the Beagle*. His synthesizing imagination, which transformed all subsequent biological thought, burst forth in *The Origin of Species* of 1859. And his proof that he was still growing and could twist the tiger's tail twice was the appearance in 1872 of his study on *The Expression of the Emotions in Man and Animals*.

Darwin was a friend of both men and animals, although it could hardly be said that the former fully reciprocated this friendship, then or even now. The wrath of the Victorian religious world gathered itself up and descended upon him with a mixture of unbelieving shock and protest that has endured until the present: even so respected a scientist-philosopher as Teilhard du Chardin was censured in recent years by the keepers of Peter's keys for his suggestion that the evolutionary descent of man could gloriously be put to God's account.

But this outrage and dismay was as inevitable as it was understandable, for the "theory" of evolution was, in itself, a revolution in the fundamental conception of man which the cultural tradition had so long cherished. Like Immanuel Kant a century earlier, Charles Darwin thrust the thinking of men into a "Copernican Revolution" whereby the world was turned topsy-turvy, where what seemed to be the center and substance of the cosmos was declared to be dependent and derivative. When men's basic understanding of themselves and their world is turned inside-out, it requires a long and painful period of adjustment before they can learn to orient themselves comfortably within such a new understanding. And it is just such a slow adaptation that has been taking place during the period of more than a century since Darwin's epochal book appeared. As an aid and spur to this adaptation there has been a continuing series of confirmations of the "theory" of evolutionary process by paleontologists, biologists, ethologists, neurophysiologists and psychoanalysts. The "theory" has finally metamorphosed into fact, and the fascinating confirmations surveyed within this section of the present book can now be gathered together to form a more coherent picture of what we are as men and what is presently happening in human history.

The cornerstone of Darwin's synthesis was the process of "natural selection." The information lay there before him, well known to Darwin and all naturalists of the nineteenth century. French naturalists had, a century earlier, begun to classify the amazing family similarities and relationships of all known plants and animals. The taxonomic, morphological arrangements of earlier naturalists had laid out a composite picture of the animal kingdom that had the simplicity of a pyramid: from the pyramidal top of the triangle, the animal kingdom branched outward and downward into the well-ordered layers of phylum, class, order, family, genus and, finally at the bottom, the species. The homologies were there, the remarkably interrelated similarities were spread out for all to see, and these data only waited for the audacious imagination of Darwin to synthesize and bring them to life. The pyramid was static, frozen into what seemed to be eternally given, statically ordered classifications. What Darwin did was to breathe the warm breath of time into the pyramid, showing it to be the living, evolving core of history.

Darwin's observations while traveling on the *Beagle*— particularly of the amazingly variegated animals he found on the Galápagos Islands—were the impetus to seeing the many species of the animal kingdom not as frozen but as evolved and still evolving. On these islands, several hundred miles off the South American coast, there were species of animals and plants which were generically related to South American species but which were new species. However, what was more astonishing about this archipelago of scattered islands was that there were new, previously unknown species of animals that were native to certain of these islands but which were not found at all on any other of the islands. It was as if a particular new species had somehow emerged from its own particular island environment and was totally bound to that environment. The Galápagos were islands of biological data loudly testifying that there is a direct relation between living things and their environment and that there is an obvious relation between the occurrence of different species and the particular environment in which they happen to appear. A process seems to be at work whereby the given possibilities within any particular environment constitute a selective pressure upon all creatures living within that environment, selecting *in* those varieties which could best exploit those environmental possibilities and selecting *out* those which were less able to do so.

But this meant that animals, rather than being eternally

fixed within a static bodily structure, underwent changes from generation to generation. Higher chances of survival selected out certain of those individual animals who happened to be structurally different from other members of their species. In fact, this was a different version of an old story known by all English stock breeders: when an occasional variant animal was born (with shorter legs, longer wool, etc.), this mutation was *artificially selected* out for breeding for its beneficial difference; Darwin saw that when the same mutations occurred among animals in a natural, wild state, the environmental conditions would *naturally select* those mutants whose differences were more advantageous to their survival than were the normal, non-mutant animals. Indeed, during several generations of nature's having selected out those individual animals whose variant physiology made them more suitably adapted to survival in their environment, such different animals would have been procreated that, structurally, they would constitute a distinctly *different* species of animals—a species of animals which would have classifiably different bodily characteristics than did their forefathers of the prior species.

The evidence on the Galápagos also meant that the species of extinct animals, which had not been able to survive, did not survive because they lacked those particular bodily characteristics which would allow them to make it within their particular island environment. So then, we have one known species of animals surviving but another similar but slightly different species of the same genus of animals which did not survive. It was evident that certain species of animals have poorly adaptive bodily characteristics which edit them *out* of their environment, and others possess characteristics which naturally and inevitably "select" them for survival, inasmuch as these happen to be the bodily structures and abilities which are best adapted for continual survival in their particular environment.

Bathed in the light of these circumstances, the pyramid suddenly lurched into time; and the remarkable similarities between species, which had allowed taxonomists to classify the animal kingdom, were no longer seen to be the clear-cut rational ordering of a once-and-for-all-time creation, but, rather, these similarities were now seen to have had a radically different origin: the species were similar because they evolved out of earlier, related species to the degree that certain fortuitous bodily characteristics selected them out for continued survival in the kind of environment in which they had to live.

"Because" is the important word. Darwin saw that there was a *cause* for the enormous variety of body types that we observe in the animal kingdom (and in the plant kingdom as well): so many different species of animals, yet all of them so basically related and similar—as if all living things were of a single, genetic family that had evolved through the aeons from one primordial life-type into the myriad different life-types that had once thrived in earlier environment-types or that now survive in certain present environment-types.

Thus, the process of "natural selection." As Darwin saw it, this was a natural, causal process of an exact and unerring mechanical nature: all individual animals are slightly different from other individual animals, and random differences of certain individuals (slightly stronger jaw muscles, slightly brighter feathers, a more supple tail, sharper teeth, etc.) would render them slightly more successful in adapting to their environment; consequently, the progeny of this slightly more successful animal would be a quick, genetic multiplication of these fortunate differences, and in increasing arithmetic progression this progeny would produce multitudes of animals which were blessed with jaws or feathers or tails or teeth which made their burgeoning new species happily adapted to the needs of their environment.

On the other hand, those individual animals not accidentally blessed with such adaptive individual differences would have progeny who were cut down more quickly by their environment, who in arithmetical diminution were progressively selected out of existence by animals that were competitively faster or stronger or more protected, etc., or by a changing natural environment whose trees were taller, whose foods were tougher, whose climate was changing, or whatever. One species relentlessly selected for survival by the accidents of individual mutations; others selected out of existence in an equally inevitable manner by the absence of such mutations which guarantee survival. With mechanical efficiency, the fittest animals were selected for survival; those not the fittest were selected for extinction.

Thus, the pyramid of the organized animal kingdom evolved out of a process of accidental mutation and mechanical selection, and yet this process—blindly devoid of purpose or telos—had evolved more complex, more physiologically adaptable animals—in short, "higher" animals with extraordinary abilities to cope with their ever threatening and challenging environment. And therewith we have an explanation for the origin of animal species and for the descent of man, both being the evolved products of random mutation and mechanical selection, yet simultaneously being meaningful and historically rooted products which had rightfully and necessarily earned their position in life through countless generations of biological adaptation.

At first blush, it all sounds so harsh. These terrible words: mechanical, accidental, relentless, unerring, struggle for existence and survival of the fittest—such words break upon the ear and evoke a scene of earthly existence that is forbidding and somehow too cruel to be credible. But if what Darwin has described is, after all, how it is, then, at second blush, this description may appear both less forbidding and more acceptable. Darwin is merely pointing out that the creatures who get along best in this world are those which are best able to cope with their world. We need not become sentimental over the "dying out" of species, inasmuch as species are not creatures which die; rather, they are body-types which no longer have any individual representatives. In the same way, we need not be maudlin over the death of individual creatures within an obsolescent species-type, inasmuch as all individual creatures nonetheless die—even those within surviving species-types.

A simple, and now classic, illustration of natural selection is found in the fate of the two varieties of peppered moth found in England. There is a variety of peppered moth with spotted wings and another variety with black wings. Up until the middle of the nineteenth century, naturalists found very few of the black-winged variety, whereas the spotted-wing moths flourished. Both types of moth typically clung to the lichen on tree trunks and, whereas the spotted-winged variety was thus beautifully camouflaged, the melanistic moth was starkly and appetizingly displayed to the wanton hunger of passing birds. But the factory system changed this situation within the space of a century: the coal smoke, belched out from the factory chimney stacks throughout industrial England, gradually darkened the lichen on trees until the melanistic variety of peppered moth was camouflaged. Then it became the spotted-wing's turn to learn how fortuitous adaptability to the environment guarantees survival. Now, a century later, the melanistic variety dominates, and the spotted-winged variety is as little in evidence as the black-wing was a century earlier.

So then, in the simplest way imaginable, Darwin managed to explain to us how—through mutation, adaptation and natural selection—it has come about that there are and have been so many different and yet similar kinds of animals. And with this explanation, men promptly found themselves meaningfully related to the entire animal kingdom, or—if you prefer—they found animals to be associates of the human race. And this explanation, eventually buttressed and confirmed by the findings of later researchers, has now become just as useful for understanding what is happening to human civilization in the latter third of the twentieth century as it is helpful for understanding what happened to dinosaurs during the Mesozoic era.

But Charles Darwin's explanatory synthesis was even less harsh than I have suggested: to the end, Darwin remained loose and cautious about the exact manner in which mutation and adaptation took place. On the question of the unerring selection of the fittest for survival, he had no doubts: it was too obvious a fact to avoid. But as to *how* these saving mutations came about, he could not finally say that they were accidental or physiologically determined or perhaps even due to the individual's ability or sheer luck in adaptative behavior. He had to construct his "theory" without knowledge of genetic laws or of the nature of environmental conditioning.

But further possibilities for understanding man and other animals were opened in his later work, *The Expression of the Emotions in Man and Animals.* In this delightful book Darwin took another leap forward with an explanation, not of how the *bodies* of animals and men came to look the way they do but, rather, of how animals and men came to *behave and express themselves* the way they do. With this leap, he moved from structural biology into the biology of behavior, thereby inaugurating the science of ethology.

All over the earth, men—when showing their inability to do something or to prevent it—will shrug their shoulders, turning in their elbows, fingers extended from the upraised palms of their hands, usually turning their heads a little to the side with the mouth open and eyebrows raised. It doesn't matter where these men live, what is their race or whether they are primitive or civilized. It is a universal and unlearned manner of expression, a form of behavior that men normally cannot avoid—unless, of course, they interrupt this programmed somatic expression by the paralyzing intervention of self-consciousness.

Ask a person if he remembers something, and as he struggles to remember, notice how he raises his chin, squints his eyes and begins moving his head slightly back and forth as if he is searching for something. It is not that men are taught to do this when they attempt to remember, nor is this something done self-consciously. Men, as somas, simply do it, because it automatically goes with the act of remembering. Remembering is searching: it is hunting, and when *you* try to remember, *all* of you as soma tries to search out the memory in the ancient way that your ancestral somas searched and hunted.

When a young man walks into a tough bar—or, for that matter, into a room filled with attractive young ladies— just as he approaches the threshold of the door his spine becomes more erect, his shoulders square and his chest comes forward. That particular environment brings forth that particular bodily expression from him. This is very "manly," but it may be somewhat embarrassing to recognize, at the same time, that toads, frogs, chameleons, various lizards and snakes also puff themselves up in order to look large and fearsome: these animals do not "think" about this action any more than does the young man; it just happens to them when the environmental situation requires that they further their best interests by an adaptation which makes them look bigger than they really are.

When a man is in extreme fear or terror of some person or thing, not only will the muscles of his body tremble but the hairs on his skin will erect. This curious, involuntary response is certainly familiar among humans, but, Darwin informs us, there is also this same erection of dermal appendages (hair, feathers, quills, etc.) with frightened chimpanzees, gorillas, orangutans, baboons, hyenas, lions, boar, horses, cows, elk, antelopes, goats, cats, dogs, anteaters, bats, birds, fowl, and, of course, porcupines and hedgehogs. Modern ethologists would extend the list much farther and would not forget to include fish. What is the somatic function of this erection of dermal appendages? Evidently, surmises Darwin, so that the animal will appear larger, and thus frighten the enemy who is threatening him. The pictorial and photographic studies made by Darwin and many ethologists after him of the fear/aggression appearances of such familiar animals as cats, dogs, roosters and geese are famous; and they are fascinating not simply in themselves but especially for the homologies we see in the various similarities of bodily behavior which we see up and down the animal kingdom pyramid right up to ourselves.

The forward leap which Darwin achieved in this book is in showing that the evolutionary process has not only produced different (but related) species of bodily skeletons but this same process has produced different (yet clearly related) species of bodily behavior. It is just this point which modern ethologists have driven home: that any animal species is as clearly identifiable through its behavior as by its bodily structure. It is also one of the prime tasks of *Bodies in Revolt* to show, through a survey and analysis of somatic thinking, that the kind of body we have and the kind of behavior of which we are capable are fundamentally the same: any given soma has a given guide-pattern of behavior, which is to say, of feeling, thinking and reacting as well as acting.

We are, each of us, achieved and still achieving somas within the pyramidal kingdom of different somas which has evolved over aeons of biological history, carrying along with it, genetically, an immensely detailed and practical body of somatic information, ready to respond to our environment and adapt with it if only we allow it. And, as will become clear, it is our aggressive achievement of a technological environment which is finally allowing us to free our somas to their full possibilities of living, growing and adapting with our world.

Darwin linked us with the animal kingdom so that we could recognize and take similar delight in the impatient pawing of eager and fine race horses or fighting bulls and the impatient pawing of eager and fine junior league baseball players as they bend their heads and worry the ground with their feet while the longwinded coach gives his last minute instructions before the game. Darwin has made it possible for us to know that when our dog fearfully yet aggressively snarls his way up to an enemy dog and raises the sides of his lips to display his sharp canine teeth, he is feeling a similar somatic experience to what we, as human somas, feel when humans contemptuously toss their heads sideways at a despicable person and curl one side of the lips upward, slightly displaying the same canine teeth. The evolved links of the pyramidal somatic kingdom assure us that the snarling behavior, the fearful/angry feeling and the biting function are similar and related—even though biting as a type of human aggression has all but mutated out of our race.

Charles Darwin opened a door, a door sufficiently wide for the entire human world to pass through into the belated discovery of what they had always been: living creatures, sprung from the womb of time and still growing within the embrace of time. Obviously, the revolutionary double significance of Darwin's discovery is that by uncovering the past of biological history, he simultaneously revealed to us the more extraordinary fact that there is also a future for biological history and a mutational, open future for mankind.

How very curious it is that Darwin should have made his discovery in the middle of the nineteenth century, just when man's industrial age first slipped into gear. It is almost as if the human creature had been finally allowed to see and comprehend the fact of evolution, adaptation and mutation *only* when a crucial stage in human development was beginning, only when we had approached the threshold of a technological age. Perhaps the evolution of knowledge in relation to our environment is such that the best of human scientists and philosophers may never know more than they need to know. It would appear that new knowledge and new theories are ways of adapting to a new environmental situation; and thus the new intellectual visions evoked from man make their appearance to the degree that a changing environment has evoked these visions and made them adaptationally relevant for human survival. This would indicate that we can only know as much as is needed to be known at any given time. If sufficient unto the day be the knowledge thereof, then our thinking is destined to be at its most authentic when it is most contemporary and relevant to the nowness of our environing world.

We are only now beginning to absorb and incorporate into our lives the full impact of the insights of Charles Darwin into the realm of living beings. Darwin, like all of the somatic scientists, loved living things. Because he was open to them, they responded by letting their ancient secrets become open to him.

The living world reveals to the loving observer a translucent beauty and purity which throws into sharp contrast the constricted limitations of human experience. Darwin recounts that Mr. Bartlett, then keeper of the London Zoological Gardens, received two new chimpanzees into the zoo. The chimpanzees were fairly old, and they had never met each other before. When he put them into the same cage for the first time, they came up and sat opposite one another with their mutually protruded lips each studiously touching the other's. Then one chimpanzee put his hand on the shoulder of the other; then they both folded their arms and looked intently at each other. After a moment of this, they both stood up with their arms draped over one another's shoulders, lifted up their heads, opened their mouths and yelled with delight.

Such fine somas. Oh, that we all might be capable of attaining such joy.

2

THE TRAUMA OF
THE EGG: FREUD

Once upon a time, there was an egg, and it contained within itself a kingdom of perfect happiness. The creature who lay dreaming and content within his membranous shell had everything he could possibly want or need already within his perfect kingdom: warmth, comfort, the immediate satisfaction of all his hungers. The perfection was not only that all he could wish for was there within his kingdom, but also that these fulfillments were so immediately linked with him that for him to wish for something (that is, for him to need anything at all) meant that simultaneously he received it: the wish itself called forth a satisfaction of the wish. It was a perfectly interlocked system of demand and supply.

But one day—never to be forgotten—an incredible

event took place: the shell-like firmament of the creature's perfect world was rent asunder, and he was projected forth into another world: a world of fantastic dimensions—so big that it did not even seem to have a final enclosing shell to contain it as did his ancient kingdom. This was a world of things and beings *other than* the things and beings that had been immediately linked to him in the ancient kingdom.

But this strange new world was no concern of his. His business was feeling happy, having what he needed and what he wanted exactly when he needed and wanted it: this was the only business that he knew, and so he had no choice but to continue it. However, he was quick in discovering that his kind of business did not work in the new world: when he needed and wished for something, the old demand-and-supply process clicked along somewhat as usual, but in a curious manner; the wish created an immediate fulfillment but it was a fulfillment of a different kind —it was not real warmth or real comfort or real nutrition, but rather a vacuous satisfaction that was dreamlike and not a real satisfaction.

Those who have dwelled in kingdoms of perfect happiness are stubborn creatures, and this creature was no exception; he knew what the business of happiness was: it was the only business he cared for, and he wasn't going to give it up. But still, he was practical enough to realize that if his pleasant business was to be kept going and if he were to have real satisfaction as well as an immediate but vacuous dreamlike satisfaction, then he would have to make a few concessions to this colossal and wretched world he had been thrust into. When one comes to a new place, one has to adapt to it and learn things about it. And so he did.

He had to learn how to feel things *outside* himself instead of only within himself. Formerly, in the old kingdom, the only things he was concerned with were those tense, overcharged, tight feelings which were most unpleasant and those loose, relieved, relaxed feelings which were so pleasant. Now, in order to preserve this wonderful, relaxed feeling, he had to feel things outside himself—not to enjoy them, however, but for the practical purpose of finding out what they were like, so he could use them and control them for his pleasure. Every possible sensitive surface of his dermal membrane was used to pick up and sense things in that outer world whose pressures and heat and particles and waves and photons were continually bombarding his external membrane.

But this process of learning and adaptation did not take place all at once; it was stretched out over a long period of time. Each time that the struggling creature came out of the egg anew, he brought with him some of the effects of his previous visit in the outer world: his fragile, malleable body bore the traces of his previous adaptive experiences. His groping, trial-and-error efforts to adapt and interact with the outside world had had the effect of stretching his tissues here, hardening them there, organizing them into units, and building connecting and supporting units.

Gradually, then, instead of sensing merely the interior of his own body, he became able to sense things exterior to his body: he became what is called "conscious." And being conscious of this exterior world was a somewhat unpleasant but eminently practical achievement of this creature who, in the long run, desired only to keep his body in happy, steady repose, as free as possible from unpleasant crampings and pressures and over-stimulations.

Consciousness was his ability to perceive the outside world. It was a grand achievement, but this creature was not one to rest on his laurels: to keep the pleasure business operating within such an uncertain environing world, one had to be somewhat aggressive. It was not a matter of sitting there passively, waiting for sense impressions to drop in; rather it was far more useful to go out and look for them, to search and hunt for these sense impressions. And so a new ability arose: that of attention. It did not feel particularly pleasant to maintain this straining alertness but, in the long run, it would result in more pleasure than displeasure.

But, while learning to be attentive to the many goings-on of the world, the creature discovered that all these energy-propelled perceptions he received left their traces inside him: a fresh sensation would zip in and leave a kind of impression in his malleable tissue. He remembered those things which were accidentally perceived, and he remembered those things which his attentive senses searched out. And now that he had attained a memory, a curious new activity began to take place. The memory began to fill up with the quiet tracings of things he had attentively observed, and when he would perceive things in the world, he could compare them with the memory of things already perceived. He knew which perceptions were new and which ones were old, and by dint of this searching out, remembering and comparing, he became able to catalogue the many things out there, judge how they fitted in, and where they belonged. Heretofore, his only concern with sensations had been whether they were pleasant or unpleasant; now he had developed the ability of judgment, by which he knew whether some new perception really did fit in with the memory-picture of the world he had built up. Even though "pleasant-unpleasant" was the only criteria he was finally concerned with, he realized that the only way to promote this deep concern was by making judgments as to whether things in the outer world were "true-false."

Without a doubt this egg-bereft creature was now definitely in business—the secondary business of dealing with
the world so that the primary and original business could
be pleasurably maintained. And so, he moved into action.
Up to this point his energies had simply been used to get
rid of unpleasant inner tensions; now his energies could be
directed outward, and he could *act* upon this strange external world which he could aggressively perceive, make
sense of and thus judge which actions would fit his known
and remembered world.

Thus, two businesses were in effective operation at the
same time: the old pleasure business which was constantly
the support and motivation for his secondary business of
being consciously engaged in manipulating things in the
outer world. But this successful and long-struggled-for
achievement made for a decidedly odd creature: because
consciousness, attention, memory, judgment and aggressive action had all been built up in response to the strange
outer world and because they were designed specifically to
deal with just this world, this meant that the creature was
not conscious, attentive, recollective or capable of judg-
mental action and thought in regard to the primary activities that continued as usual within his bodily core. By the
very history and reason for its development, consciousness
and its attendant abilities were directed resolutely outward, conscious of every thing but one: the needs and activities of the primary process which it had been developed
to protect and enhance. Conscious action was an out-
wardly-directed, aggressive movement into a worldly environment, designed uniquely for the practical task of the
survival of the original core of the creature. Because these
conscious abilities and bodily structures had evolved by
turning toward the environment and by adapting to the

contingencies of that environment, they could in no manner focus upon the inner fragile needs that were the secret motive behind their development: knowledgeable of the external, oblivious to the internal, they were blind instruments which stood mid-distant between an inner creature, ever needful of pleasure and peace, and an outer world ever threatening pain and turmoil.

This, in its simplest form, is Sigmund Freud's understanding of the nature of man. In the purest sense, it is a somatic understanding, seeing man as an autonomous, needful organism which has evolved, struggled with and adapted to its environment through the long skein of biological history. Man is one of the somas which has survived. He is the most magnificent of all somas because he has so well learned his environment and so well adapted to its elements that he has unequalled aggressive abilities in controlling and manipulating his environment.

Along with his magnificence, man is also the unhappiest of all somas: this, because the magnificent development of his abilities of conscious, aggressive action have led him to conquer his environment without knowing why he has been driven to do so, and thus his conquest seems empty and pointless. At the supreme moment of his technological transformation of the earth, he is comically stopped short, wondering what is the point of it, the why of it all. And the best of men strive to give conscious, rational explanations of the why of it, and the words ring hollow. He tries to understand and explain *himself* in the same manner in which he has so magnificently learned to understand and explain the world, and somehow the explanation never touches the hidden secret that lies throbbing within him. It is as if all his conscious, rational abilities were only the blind instrument of something else. It is as if Heidegger were exactly right in saying that mankind is "oblivious" to some basic and immediate aspect of being.

But man is not only the magnificent and unhappy soma; he is also the supremely lucky soma, for by being blindly driven to attack and transform his frightful environment, he has created a new environment that has lost its biological frightfulness; and he now has no choice but to adapt once more to this radically different environment. Man is the unhappy soma who spent aeons developing a magnificent mind for a threatening environment, and now, with his achievement of a benign environment, he will adapt and survive only by, in large measure, losing his mind.

Man, the magnificent, unhappy and lucky soma—this was Freud's evolutionary-revolutionary vision which joined solidly with Darwin's vision with a shock that is only now beginning to be appreciated and absorbed.

Like most of the somatic scientists and philosophers, Freud has been poorly understood, even by his well-known commentators. All this odd business about the unconscious, repression, cathexes, libidos, ids, egos and superegos—the reaction of most persons is that it all seems somehow mysterious and not really human. Precisely so, and this is the ground for the misunderstanding. Freud, in his works, is not addressing himself to the subject of individual human beings like Mary and Mike and Wendell; he is giving his observations on the structure and development of a biological organism. There is nothing at all "humanly personal" about it, and that's why we cannot directly identify ourselves with this bag of somatic mechanisms which he describes.

For one thing, Freud was not a psychologist; he was a laboratory physiologist, who, by dint of financial circumstances, ended by becoming a practicing neurophysiologist. He was a physician who treated people with neurophysiological illnesses, but he brought to this practice a mind which previously had been thoroughly disciplined in the matter-of-fact, impersonal attitudes proper to physiological research. He was also, by virtue of this earlier training, quite familiar with the obvious presence of evolutionary forces in the structuring and functioning of animal bodies. Although preferring a career of physiological research, once the need for money prodded him out of the lab and into the neurophysiological wards, he knew that it was his scientific duty to understand the humans he treated as neurophysiological organisms. It is clear, at least to me, that when Freud looked at a patient, his transparent gaze saw completely past the particular personality of that individual into the structured "impersonal" organism which accounted for what was taking place. This is why, in my recounting of "The Trauma of the Egg," I spoke in non-human impersonal terms; if one reads this account thinking of it as the history of a cell or organism or non-human creature, then one is thinking in the way that Freud thought. Freud, then, did not think in personal human terms but in somatic terms; and as one learns to think somatically, one sees how amazingly obvious are so many of Freud's insights into what we human somas are all about.

Freud had a term for this concern and method of gazing transparently into the somatic depths of the human individual: he called it psychoanalysis. And the science upon which the analytical task finally rested was termed meta-psychology—meaning a study of the evolved somatic structures and processes operating behind individual human behavior. In varying degrees all of the somatic thinkers we shall discuss had this in-depth, transparent view of humanity, and rather than use the somewhat negative term meta-psychology, it would be more positively descriptive to speak of it as somatology. Somatology entails just this method of perceiving other humans or of perceiving oneself. It is the method which phenomenologists have sought to develop and which Heidegger, among philosophers, has employed with perhaps the greatest success.

The program for Freud's research into the somatology of man was spelled out as early as 1895 in his *Project;* then for more than twenty years he explored the phenomena of dreaming, of sexual development both normal and deviational, of repression and its various somatic and behavioral effects, and the general light which psychoanalysis shed on human culture both primitive and advanced. By 1917 these explorations first began to be summed up in a positive somatological manner in the paper "Formulations on the Two Principles of Mental Functioning," probably the most concise and brilliant paper ever written by Freud. Then, in the early 1920's, he continued his effort to put together a comprehensive somatology of the human being in *Beyond the Pleasure Principle* and then, a bit later, in *The Ego and the Id*—the former book attempting to reach through human biology and formulate the nature of life itself as it arose out of inorganic processes (which Reich, also, took as his task); the later book attempting to summarize Freud's mature views on the many-faceted structure and processes of the human soma.

Freud had come to understand the human creature to be an ancient and complex organism whose primary and primordial nature had evolved and adapted to the challenges of the environing world by building up secondary structures and processes which could successfully cope with this world. The primordial core of man was a bodily system of energy patterns whose autonomic ebbing and flowing was *felt* alternately as unhealthiness and healthiness; unhappy over-accretions of stimuli and happy discharges of surplus stimuli; tension and release; or—in its most typical statement—as displeasure and pleasure. This primordial soma was, at the beginning, a blind and helpless creature which was *not yet* conscious of itself but only *felt* itself, as its body autonomically discharged the occasional hyper-concentrations of energy stimuli from its tissues.

But in order to survive in the earthly environment, this helpless, inwardly dreaming organism was compelled to respond in whatever ways it could to the threatening waves of energy which collided with its outer surface. Appropriately, it was this outer membrane which began first to adapt to the challenge of the world; it became more and more sensitive to the different kinds of energy patterns that bombarded it. And the development of this sensitivity was quite simply the gradual development of the *organs of sensitivity*. For Freud, as for the somatic philosopher Merleau-Ponty, to be conscious means to perceive; consciousness is the somatic activity of perception, which involves all the complex apparatus of sense perception. Every millimeter of our bodily surface is in the business of perceiving, and thus every portion of our bodily surface is conscious. Our whole sensitive body is conscious; it is constantly "attentive" to stimuli.

And this is why those who do not think somatically cannot understand Freud when he speaks of the "mind" and the "mental process" as if he were really talking instead about what we traditionally call the "body" and "bodily process." You, as soma, are constantly perceiving; from head to toe your sensitized body is receiving and recording data from the environing world. This is why you continue to perceive even when sleeping; you can learn the basics of a language while sleeping, because even though you are not "conscious," your (in Freudian terms) mental apparatus is "unconsciously perceiving." A bell rings while you are sleeping, and your primordial somatic core—blissfully engaged in its ancient business of dreaming of pleasant-unpleasant things "as if they were real"—incorporates that perception of the bell tone into its dream-reality without the slightest hesitation. Even without the presence of the secondary activity of "consciousness," the sound of the bell is heard and smoothly folded into the flowing context of one's inner experience.

Might as well forget about the primacy of the "self-conscious mind"—which is merely secondary—and try to train oneself in the "primacy of perception," which entails a somatic understanding of oneself. Then when Freud speaks of "the unconscious," you will understand that he means the primary, primordial, bodily core that has always been within the heart of our soma but which has, during the course of evolution, been covered over with the secondary structures and processes involved with the practical business of being conscious of the external world which lies just beyond the membrane enclosing our bag of muscle and bones.

What Freud entitled "psychoanalysis" was, then, a study of the interrelationships of this primary core of the soma with the secondary overlay of practical functions, as the entire human soma developed and adapted to the immediate environment within which it lived.

This immediate environment of the human soma is, at its earliest age, the mother, nurse, father and general family into which the young and fragile soma has been introduced. At this early stage the practical, protective secondary abilities which the young soma has inherited have not yet had a chance to develop and mature—because they developed late in the evolutionary history of the human soma, they will develop later in the history of the individual human soma: hence, the general law of biology that ontogeny (individual development) recapitulates phylogeny (the evolutionary development of the species).

So then, with its protective secondary abilities latent and undeveloped, the infant human soma lies fragilely exposed to its environing family world, with its ancient core of primary bodily processes nakedly revealed for all to see: it is a pulsing little creature of alternating bodily constrictions and dilations which unashamedly expresses its displeasure over its felt bodily tensions and unashamedly expresses its pleasure over its felt bodily repose and satisfaction.

This neonate soma, this infant human being: look at it, and you are seeing your primordial, somatic core, which has never ceased to exist and dominate your somatic being, but which has only been covered over with the later developing somatic abilities of consciousness, attention, memory, judgment, practical action, thinking, use of language, etc. This is the simple and, in the end, rather obvious description which Freud has given us. And if we have deeply resented this description and have failed to understand it, it is not only because during our maturation we have become oblivious to our original unconscious core but also because the traditional culture which our practical, aggressive consciousness has created is a culture which refuses to entertain a conception of man other than of the "secondary" practical aspect of him. This traditional cultural definition of man is false; it is a repressive falsehood which evolving, fearful man has kept from himself for the very practical reason that his initial evolutionary task has been to aggress upon his environment, learning to control, manipulate and subjugate it to his needs. But once man has finally completed just this task of subjugating a threatening earthly environment, he will no longer need to hide from himself and be repressively oblivious to the ancient, primary core that has always pulsed within him and motivated his practical outward surge toward the world.

If Darwin opened the possibility of understanding ourselves in terms of the somatic history which brought us where we are, Freud enabled us to understand something of the specific somatic human creature which evolved and how the very nature of our two-sided soma constantly incurs an unhealthy development in its relations with the human environment.

From an evolutionary and somatic viewpoint, the situation seen by Freud was this: the history and structure of the human soma indicates that, ideally, the primary inner system of the soma should remain healthy and integral in its development while the secondary, outer-directed bodily systems smoothly mature and achieve the practical ability to protect and serve the driving and unquenchable needs of the primary human system. Biologically, this is the kind of phased, complementary development which seemed designed to take place; and if it did, the human being, thus matured, would be healthy, adaptive and—most importantly of all—would be a human who was able continually to achieve states of satisfaction and inner repose during his day-to-day encounters with the world of men. That such a happy, successful human being is possible is clearly indicated by the evolved somatic structure of man; but that such inwardly contented human beings are rarely achieved is equally clear, and it was Freud's understanding of the evolved inner-outer soma that allowed him also to understand the psychopathology (or, in our terms, the somapathology) of man.

In the main, Freud saw that "mental" (i.e., somatic) illness was *not* due to inadequacies in the human soma (unless, of course, there was actual organic damage of the individual), but to inadequacies in the environment within which the human being had to develop, particularly the very early development up to four or five years and then less importantly from the fifth year until the beginning of puberty. There is no question but that Freud saw many pitfalls and difficulties during this period from birth to puberty, even for the most fortunate of humans, but it is also without question that a normal, healthy human being could, in his view, develop if the environmental circumstances were right. Later, Freud's disciple, Wilhelm Reich, was even more vigorous in pointing the accusing finger at the child's early family and cultural environment. In traditional terms, suffice it to say that Freud saw the just-born human soma as "sinless" and "uncorrupted." And in most un-traditional terms, suffice it to say that the sinful and corrupting influences were in the traditional culture.

I will not embroil the reader in the labyrinthine Freudian analyses of the myriad things which can go wrong during the infanthood of a human being, creating "mental" illness. Staying within the main outlines of what we have discussed, it is enough to say the following: because the primordial soma is the primary motivational and energy source for what takes place in the secondary processes of human life, if early events in the life of the child either cut off the needed satisfactions of the inner soma or if they create secondary conscious structures which cut off these needed satisfactions, then the human being as a whole will be sick, unhappy and ill-adapted to the contingencies of his human environment. Weening at three months of age would be a clear example of "cutting off the needed satisfactions of the inner soma." Allowing the child dimly to understand that his beloved mother was someone who, like him, once had a penis but had somehow had it removed so that she bled from the crotch—this would be a clear example of "creating secondary conscious structures which cut off these needed inner satisfactions." Once the somatic channels for the satisfactions of the primordial human core become blocked, twisted or diverted, then the manner in which the inner energies of the human flow out and express themselves in conscious, active behavior will be deviated, inefficient and will be continually *felt* within the human *as actual organic tension,* anxiety and unhappiness. In its simplest statement, this is the psychopathology of Freud. The question as to the many *ways* in which this somatic blockage between the inner core and the outer layer may take place—this is part of the labyrinth of Freudian research. And the various *developmental stages* during which this unhealthy blockage or deviation can take place are also part of the maze of Freud's explorations, which were the ever shifting, never final theories and insights which can confuse even the canniest of readers who might venture to put all of Freud's insights together in one neat package.

The enormous legacy of Freud's writings for the late twentieth century is not his technique of psychoanalysis, but his evolutionary somatic vision of the human creature. Freud's technique in psychotherapy seems now like an early horse-and-buggy attempt to relieve emotional illnesses—the therapy was far too long, too limited in its applications and too often attended by relapses. But the enduring Freudian legacy is the complex somatic understanding which he brought to our understanding of the nature and development of human health and illness—not "psychic" health and illness, but simply human health and illness; not "psychosomatic" either, but simply somatic human health and illness. It isn't that medicine is not somatic, but rather that it is hardly somatic enough: it has not yet had the courage to develop a comprehensive science of man which understands how the evolved human soma can develop healthily and unhealthily in exchange with all aspects of its environment, both with the *actual* physical and human factors as well as with what the patient *believes* are the actual physical and human factors. All insightful physicians must suspect or know that such a comprehensive medicine is not only possible but is just over the horizon, waiting for men of unexpectedly broad knowledge to appear (and such are particularly lacking in American medicine) as well as for men of great courage and fortitude (inasmuch as the traditions of Western medicine are deeply a part of the cultural tradition which now stands challenged and will battle with force and epithets any revolution in medical science).

I am aware that many younger physicians, especially in Europe, suspect and anticipate this transformation. They know that men still die "from broken hearts" and from "fried eels in fresh butter," i.e., from very actual human interactions as well from very non-actual but "believed in" physical interactions. Only a somatological medicine can comprehend these events within a context which will include the copious data we already possess of some of the structures and processes of the human organism.

Ultimately, it is not more data that is wanting; it is a comprehensive medicine that is wanted, and such a comprehensive program will mean that we can live in a society where medicine means preventive, constructive medicine before birth and from birth onward, rather than the current absurd system of terminal medicine where the enormous energies and monies of medicine are primarily focused on what to do to cure or save the already-ill human being. This kind of a revolution entails an upheaval in the structure of medical schools, of the profession and of the traditional role of the physician; and it will come about at

the same pace that the evolution-revolution in late twentieth-century society gradually takes place. Within such a
society and with such a medicine, we shall then find out
whether it is, indeed, necessary or inevitable that human
beings should ever become ill. For we must ask, why
should they? If Freud is correct in surmising that the
healthily born human soma should not be itself the cause
of illness; if I am correct in surmising that technological
control and manipulation of our physical environment will
eradicate physical, chemical and biological causes of illness; and if I am finally correct in surmising that the evolutionary-revolutionary changes currently at work will
possibly mean that social, economic and political structures will no longer be the strange "psychological" causes
of illness; if these three things—these three not impossible
conditions—then we shall finally know whether human
beings must inevitably become ill (in any somatic sense) or
whether illness and the business of patching it up too late
have merely been the unhappy consequences of an ancient
human culture that is mutating out of existence. This is
just one of the many questions which men of the twenty-
first century will enjoy finding the answer to. And if the
answer is yes, then it seems only likely that they shall inevitably ask, "Then, is it inevitable that men must die?"

That such "dreams" are very real possibilities, which
men can and are already thinking of and planning for, has
been made possible in large measure by Sigmund Freud: it
was he who radically transformed our understanding of
the human soma and, consequently, it is he who opened
the door to radically new possibilities in all branches of
human medicine. From the point of view of our moribund
culture, the twenty-first century is the century when anything is possible, not simply the things we do not dare to
dream of but the many more things which we are not even

able to dream of. Even dreaming itself may radically change—and about that, Freud would be profoundly happy. He would have been delighted to know that, during the generations which followed him, men finally either ceased to dream or, better, that they only dreamed the sweet and wish-fulfilling dreams of infants: for this would mean that men had learned to grow to adulthood without ceasing to be the sinless, honest and anciently wise infants which we were from our beginning and within our hearts.

Freud taught us that we are much more than that aggressive, fractional part of ourselves which is the conscious mind. He was absolutely right: we are much, much more. And we now *know* we are much more, because we are now *becoming* much more: we are becoming the full and splendid somas which heretofore have lain repressed and waiting in the warm body of our dreams.

3

THE BIOLOGY OF BEHAVING:
LORENZ AND THE ETHOLOGISTS

In the district of Altenberg, whose inviting flats and crevices straddle the turbulent Danube and drink in its annual flood waters, there is an unexpected wilderness in the heart of old Europe. The backwaters, marshes, scrub brush and willow forests stretch away from the broad, undisciplined river, gradually changing into rolling hills and quiet vineyards where an occasional medieval *Schloss* stands gloomily picturesque on its summit.

If you were to fly over this isolated wilderness in the middle of Lower Austria, you would likely think it an excellent spot for a naturalist to pursue his studies. And if, one Whitsunday, when the field grass was young-green and tall under the spring sunshine, you had looked out into one of the fenced-in meadows of this district you would have seen a spectacle that was not only mystifying but might, perhaps, have been a little disturbing. Out in the field was a large, portly man with a full beard, squatting down in the grass and waddling along, making a large figure eight pathway and mummering, "Quahg, gegegegeg! Quahg, gegegegeg!"

One of two things: either a madman or—something closely akin—a somatic scientist. In this case, it was the latter. The portly, bearded waddler and quacker was the ethologist, Konrad Lorenz, and what you could not see hidden there in the meadow grass was a crowd of recently hatched mallard ducklings who were eagerly and anxiously keeping up with the ethologist as he waddled and dragged himself around in the field, speaking to them in the ancient and not unlovely language of mallardese. And if you had also realized that the ducklings thought that the waddling man was their mother, and worst of all, that the waddling man himself thought that he was their mother, then you might have felt that there was no choice between madman and somatic scientist: that both were quite the same.

Konrad Lorenz was engaging in a laboratory demonstration—or, if you will, a field study. And he was in the process of confirming something most remarkable. He had known that some geese and ducks, when initially hatched, would "imprint" upon the first moving object they saw and immediately adopt that person or thing as their parent. Lorenz had already, through the years, been "mother" to countless geese and ducks, but he had also noticed that mallard ducklings, when first hatched, would not "imprint" upon him but, instead, would run away and cower in a corner. What were the factors that allowed some geese and ducks to imprint at first sight and yet prevented the mallards from so doing? At one point Lorenz had set a domesticated farmyard duck (which looks quite different from the mallard) on some mallard eggs; when the eggs hatched, the mallard ducklings immediately imprinted on the common duck and scurried after her, despite the obvious differences in both the color and shape of their "mother."

What was the missing factor? Or what charm was it that the farmyard duck had that Lorenz, in this case, didn't have? Lorenz hypothesized that it was the call note made by the duck. He knew that the domesticated duck had been descended from the wild mallard and that although its physical appearance had gradually become markedly different from its progenitor, the particular mallard quacking sound had not been modified. So he practiced mallardese and waited for the next brood of mallard ducklings. And when they hatched, he was there, patiently waiting; and he mummured the call note of the mallard, "Quahg, gegegegeg!" And yes, the little mallards immediately came to their "mother."

Lorenz had thereby added one more fascinating discovery to the fascinating science of ethology. He had found that some geese and ducks imprint visually on the immediately found "mother" and that the mallards imprint aurally. At the moment of their birth they already "know" the sound of the mallard mother: this is the sound they want, and no other sound will release this fixed pattern of imprinting behavior. When we saw him out in the field, Lorenz was engaged in confirming this secret of mallard imprinting by varying his height as a visual object and by testing the effect of stopping the quacking sound. Unfortunately for Lorenz, he discovered that if he stood to his full height, the ducklings visually "lost" him and stretched out their necks anxiously while weeping out their distress call. And doubly unfortunately, the ducklings also felt "lost" from their "mother" if the quacking did not continue as an uninterrupted sound. And thus, the Austrian ethologist waddling in the grass and quacking unceasingly.

Konrad Lorenz is not the first of the ethologists and most certainly will not be the last; but he stands as the spokesman for this science, which he calls "the biology of behavior." Scores of other ethologists have patiently gathered exciting and momentous data as significant as that discovered by Lorenz, but it is Lorenz who, appropriate to his special importance, has constantly synthesized his and others' research into general theoretical statements that have been coherent, consistent and lucidly expressed. Moreover, Lorenz's role as the spokesman for ethology is buttressed by the fact that, in his writings, he has always been generous in including all other ethologists—even his detractors—as fellow scientists in a common task. In the same way that Darwin, because of his synthesis of theory with an extraordinary range of data, is considered the father of natural selection and evolutionary science (even though Alfred Russel Wallace and others should share equal credit for its "discovery"), so will Konrad Lorenz for similar reasons be thought of as the father of ethology.

The science of ethology is, in a fairly exact sense, the missing link between the Darwinian science of evolved species-types and the Freudian science of the neurophysiological development of the human organism; as the science of comparative animal behavior and its innate, fixed motor patterns, ethology links the neurophysiological insights of Freud concerning the human species of animals with the evolutionary insights of Darwin concerning the origin of the bodily structures of all species of animals, including man. Put in somewhat different terms, the discovery and confirmation by ethologists that all species of animals not only inherit fixed bodily structures particular to their species but also inherit fixed motor patterns of behavior that are particular to their species—these discoveries constitute a direct linkage between the fixed neurophysiological events which Freud saw within the human soma and the fixed patterns of bodily structure which Darwin saw to have evolved into the different species of the animal kingdom.

We have already seen an example of behavior which is an "innate fixed motor pattern," a pattern which is obviously made possible by a particular coordination of neurophysiological components inherited by all the members of a certain species. The mallard ducklings did not "learn" the sound of the mallard call note; rather, the call note heard by the neonate ducklings released an inherited pattern of behavior which had been genetically coded into the specific neurophysiological structures of each mallard: the innate, fixed motor pattern of imprinting upon the first and nearest body which emits the mallard call note.

The ducklings did not have to be taught this behavior—behavior of such obvious survival value, inasmuch as baby mallards in their natural habitat would imprint upon the nesting mother duck and follow under her protective wing; they did not need to be taught, inasmuch as they had *already* been "taught" through myriads of generations of mallards who had survived early life via this form of behavior. The ducklings will vigorously fight their way out of their shells and then lie forlorn and dripping with their heads down, waiting; but when the little messes of feathers hear the marvelous, ancient sound "Quahg, gegegegeg!" they raise their heads, stretch their small wet necks and stutter out an answering call: their first act is to greet the world that has in it such beautiful and familiar sounds.

They did not learn these things, so essential to their survival, any more than the human neonate learns to take the nipple of his mother's breast into his mouth, position it in just the correct manner and then proceed, on the very first try, to suck the milk which (he was not taught) was there and to successfully manage to coordinate the complex and mutually interfering actions of swallowing and breathing so that he does not choke. All this on the first try appears to be highly "intelligent" behavior for the survival of an infant who has not yet learned anything of his environing world. But such programmed, fixed behavioral patterns are the common coin of all animals, inasmuch as the anatomy and neurophysiology of all species of animals have, through natural selection, been increasingly adapted to their common environment through skeins of generations.

The reason that ethology is so startling, particularly on the American scene, is that it is concerned with the comparative study of animal behavior in its fixed patterns and is thus concerned with many types of animals. The more different types of animal behavior studied—especially among the vertebrates—and the more similarities and differences discovered in these species-specific forms of behavior, the more enlightening this is for our understanding of why the animal, man, behaves as he does and in what ways he can honestly be said to differ from other animals.

This is startling to Americans because their behavioral psychologists have been telling them that they already knew more or less the basic truth about animal behavior long ago. The truth, which was discovered around 1920, was the amazing revelation that the Norwegian rat was the king of the beasts. When one remembers that there are in the animal kingdom approximately 1.25 million different species, then one can only marvel at the thought processes which led psychologists of the United States to this conclusion. It is perhaps unkind to suggest that they all suddenly decided that, "When you've seen one animal, you've seen them all," and so proceeded to choose the most easily bred and easily handled vertebrates around. It is perhaps also unkind to suggest that in some *a priori* or semireligious fashion they already anticipated everything about comparative animal behavior and could therefore concentrate their experimentation on rats for the purpose of answering other questions. Yet both suggestions are, by and large, the unkind truth. American psychology has typically been the most tenacious defender of its activities as a "Science," and this is so for the very important reason that as an establishment it has not been a research science so much as a doctrinaire technology. The "doctrines," which spared them the effort of basic scientific thought, was the nineteenth-century doctrine of positivism and that of behaviorism. The "technology" to which they gave themselves was not the business of understanding animal behavior but, instead, of finding out what the animal could do and under what conditions it could or could not do it; by extension this meant that their research information was technologically important for finding and pinpointing the conditions under which man or any other animal could be expected to perform or not to perform certain actions.

In brief, what Americans term "psychology" has achieved its spectacular growth and support from government and industry for the very good reason that the information it supplies can be used for the engineering of human beings for whatever purposes government and industry might have in mind. In their own terms, our psychologists are concerned with "the control and manipulation of behavior." Precisely so; and the research done upon human beings is sold to the establishments in our society so that they will be able to control and manipulate human behavior, engineer human thinking and, in general, exploit every human blind spot.

I am acutely aware that this kind of lucrative exploitation is not the case with all psychologists, particularly educational psychologists; it is simply generally the case. Many are the men who, since the 1920's, have struggled against and decried this runaway trend of moving away from the patient, nondoctrinaire business of *scientia* (knowing) and toward the very different business of *ingenium* (automata which do something) and *techne* (the art of doing it): but they have decried this only to become professionally ignored or ostracized.

I am also aware that among contemporary behavioral scientists a movement is rapidly growing to revolutionize the psychological establishment. Humanistic psychologists such as Abraham Maslow and Sidney Jourard understand only too well the anti-human exploitation which human engineering represents; and thus Jourard invites the new generations of psychologists to engage in a mature psychology that is not only *of* man but *for* man also. Or neo-Marxist political thinkers such as Herbert Marcuse or the much younger man, Kenneth Megill, both point out that the use of research in universities, industries and government for the exploitation of men is clearly the result of socio-economic structures that are part and parcel of a dying cultural tradition; and they, as neo-Marxists, see these traditional establishments as just as obvious in the Soviet bloc as in the capitalistic bloc of nations. A proportion of the younger generations within all of these technologically advanced nations lucidly see the nature of propaganda, thought control and the engineering of human learning and motivation by governments and industries *against* the individual interests of the populace which they falsely claim to represent and serve.

In its broadest terms, this is that so-called establishment and its blindly habitual traditions which are now coming under fire from the proto-mutants of both the Eastern and Western technological nations. And the salvos against such "establishments" are only in their early, groping maneuvers. The evolution-revolution within the achieved technological societies has not yet even turned the corner. The constantly growing and changing communities of rebels have a very simple perception of their society: they see that the aggressive technological accomplishments of men need not, at this point, be used against men but can more practicably be used *for* all men within such a society, inasmuch as this very technology has not only subdued the environment but has released sufficient energy so that all individuals can themselves be released to greater freedom of thought and behavior within a society of greater democracy and individual control.

In sum, inasmuch as the fundamental drive behind technology has been to subdue and control the non-human environment for the protection and greater good of humans, then there is no practical reason for now using this human technology to subdue and control the human needs which it was designed to serve. The adjustment to this simple truism has been the major political adjustment of the twentieth-century technological nations during their futile wars.

This expanding series of observations which led suddenly from considerations of American psychology to broad remarks about the political life of our century is a typical progression in thought for those who think in evolutionary-revolutionary terms; and I shall bridle myself to protect the reader from such telescopings, at least until Section Three of this primer in somatic thinking. Such expansions are typical for this reason: those who begin to think in terms of the coming mutational culture, begin at the same time to see the traditional culture at a distance and as a whole, all of whose many parts clearly connect with one another to form a uniform pattern. One sees how each part connects with each other part, and one rushes to make observations concerning these connections.

The science of ethology, on the other hand, is a fresh, tonic breeze which does not draw its sources from our traditional culture; rather, it is a patient, authentic science of somatic behavior whose very methodology rests within the shifting context of mutation and evolution. The breeze is fresh, also, because it raises man to the height of authenticity by humiliating him within his forgotten and scorned family, the kingdom of animals. The study of ethology is like coming home again after a long and difficult voyage. Only among one's own kind does one know who he is.

Lorenz, like both Darwin and Freud, sees all animals as complex, evolved organisms which accrue and discharge energy in particular ways, according to their species. When an animal discharges energy in expressive or active behavior, he does so through neurophysiological channels and coordinations that are specific to his species. For decades the question has been, How is organic energy discharged in so many different ways? Are there different kinds of channels, different kinds of energy or what? On this point, Darwin had only a general mechanical theory. Freud, for his part, worried over this question throughout his life and debated with his disciples, particularly Jung, over it. At first Freud surmised that all energy was libidinal in nature; but then, toward the 1920's, he began to suspect it was more complex than this and postulated the workings of a "thanatos," which was an organization of energy that was minimally biological and more physical in nature.

But it is Lorenz and the small army of ethologists who have made most sense of this question of how organisms discharge energy in their behavior. As they see it, the four basic energy drives of organisms are flight, aggression, feeding and mating; expressed subjectively (i.e., from the point of view of the animal's experience of these drives) these four are fear, anger, hunger and lust.

For ethologists, then, it is not a question of speaking vaguely about energy drives but rather of studying what Lorenz calls the "big four," which are the four primary drives of all animals. Just as Darwin, in *The Expression of the Emotions in Man and Animals,* saw that, when a man is angry or terrified or loving, these "emotions" are physiologically "expressed" in very exact and characteristic ways in the face, shoulders, arms and entire body, so have the ethologists confirmed and clarified the workings of these fixed modes of expressive behavior in the animal kingdom.

They have noticed that each of these four drives will occasionally appear in pure expression, for example when in extreme terror and flight an animal's body will appear to be totally driven and motivated by the single drive of flight. But it is generally the case that in various kinds of behavior, the big four drives work with each other or against each other in varying combinations. These varying combinations are "secondary drives," or "ritualized drives," which constitute the varying kinds of fixed motor patterns of behavior inherited by each species of animals and which are the recognized characteristics of a species. What the ethologists have done is to confirm Darwin twice over: they have discovered that the fixed patterns of behavior of every species of animal are so exactly identified with each species that, even without looking at an animal, one can precisely identify him by knowing how he behaves in different situations.

The way in which these "secondary" combinations of the flight, aggression, feeding and mating drives are expressed is highly interesting. For example, a male stickle-back fish, grown to young adulthood, leaves the family territory and goes out to establish his own territory. His new home is centered around the "nest" which he nuzzles into the sand or muck and covers over with leaves or moss. He is settled and ready for business. Working from his centrum outward he forages for food, always coming back to his main territorial point. Frequently, other male sticklebacks, while foraging, will swim into his territory; this automatically triggers an angry flush of aggressivity, and the home defender flairs out his fins to their frightening dimensions, turns an angry pink and rushes straight at the intruder to attack and repel. The nearer the intruder is to the nest the more violent is the anger released, and such an intruder normally recognizes this violent anger and himself automatically displays the submissive signs of fear and immediately flees the other's territory.

But if the aggressing stickleback continues the pursuit and makes the error of chasing the intruder into the intruder's *own* territory, a sudden reversal takes place: the pursued stickleback stops, flushes with an angry color, erects his fins and turns on the pursuer, who just as suddenly goes pale, relaxes his stiffened fins and flees back to the haven of home.

But if two male sticklebacks of roughly equal size meet in the no man's land between their territories, this roughly balanced situation brings forth a peculiarly balanced combination of drives: in terms of both their behavior and their appearance both fish obviously want to attack each other and just as obviously want to flee one another. They are caught in a stalemate of two drives, each one counterbalancing the other. They may eventually drift away from each other, each saving face, or sometimes the energy that is built up within them will express itself in a "displacement drive," i.e., rather than either attack or flee, both fish may, surprisingly, turn vertical, swim to the bottom and begin casually nosing in the sand or muck as if they were looking for a good place for a nest. Such a displacement drive is much like two boys facing each other and ready to fight, yet each afraid to start it by landing the first blow, and so, instead, they turn their heads down and glare at the ground while nervously scuffing a foot against the turf.

However, a far more interesting combination of drives takes place when the territorial invader is not a male but a female. In all innocence a female stickleback sashays into the territory of the young bachelor stickleback. Because she is an invader, the behavior of aggression is automatically triggered in the male, and he accordingly flushes and flairs and charges the female. But because she is also a female, another drive is triggered, so that as he ferociously charges at her, his aim is slightly off; and he rushes by her with a grand and powerful push of water, so that she will indeed see just how ferocious and brave a fish he is.

So his aggression and mating drives are phylogenetically programmed to cooperate when the environmental situation is that of a female stickleback intruding into his territory. And he repeats this courtship behavior over and over.

The female stickleback for her part is undergoing a different kind of secondary drive behavior. When the very brave and manly (or fishly) male rushes at her, she shows the signs of fear: she pales before the onrusher and turns to flee; but, unsurprisingly, she does not flee very far. The male grandly rushes by her, pushing his mighty wave at her, and she in turn flees for some distance and then pauses: she may be afraid of him, but she's not *that* afraid. So she stays, waiting for another courtship charge by the fearless male, both the drives of flight and mating balancing her behavior into what is called a "coyness." Sometimes the male may chase her all over the pond, she seeming to flee for her life; but if she gets too far ahead, she always waits for him. But, on the other hand, if the female is quite large and the male small, with unimpressive fins and with an impotent wave-push, it is predictable that she will turn the aggressor. And heaven hath no fury like a woman stickleback who scorns her suitor.

These examples of secondary drives are not, of course, typical only of sticklebacks, nor only of fish, but are rather commonplace ethological phenomena which no human being can observe and study without experiencing a peculiar identification with the animals in question. And the fact that one feels this identification rests upon the fact that humans, too, are animals and, as animals, they have experienced similar secondary drive patterns. It does not take long to realize why an ethologist might be one who loves animals: it is a form of self-love. Human children, who have considerable narcissistic self-love, are forever the finest natural ethologists; without the least effort they discover themselves in cats and dogs, sheep and horses far more easily than they can in civilized adults whose identical drive patterns (or, as termed in the previous chapter, "primordial core") are hidden under the rigid controls of inhibition and repression. The more repressed a human being, the more mysterious or repulsive seems the behavior of a child. And for his part, a small child is very clear on the point that he loves his parents, but that they are not his friends as are his cat or dog or stuffed animal.

Even though the general example of stickleback territorial defense and courtship has homologies throughout many species of animals, it is the specific manner in which a particular species of animals with their own particular bodies and environment perform these fixed drive patterns

that make the substance of ethological studies. Just as
there are animal skeletons from birds to primates that are
different yet generally similar, so are some forms of secondary drives spread through hundreds of species in a different but similar way. But as in morphology, where a
duckbill platypus differs widely in body structure from a
sea urchin, so in ethology the evolved and phylogenetically
inherited behavior of an ant is strikingly different from
that of a bat.

Because they are concerned with the kinds of behavior
that are specific to each animal species, the focus of ethological study is evolutionary: it searches for those fixed
motor patterns which are genetically transmitted within
the neurophysiology of the species and is not searching for
behavior which has been learned. Throughout much of the
last few scientifically oriented centuries, the assumption of
behavioral scientists as well as philosophers has been that
animal (including human) behavior is learned through
adaptive experience in the environment. This, however, is
simply not the case: some ways of behaving are learned,
some ways of behaving are innate and most ways of behaving are a gradual accommodation of innate "blueprints" with the specific features of the animal's environment.

There can no longer be any argument about the existence of phylogenetically inherited behavior patterns. Men
and all other animals are born with them; they are part of
the storehouse of survival-value information acquired by
the somas of every species concerning their environment.
The question is simply this: if a living organism shows that
he has certain information about his environment, then
did he come into possession of this information ontogenetically (i.e., through experience after his individual birth) or
phylogenetically (i.e., through a genetic "blueprinting" of

this information within the neurophysiology of all members of his species)? And the method of answering the question is equally simple: rear the animal in total isolation from the information in question, and then test him to find out whether he does have this information even though he did not have a chance of learning it from his environment. By this method ethologists have isolated and discovered many forms of fixed behavior and encoded information which are already adapted to the particular environmental situation before any learning has taken place.

Examples of phylogenetically acquired information and behavior are almost endless. A few instances would be K. Hoffmann's discovery of a kind of computing mechanism in the starling which enables him to guide himself by deducing the points of the compass from the sun—when this same starling has not up until that time been allowed to see the sun. Another instance is the unerring surgical precision of the mantid in the manner in which it attacks or seizes its prey. Another is the invariable courtship movement of the drake which releases a specific answering behavior in only a duck of his own species. Or the flight response of the greylag goose to a silhouette of a certain size and movement against the sky. Or the "mobbing" response of geese who will attack the feared fox when he is stalking the water's edge.

More striking are the phylogenetically acquired abilities of ants to steer their course to and from their nest by taking their bearing from the sun. Or the way in which a male salticid spider, reared in total ignorance of the larger ferocious female, already "knows" whether or not she is of his same species and already "knows" exactly the kind of movements he must make in his courting dance, otherwise either mistake would see him devoured forthwith by the female; but even though environmentally unlearned, he makes neither mistake. Also, a young swift reared in obscure light where he cannot learn to focus his eyes and in a confinement where he cannot spread or beat his wings to test them, will, upon his release, be able immediately to judge distances of objects, handle all the subtle flight adjustments of air resistance, upcurrents, etc., *can* recognize and capture prey and *can* come in for a perfect landing in a perfectly suitable place.

A marvelous example of pre-programmed "blueprinting" of environment is that reported by Braemer and Schwassmann concerning the way in which certain sunfish (*Centrarchidae*) orient their travels by the sun. Sunfish are found only in the Northern Hemisphere, and they take their orientation from the motion of the sun. When reared in artificial light and then later allowed to swim in the open, they immediately know how to orient their position. But these same sunfish if taken to the Southern Hemisphere and set in water under the open sun have a reversed orientation: from their compass direction the sun "should" be moving from left to right, but in the Southern Hemisphere they are oriented so that it moves for them from right to left. Their phylogenetically acquired complex of information was for a northern hemispheric environment and not a southern one.

These and a host of other ethological studies make it manifestly clear that no animal comes into this world as an empty shell, as a *tabula rasa* waiting for experience to write its lessons on it. Indeed, no neonate animal is "new"; he is, instead, infinitely old with a continuous history as deep as biological time itself, if not deeper. Every man, every animal is born into this earthly environment already armed with a somatic wisdom encoded neurophysiologically into its living body. The particular combinations of drives that are fixed genetically within each species are the accrued residues of practical behavioral patterns which have allowed that particular species to survive and thrive in its particular kind of environment. These genetically encoded blueprints may be as specific as a mantid's or hornet's deft precision in killing a certain prey or they may be general patterns such as opto-motor responses to certain silhouettes, shapes, color spots or types of movement. Certainly all animals will also learn (i.e., adapt) with their environment; they will interact with the specific conditions they must deal with in order to survive, and this acquired experience will sharpen the effective use of their somatically-based fixed motor responses. Those who adapt best will have the best chances of survival, and these better adapted somas will multiply themselves through a progeny who will be better adapted to their environment than the progeny of those other animals who were less well adapted. And thus, all species of animals bear within them a structured past, and they are currently adapting their structures of behavior to the particular present environment and thus are also genetically transferring these past and present structures into the generations of the future who, themselves, will continue the same process. In advanced species of animals, these inherited structures are more and more "plastic," more generalized for purposes of adaptation and environmental learning. Man's unlimited ability to learn is a phylogenetic inheritance and his "plasticity" bears out the thesis that the more complex anything becomes, the less specialized it is: it becomes more generally adaptable. On this point both Ernst Cassirer and Marshall McLuhan would rush to agree with Lorenz.

Ethology, then, shows us that no creature is empty; no soma is a shell waiting to be filled with environmental information. Rather, every soma is an organized neurophysiological organism, ready to engage and interact with its environment and further sharpen and adapt its behavior. These fixed motor patterns do not wait for the environment to supply the stimulus; no animal is like a machine waiting for the world to press its buttons. Fixed motor patterns *seek* the stimulus which will release them, and if the stimulus is not there, an inner releasing mechanism will trigger the "response" without the stimulus. Domestic dogs and cats, which are overfed and do not need to hunt for their food, will nevertheless do so because inner releasing mechanisms drive them to stalk, chase, grab, bite and shake to death either real or imaginary animals. They are driven to do this, not by the primary drive of hunger but by the secondary phylogenetic drives of hunting, which, as drives, are self-releasing even without the stimulus which in ancestral dogs and cats would have triggered hunting behavior.

Lorenz had a starling, hand reared in total isolation from other birds, who had never before caught a fly nor, obviously, seen other birds do so. And also, he was quite well fed. One day Lorenz saw the little fellow, while out of his cage, gazing up at the high ceiling, head cocked and showing signs of searching for something. Then suddenly he flew up to the ceiling, pecked something off, returned to his perch, went through the motions of killing his prey, then swallowing it and finally giving the happy satisfied shudder that some birds will give after a good morsel. Lorenz fetched a stepladder and climbed up to look at the ceiling: there were no flies there. The starling performed the same act again and again, but there were never any flies. Hungry or not, the secondary drive of hunting, seizing, killing, swallowing and shuddering had to be released within the starling; the internal tension within this fixed motor pattern had built up to the point that an inner release took place, the energy and patterned movements efficiently took place even without benefit of prey. In this incident there lies a compelling lesson for psychiatry about the etiology of some human hallucinations.

Lorenz, like Freud (and also like Piaget), understands that all living bodies tend to seek an equilibrium of bodily energy, a homeostasis whereby the entire soma functions easily and efficiently at a steady state of energy flow. If this steady state of energy dispersal becomes imbalanced, then a tension arises within the animal. Freud called this tension "unpleasure." This organic tension automatically leads the organism to behave according to the pre-programmed pattern of neurophysiological events and overt behavior which are appropriate to the relief of this tension. In ordinary human terms, the animal "feels the desire or need for something and proceeds to satisfy it." In Freudian terms, the animal experiences a hypertension of energy in some area of its organism and moves to discharge this unpleasant energy accumulation so as to regain the pleasure of organic balance and repose.

Desire and satisfaction, unpleasure and pleasure, imbalance and homeostasis: these are three ways of saying the same thing and of saying them in somatic terms which cover the behavior of all creatures of the animal kingdom.

You and I are creatures of the animal kingdom. You and I are somehow driven constantly by desires that well up from within us and are not of our own "conscious" choosing. You and I are compelled to act to satisfy and satiate these desires, and we must grapple with our environment in certain ways in order to satisfy these desires in the certain ways that they require. And when they are satisfied, you and I—like all fine animals—feel repose, a happiness and peace which will last but a while. As our soma pulses its way through time and as the surrounding world changes and throws new situations and new stimuli at us, we feel new surges and moods and regroupings of tensions, and we are compelled again into action and the search for further satisfactions without end. There is no final happiness—it is always mutating—but there is no final unhappiness—it, too, is always mutating. And existence is just this ever renewed pendulum swing between the satisfactions which lull us and the pangs of need which arouse us. But with each swing of the pendulum, minute adjustments take place: we know a bit more about that gnawing dissatisfaction which moves within us and we know a bit more about the ways in which we can move and manipulate our world to bring satisfaction. At least if we are healthy somas we learn and adapt; if we are unhealthy somas we do not learn and adapt to our inner imperatives and to the world's many possibilities: the ancient gift of living becomes heavy and we can scarcely drag our way through survival.

You and I are somas, magnificent somas of an ancient and accomplished species. We bear within us infinite richness and wisdom to which we have not awakened. Ethology has taught us that our consciousness is only a fraction of our somatic being, and it is a fraction which is unfortunately unaware of the massive body of intricate wisdom out of which it has evolved. Other animals do not even have this conceptual-verbal ability of being conscious; they are undivided somas, but somas which live with the same basic drives and needs that we experience. However, these other somas—undivided as they are—handle their pendulum-like somatic cycles with much more aplomb and much less fumbling and unhappiness.

The great and much abused Nazarene, who has never ceased to be crucified by his disciples, said two things of profound ethological and somatic insight: "The Kingdom of God is within you," and "Except ye be converted, and

become as little children, ye shall not enter into the kingdom of heaven." For "God" read "soma," and for "children" read (although it is not really necessary) "animals,"
and very likely you will have a fine sermon to guide us
toward the coming century.

4

MENTAL EMBRYOLOGY:
PIAGET

Jean Piaget is an imperturbable man: he has gone his own way, doing exactly what he wanted and doing it in the way he wanted to do it. Such men are always offensive, inasmuch as the majority of men insist that things be done the way *they* have been taught slavishly to do them. And, accordingly, the psychological establishment has, over the decades, railed at the unheeding Piaget for conducting experiments which are not clear enough in their description, not controlled enough in their procedure, not precise enough in their data and not double checked in their results. Besides that, he theorizes too much—a sure sign of heresy. For the graduate student in psychology Piaget is a godsend; for they can compare their constricted little methodologies to his loose rambling procedures, and it makes them feel proud and grown-up.

But like a venerable old grizzly bear, Jean Piaget just rambles along into his fiftieth year of research, too preoccupied to notice the feists yapping at his rear flanks. The problem with Piaget is that he is a revolutionary; moreover, he is a genius in the art of observation and the discovery of human secrets—a double offense. The work of Freud suffered the same condemnation; and this similarity in their fate is no happenstance: Piaget stands with Freud as the second towering figure in the revolution of the science of man.

In general parlance, Piaget is called a developmental psychologist; in his own terms he is a "mental embryologist"—one who studies the way in which human intelligence develops and matures into its adulthood.

His work is an exact complement to the work of Freud: whereas Freud explored that 90 percent of the human iceberg of primordial processes which lay submerged, Piaget has made it his task to study the top 10 percent of the exposed iceberg which involves those later evolved "secondary processes" of consciousness and conceptual thought. Only partially concerned with human perception, he is primarily interested in the development of human intelligence, that very practical mechanism which we use to make sense of and actively control our environing world for our own survival and betterment.

Jean Piaget is a somatic scientist, and no one need be surprised that, like Darwin, Freud, and Lorenz, his concerns are biological. Some of the earliest experimental work done by Freud was the location of the sexual glands of the male eel. For his part, Piaget's earliest work was with mollusks, and even some ten years after beginning his work on mental embryology he was still publishing papers on malacology.

Born in the French section of Switzerland, Piaget received a doctoral degree in natural science in 1918 from the University of Neuchâtel when he was twenty-two. Shortly thereafter he was in Paris doing research with school children in the famous laboratories of Alfred Binet, the developer of intelligence tests. For two years, Piaget worked with children, studying their responses to varied types of test questions. But what captured the fancy of Piaget was not the ranking of children's abilities to answer these questions but, rather, their inability at certain ages to answer certain questions—simple questions which would appear obvious to a child somewhat older but which were quite baffling to a younger child. It was clear to Piaget that what the adult human being believed to be automatically "obvious" to everyone, including children, was not at all "obvious." Indeed, the ability to recognize simple "facts" about space, time, quantity, movement, velocity, and even the ability to do the most "obvious" elementary reasoning, were not natural abilities which the young human possessed from the very beginning but were achievements which the child slowly attained over a series of developing stages. By the time he was thirty, Piaget had become famous for the ingenious and eye-opening studies he had made on the manner in which children saw and understood their world. And he has continued and developed and expanded and theorized about these developmental stages ever since.

Like Darwin before him, Piaget made studies on his own children, and these early studies were fascinating discoveries. At about eight months of age his daughter, Jacqueline, would reach for and grab her toy duck when she saw it, but when it tumbled behind a fold in the blanket on her bed, she would not reach for it even though it was within reach, although out of sight. Piaget would hand her the duck, let her touch it three times and then, while she was still looking at it, let it drop again behind the fold in the blanket; Jacqueline would not reach for it, inasmuch as for her, at eight months, the toy duck ceased to exist when out of sight—it simply *wasn't!*

But the intelligence of Jacqueline develops. By ten and a half months she will look for her toy even though it goes out of sight; but still there is something curious about her searching habits. Piaget would take her toy and—while she was looking at it—place it just under the mattress of the left side of her crib. Thereupon, little Jacqueline would "intelligently" reach over and seize the hidden toy from under the left side. But then—still with her watching—he placed the toy under the right side of the mattress and waited to see what she would do. What Jacqueline did in response to this was to lean forward and reach under the *left* side of the mattress where he had first hid the toy. Over and again Piaget would make a show of hiding the toy under the right side of the mattress, but no matter how many times she saw him do this, Jacqueline still searched for the toy under the left side. Clearly, she seemed to understand that, having found it first of all under the left side the toy should always be found under the left side of the mattress, no matter where else it was hidden. And, just as clearly, the perception and intelligence of young humans is not as "obvious" as we had thought it to be.

More will be said about these eye-opening and ingenious experiments of Jean Piaget, but I think you may find it similarly interesting to know *how* the imperturbable Piaget thinks about human beings and the development of their intelligence—this top 10 percent of the human iceberg. He thinks purely somatically. Exactly as Freud did,

Piaget looks at the human being, not as a "person" but as a biological organism which has been a product of evolutionary selection and which is continuing to change, develop and adapt to its environment. In the most fundamental biological sense, Piaget realizes that he cannot allege anything about the basic nature of the human organism which he could not equally allege about all other living organisms. Like all somatic scientists, he knows that the only way we shall come to understand the human animal is to see him alongside all other members of the animal kingdom; only by this flat and clear-sighted comparison will we ever discover what is truly different in the species man as well as what is shared in common by man with all other animal species.

In going from mollusks to man, Piaget did not go from biology to what we think of as psychology; he remained a biologist. There are given biological processes that are true for all animal organisms, whether they be mollusks, men or Norwegian mice (in this equation of all animals, American psychology is on the right track); but the manner in which each given species, sharing common biological functions, develops as a species is varied within each species (it is by not recognizing this second biological fact that American psychology drifted into insularity, leaving the field of behavioral studies to ethology).

What are these "same" biological processes which human somas share with all other somas? Piaget sees them lucidly as the possession of an organic structural organization and of organic functions by which the organism—human or otherwise—actively adapts with his environment. Piaget's studies are founded on a strictly evolutionary and biological view of the human creature, and it is because of this solid grounding that his work has such far-reaching importance.

Like all other living phenomena, intelligence has a certain *organization* and it has certain *functions;* it also has a constantly changing *content,* but because this latter is fluidly developing, it is of less immediate interest to Piaget. From birth onward, the invariable function of human intelligence is to adapt to the environing world. But adaptation is a to-and-fro process of give and take between the somatic organization of the human and the environing structure of the world. The neonate human begins his business of adapting to the world with the fragile young bodily organization he has inherited, and he takes this early structure and, via the give-and-take process of adaptation, gradually changes, adjusts, grows, enlarges and enriches this early somatic organization. He gradually becomes more adept at sucking, at reaching, at grabbing and at visually locating and following objects: this is his process of adaptation to his world.

But because this business of adaptation is give and take, it is a two-way street. Sometimes the developing human must "give in" to the things in his world and *accommodate* himself to them: the baby cannot suck and bend the hard plastic ring hanging down from his crib; he must give in to it and learn (i.e., adapt to) *its* hardness and its smooth circular contours. At other times the developing human makes the things of the world "give in" to *him,* and he *assimilates* them to himself and his bodily structure: the baby molds and positions the nipple to fit *his* inherited sucking motor pattern, and once the milk or other nutrient reaches his stomach, his body's gastric juices break down the chemical structure of the food, forcing the food to give in to the needs of his bodily organization and become assimilated into it.

So, then, these are Piaget's working terms: organization and adaptation (accommodation or assimilation), and these terms not only account for the development of all living organisms, they account, as well, for the development of human intelligence. Fifty years of experimental work have filled in these developmental stages whereby the organizational structure of human intelligence grows, changes and adapts to this world by the invariable give and take of accommodation and assimilation.

The first organizational structure which the just-born infant has to work with is that of sucking: the infant can at first learn about his world only through sucking his world. And so he sucks upon nipples, fingers, sheets, blankets, pacifiers, toys, plastic rings; and he learns that some things are suckable and nourishing, other things are suckable but non-nourishing; also he learns that some things are suckable and softly yield to the orbicular comforts of his lips, gums and tongue (he assimilates them), and other things are also suckable but they are harder, unyielding and so he must accommodate his lips, gums and tongue to their stubborn shapes. What the infant is doing is learning: in accordance with his sucking organization he is adapting to various objects in his world. He is gradually classifying these things into "nourishing and non-nourishing," "soft and hard," "shaped-like-my-mouth and not-shaped-like-my-mouth." Given the minimal biological organization he had to start with, he is using it to adapt to his world; he is making sense of the world, using the only organizational medium he has to make sense of it: his inherited fixed motor pattern of sucking.

But as the body of the infant matures, new organizational structures awaken within him, and he thus has new ways of adapting to his world. He learns to touch, feel and grasp objects. These later talents of "prehension" are now tacked onto the talents of "sucking"; for example, the plastic ring dangling over the crib not only sucks in a certain non-nourishing way, but it also has a smooth, hard, resistance and it jiggles independently, jumping out of the hand sometimes. As Piaget describes it, the "schema of sucking" is now combined with the "schema of prehension" to give two coordinates, two ways for the infant to fix on objects. Then, eventually, the "schema of sight" is added, and the infant learns that the ring not only sucks a certain way and grasps a certain way but also looks a certain way: it has visual shape and specific color. The infant now has three ways of identifying objects, and his talents of identification are becoming more efficient, more practical, more adapted to his immediate world. He is, in short, becoming more intelligent.

This is the simple, biological view which Piaget and his colleagues have of the development of human intelligence. At this early, infantile stage it hardly seems to qualify as intelligence; but intelligence it is: primitive and so necessary that without this building up of more and more sensory-motor coordinates, the later conceptual and verbal intelligence of adolescence would never be possible. It is with infants as it was with Helen Keller: the vibrations of human words had no significance to her until they were linked together with all the sensory-motor talents she had already developed; but then, once they were linked, something stupendous took place: a meaningful conceptual world leapt up all around her and Helen Keller moved to possess it and love it.

Piaget and his associates at the Jean-Jacques Rousseau Institute in Geneva have, over the years, come to see the development of human intelligence spread out through three fairly distinct periods. The first is the period when sensory-motor intelligence is developed; it is this period from birth until about two years of age that we have, in part, just been discussing. The next period is that stretching from two until about eleven years, when the child begins to learn in a delightfully confusing way how to understand, judge and describe his world. By eleven, with the beginning of puberty, he goes into the last period, which is normally completed around the age of fifteen: the period of "formal operations," when the adolescent human can think efficiently not only about things he sees but can also think abstractly about things he doesn't see, or which might possibly be the case. This last period can be continued toward infinite refinements of intelligence of which Jean Piaget, still exploring in his seventies, is a prime example.

Now there is no escape from the fact that when a man of the ambitiousness of Jean Piaget is given an institute and the support of colleagues and is allowed to experiment and theorize for a period of fifty years, the resultant material is staggering. Similarly, Piaget's resultant conception of the development of human cognition and intelligence and the grand project of what he terms "Genetic Epistemology" are equally formidable and are not matters to be summed up in a nutshell. In the demanding complexity of his work, he bears still another comparison with the extraordinary Freud. In the light of this, what we have wanted to do is to give a most general outline of his methodology and his general conclusions in "developmental psychology," suggesting along the way a few examples.

There is but one further remark that should be made concerning Piaget's theory of human cognition and this is what he sees as the constant biological drive toward attainment of "equilibrium" during the ongoing development of human intelligence. Piaget has come to understand that as human intelligence develops from one stage to another, it attains these rather clearly observable stages at those times when the functions of accommodation and assimilation are in balance, when the human being reaches the happy equilibrium where he "gives in to" his environment only to the same measure that he compels the environment to "give in to" him. This is an optimum state of human balance in its constant intercourse with the environing world. And this is worth mentioning, inasmuch as Piaget's insistence that human intelligence (the top 10 percent of the somatic iceberg) strives for an equilibrium of its functions, corresponds squarely with Freud's insistence that the "primary processes" (the lower, non-conscious 90 percent of the somatic iceberg) also stubbornly seek to retain a steady homeostatic state of energy, which is the reposeful, optimal state of pleasure. Of course, when we recall that Lorenz, as well, has stated that the bodies of all animals tend to maintain homeostasis and that fixed motor patterns are triggered when there is an imbalance and tension within the animal's body—when we recall this, then we have before us an impressive triumvirate of somatic spokesmen, whose general complementarity cannot be ignored: all somas tend toward the optimal state of homeostasis, and when this is lacking, the soma is driven into adaptive activities whose function is to achieve homeostatic balance.

What Piaget has shown us—with experiments that are as fascinating as those of his brothers, the ethologists—is that what we adults believe is "obviously the case out there in the world" is not at all obviously the case; that the way in which we see and understand our world is a slow, developmental achievement, and that all of us, as children, saw and understood the world in quite different ways, surprisingly different ways. At certain stages the world *is* one way to us, at later stages it *is* another kind of world and at so-called adult stages it *is* another kind of world; so that if one asks, "What kind of world, finally, is it?" then the stunning answer comes back, "What the world out there finally *is* depends on the stage of perception and cognition which humans have attained in relation to their world." Within this reply lurks the vertiginous implication that if human beings and their cognitive structures are mutating into something new, then their known world is likewise mutating into something new. In this connotation is the final twist of somatic thinking, a wrench away from the naive "objective minded" thinking which is characteristic of our traditional culture. Piaget has, by and large, ignored the difficult-to-test business of perception and has properly concentrated on intelligent cognition, which is more amenable to laboratory procedure. The only such work dealing in a similar manner with modes of perception of "what is" is my exploratory book, *The Other Is: An Essay on Ontic Projection,* which was completed just before this present work.

I remember very clearly that when I was very young my friend, Bubba Davis, and I found an electric switch out in a field behind my house, a big metal switch—the kind with a handle that moves back and forth to cut off the main current coming into the house. The morning we found it, we sat down in the shade and proceeded to exercise our new powers: we used the switch to turn the wind off and on. Sometimes the wind was a little slow in obeying our switch, but it would finally stop, and then we would flip the lever up and wait for it to blow again. We were about five or six at the time, and our understanding of the causes of winds were typical of our age.

Piaget has carefully investigated the developing stages of a child's understanding of causality. The first stage is magical: the wind moves because we move. The next stage is "artificialistic": God or men (or little boys with wonderful switches) make the wind and the clouds move. By about seven, there is a third stage of understanding when we know the clouds somehow move themselves, but we do not really know why—maybe the sun and the clouds work together. But by about eight, a fourth stage of understanding develops, and we have the notion that the wind must push the clouds, but at the same time we figure that the clouds carry along their own wind so that it can push them—a kind of self-causality. By about nine, most children can think of the wind as one separate thing, and the clouds as another, which are pushed by this wind. This is a simple example of the development of a young human's intelligence in respect to causality; the ages mentioned are not fixed—there is always variation—but the progression of stages *is* fixed, and the child progresses from one stage to another until he eventually reaches the "correct" adult understanding of causality.

Even more interesting is the gradual development of a human's understanding of quantity. Piaget would take a ball of clay and ask a child to make another ball exactly the same size. When the child had done it, Piaget would put one of the two balls of clay down and then flatten out the other ball into a pancake. He would ask the child if there is now just as much clay in the flat one as in the round one, and at an early age children would invariably say that there was *less* clay in the flattened piece. On the other hand, if he then takes the clay and stretches it out like a long sausage, the child will then reply that there is now *more* clay in the sausage-shaped one than in the round one. What this means is that at the early stages of our understanding of the world, we have no fixed notion of the conservation of matter. Even when the child participates in the experiment and sees everything directly before his eyes, he is unable to think of the quantity of matter as something constant.

Piaget has done the same experiment on the understanding of quantity in other ways. He shows the child a scale balance, puts two equal balls of clay on each of the trays of the scale and shows the child that they have equal weight: they are balanced. Then he takes one of the balls of clay, changes its shape and asks the child whether the scale will tip this way or that way with a sausage shape or a pancake shape; and the child will predict that the sausage-shaped clay will weigh heavier and the pancake will weigh lighter!

A third aspect of these conservation of quantity experiments has to do with constant volume. Piaget takes two identical glasses containing the same amount of water and then drops two identical balls of clay into them; the water level rises equally in the two glasses. But, again, he changes the shape of one of the pieces of clay and, again, the child predicts that the water will rise higher when the clay is sausage-shaped and will remain lower than the other glass when it is pancake-shaped.

The findings of these experiments concerning conservation of matter, weight and volume are not only that a Western European child shows gradually developing stages (equilibrium states) of understanding these three aspects of quantity, but also—most curiously—that a young human does not come to understand these three things "correctly" at the same time. He gets the idea of conservation of matter from about eight to ten years; he then understands conservation of weight at about ten to twelve; and, lastly, he is twelve or more before he catches on to the notion of conservation of volume.

In another direction, Piaget has tried to pin down the developing stages of a child's ability to think logically, and some of the results are most surprising. To see how the younger child thinks when he tries to classify different objects, Piaget would give a little fellow two red squares of plastic, two blue squares and five blue circles. Now the child would seem to have two ways of classifying these objects: (1) as red objects or blue objects (the blue objects being either circles or squares) or (2) as square objects (either red or blue) and round objects. When younger children are then asked, "Are *all* the blue objects circles?" they generally give the "correct" logical response, "No." So far so good. But then when they are asked the very "obvious" question "Are all the circles blue?" even though the only circular objects in front of them are the blue ones, they generally answer, "No, all of the circles aren't blue, because there are also squares that are blue." This example of "illogical" classification by younger humans is a splendid instance of how what a human "understands" can run counter to what he "sees" directly before him.

Similar results were obtained in Piaget's study of a child's understanding of movement, velocity, time and space. For example, with younger children, if two toy trains move from one side of the table to the other, one moving on a straight track and the other moving on a constantly curving track, they invariably understand that the two trains have covered the *same distance,* even though the train on the curved track has covered twice as much distance. For the child, it is the terminal point that is the point of comparison; what happens in between the beginning and the ending point simply cannot enter into his calculation. It is the same with a child's understanding of time: the bigger a thing is, the older it is; if one's sister of nine years is bigger than the sister who is eleven years, then the nine-year-old sister is older.

Some grand examples of how our understanding of spatial relations is not given at birth in some *a priori* fashion but is slowly acquired were obtained in experiments done in the late 1950's. Children were shown a transparent bottle filled with colored water, and they were asked to draw a picture of what the bottle and water would look like if the bottle were tilted. The younger children drew pictures of the bottles slanted and with the water level inside rigidly at right angles to the bottle, as if it were frozen. Or a string with a weight on it was hung from the top of the bottle; the child was asked to draw a picture of how the weighted string inside would hang if the bottle were tilted. Again, the children would show the string slanting along with the tilted bottle, as if they could not correlate their understanding of gravity with that of space. Another good instance of this was when the children were given the soft plastic model of a mountain and asked to take some sticks and poke them in, so that they were good and straight: the younger children carefully placed each stick at right angles to each spot on the mountain—only the sticks at the very top were vertical.

The experimental examples of the development of these various aspects of human intelligence are seemingly endless; they are spread out through more than twenty-five books and more than one hundred fifty articles published over the years by Piaget and his resourceful colleagues in Geneva. Some are as simple as placing two sticks of identical length side by side and asking a child of about six years if they are of the same length. He will say yes. Then the top of one stick is moved slightly aside and ahead of the other, and the child is asked the same question. Now he says that the stick that is ahead is "longer." Thereupon, the experimenter moves the other stick up so that its top edge is level with the other's top edge. Question: "Are they the same length or not?" The child's answer: "No, they're *both* longer."

Others of the experiments are more complex and involve an amazing ingenuity in the way they are devised to get at certain aspects of a growing child's understanding. But, in general, what all these experiments make unquestionably certain is that our perception and understanding of our world is not at all automatically given to us but is attained only gradually and in developmental stages which are fairly obvious to the trained observer. And Piaget has presented a convincing case for understanding this in strictly evolutionary biological terms as the way in which the human soma takes what organization it has inherited and, in the process of adaptive interplay with his environing world, slowly builds new organized abilities which at successive stages achieve a balanced, equilibriated level of accommodation and assimilation of one's environment.

As was suggested earlier, it is not only that we now know that what we call the "real world" is not necessarily "out there" in the final manner that we understand it to be, but also that this "real world" that we cognize is the product of the development of perception and intelligence.

But what are the limits to the development of human perception and understanding? If we recognize that, at this exact moment, you and I and our race are still involved in the mutation and evolution of our somatic beings, an evolution which has brought us to where we are and is continuing to take us beyond this—when we recognize this, then we are compelled to recognize that these organized structures of perception and understanding studied by Piaget are not fixed and final; they are mutable. And, as mutating somatic structures, we have been perceiving and understanding a slightly different world with each successive generation of humans.

And if we have reached a moment in our history when the achievement of a radically new environment compels us into radically accelerated mutation, then without question there looms before us in the near future a radically different world. The extraordinary conclusion appears to be that it is not only human biology which undergoes evolutionary mutation but—and this is what Piaget's monumental work forces us to accept—also this "real physical world" in which we live is, thereby, undergoing an evolutionary mutation. Because the organic world evolves, the inorganic world evolves step by step with it. A strange conclusion: not only is there a new man on the horizon but he brings with him a new world.

Such conclusions are only reached by somatic thinking and can only be fully accepted within the shifting, evolving nature of somatic thought. Without the trail-blazing work of Jean Piaget, we should find it far more difficult to think in this fashion, and it would be enormously more difficult to understand what is happening to us within the technological societies of the earth. For my own part, I can only feel grateful for the imperturbability of Piaget and that he never looked back at the yapping feists of the old, dying forest through which he was passing as he rambled patiently toward a different and a greener environment.

5

ON REMOVING YOUR
MUSCULAR ARMOR: REICH

For those in the profession of psychiatry, the reading of Wilhelm Reich is similar to the reading of *Fanny Hill* in a Southern Baptist women's college: it is done under the dark of the moon and with fascination, but when the light of day comes it is not proper to speak of this fascination with one's peers. This comparison of Reich's books with pornography is not at all inapt, since it is generally the case that anything which excites a human simultaneously with both delicious thrills and fearful shame is something as vitally important for his own life as it is equally important not to mention to others.

The whole machinery of social morality and repression has always been a most practical device for the protection of the human community against real dangers which were very much to be feared. But if a society succeeds in conquering the dangers it faces, then there is nothing any longer to be feared, and thus the repressive rules cease to be relevant—first of all to the rising generation, inasmuch as they have not known the real fear of the real dangers felt by their elders. For the younger members of a mutating society, not haunted by the nest of memories embedded within their cultural tradition, there is no danger to be seen or feared and, therefore, no practical relevance of certain moral codes for their behavior.

This is to say that behind every specific moral restriction in the history of mankind, there was originally an eminent danger to feared and guarded against; and to the measure that each such danger is eliminated, each such behavioral code is rendered irrelevant to those who have never known the danger. Hence, when ease of movement, communication and location is achieved, along with contraceptive pills and the affluence to employ these technological boons, then not only is traditional Western sexual morality about to mutate out of our society but so is its prime product, pornography. Who needs the moral code when the dangers are vanquished? And who needs pornographic substitutes when one can have the real experience without the danger?

Now Wilhelm Reich seems to have been read by the dark of the moon for two very good reasons, both of them, indeed, grand reasons: for one thing, he was radically "unprofessional" in his research and theorizing (compliment no. 1), and, for another thing, he insisted even more pointedly than Freud on the prime importance for humans of genital sexuality and orgasm.

The "unprofessional" aspect of Reich's work and theorizing is his marvelously reckless ambition, not simply to unriddle the human soma, but to unriddle the universe, which he came to see as an ocean of cosmic energy. It is surely an impossibility to become a Renaissance Man of Science in the twentieth century, and it is pushing the matter a bit to try to become this with almost no assistance and with relatively unsophisticated laboratory equipment. But the marvelous Reich was not one to bridle at the mere barrier of impossibility; given what he had already discovered in the somatic sciences, he felt it would be foolish not to break out of the enclosed world of somas and see if he couldn't do equally as well with all of the physical sciences. And, given the limitations under which he worked, there is no question that he gave it a damned good try. No adventurous man of science can read of Reich's experiments and his theories about orgone energy and its functions without being alternately appalled and exhilarated with what sometimes appears wild nonsense and what at other times just might wildly be true. But psychiatrists and psychotherapists familiar with Freud know and understand (and, I trust, forgive) Reich for doing what his older colleague, Freud, was doing after the 1920's: they both were attempting to see *through* the structure of organic matter into the supporting structure of inorganic matter in order to see the common secret of each. A colossal ambition—but, then, why not? for any man of supreme confidence in his abilities.

I shall say no more of this aspect of Reich's work. You yourself can read these later soarings of Reich and decide whether he became, finally, Leonardo da Vinci or Don Quixote—in either case, a grand and unforgettable reacher for stars who shows us just how paltry it is for any man to be afraid of attempting the impossible.

But it is the earlier, somatic work of Wilhelm Reich that I wish to speak of here; and it is this revelatory work that extended, pinpointed and, if you will, *somaticized* the insights of Freud considerably beyond that great master's initial discoveries.

Like Sigmund Freud and the other somatic scientists, Reich saw the human being as an organism, basically like all other living organisms, whose bodily structure and neurophysiological organization had evolved in practical adaptation to an earthly environmennt over aeons of organic history. Also, like Freud, he understood that the energy source of the human soma came from within the primordial, central somatic organization of humans (i.e., the unconscious primary processes). Finally, like Freud, he understood that when a human soma was functionally unhealthy (neurotic or psychotic), the functional reason for this was some blockage or deviation of these primary energy patterns from their normal channels of efficient, easy flow outward into practical behavior within one's environment.

The somatic discoveries which Reich added to these basic Freudian insights were centered in Reich's findings about "muscular armor" in human beings. And the importance of the discovery of muscular armoring is that it took Freud's rather general notions of the operations of "repression" (or, as earlier termed, "resistance") and saw these crucial human events to be observable, accountable events within the body of any human being.

After Freud, psychoanalysts knew that the blockages which had taken place in neurotic patients were some kind of neurophysiological event, but this "repression" was not a clearly locatable happening in the human soma; it was vaguely "in there," somehow operating. And the hanging question was obviously, What is happening within the human organism when repression takes place? And it was Wilhelm Reich who supplied the surprising answer: the manner in which human beings repress themselves is through muscular contraction, and when this muscular contraction continues for a long period in a human's life, it becomes habitual and gradually passes under the control of the autonomic nervous system. And, once these muscular contractions pass into the control of the autonomic nervous system, they become spastic, i.e., they remain in a constant state of contraction, and the person himself is quite unconscious of this spastic condition, inasmuch as he is not at all "aware" of exerting any effort in contracting the muscles in question—the autonomic nervous system does this work for him, "unconsciously," just as it also does the work of pumping his blood, digesting his food, triggering his breathing and a thousand other functions.

What is obvious is always the last thing to be noticed, whether by detectives or scientists. And how obvious it was that the agencies within the human body for repressing, holding back and controlling energy flow were the interlaced bands of muscle which surround and bind together our bodies from the crown of our heads to our toes. Darwin himself had laid the answer out for later somatic scientists to use: he knew that the way in which the nervous energy of human emotions *expressed* itself in outward behavior was obviously through complex muscular movements. An emotion was, indeed, a "motion outward" of nervous energy triggering the release of various innate neuromuscular patterns. Without realizing the full import of it, Darwin even described the operation of muscular repression when he pointed out that people who disapprove of another person (say, a mother piqued with her naughty child) will sometimes be so charmed by the disapproved person that they will be on the verge of smiling; but then when they *remember* that they are *supposed to look disapproving*, they fight the automatic inner urge to pull up the corner of their lips and smile by a counter muscular reaction of exaggerated pulling *down* of the lip margins into an odd kind of grimace. Think of every kid you have seen in school in the desk next to you who has suddenly thought of something uproariously funny, and who fights this forbidden outburst by that strange, puckered down-tug of the mouth—and you have seen the simple mechanism of repression in the human soma. Think of all the times you have done the same thing yourself: the inhibiting, counter-reacting muscular tension you felt is the feeling of the mechanism of repression: of "pressing back down" the natural response which your soma has to a situation and, because of fear, fighting it with an opposing muscular response.

It has been so obvious that once we come to recognize the obviousness of somatic behavior, we realize that we have all been seeing the results of repression all our lives (and, perhaps, feeling the results within ourselves). If that simple countering contraction of disapproval has been fighting the upwelling feeling of approval for an extended period of time, the disapproving "look" becomes spastic and permanent. For example, the many, many unfortunate American children who have been reared in a family and community environment of stern, serious disapproval of frivolity generally show the spastic results of this disapproval as an adult: one look at those hard, dry, tensed brows and cheeks and, especially, that straight, forbidding mouth, whose sides turn more deeply downward with each year, and you know the somatic results of repression. Sidney Jourard, a superb somatic psychologist and less than superb handball partner, has impiously termed this common spastic condition "Presbyterian mouth." He will permit you to substitute your own adjective.

But what Reich has made clear is that a person who has, for example, "Presbyterian mouth" does not *know* he has it; because the contraction has become spastic, he isn't aware of "consciously doing it" but believes that this is the way his mouth "naturally" is. But the unfortunate twist of contractile repression is that this spastic and, thus, unconscious constriction of his facial muscles is *felt* by him constantly as he deals with his world. Such a man feels muscular disapproval of persons and things in his world as a "natural" state of his emotional tone; it "feels natural" because *he* (the conscious, well-trained 10 percent of the somatic iceberg) isn't doing it. Quite right, this "he" isn't doing it: the autonomic processes of his soma are doing it for "him."

Facial repression (i.e., spastic counter-muscular contraction) is obvious, and that is why Darwin pounced upon it. It is so common and we have for so long taken these odd facial distortions as "just the way he (or she) happens to look" that we take any person's face as a purely *given* appearance and not also as an *achievement.* As Albert Camus wryly remarked after reaching two score years: after forty, everyone is responsible for his own face. However, the timing may often be much earlier in life, and the responsibility is so frequently that of the environing family or community environment. I have seen the faces of far too many preadolescent children whose visages look like the early moldings of a Greek tragic mask.

But this obvious—and, usually, less serious—symptom of repression through the face is a phenomenon which allows even those most in ignorance of somatic science and the psychoanalytical tradition to understand what repression is—and, perhaps, to realize that they have always *sensed* exactly this in looking at others without "being conscious" of it through words such as these. Darwin opened up the possibility for seeing the obvious, Freud created a way of understanding this common human event, and the ethologists and Wilhelm Reich brought it to life and made it self-evident to us through their confirmations of neuromuscular expression and repression in animals and men. And the tough-minded, successful and wealthy businessman you saw yesterday getting out of the taxi did not necessarily come equipped with that pugnaciously thrust lower jaw and those hard, aggressively "manly" jaw muscles which look like cables; perhaps he is a little boy who felt so stricken at the loss or lack of something in his childhood that the only manner in which he could keep from crying and could counter those muscular feelings of defeat and surrender was to fight them with the counter-contractions that make him appear and feel angry and aggressive. Some little boys have to fight tears for so long that the benign autonomic process takes over for them and they don't need to *try* to fight disappointment with the cover of anger. And, of course, the "manly" facial expression is only a minor somatic symptom of the disappointed infant's constrictions. Within other regions of his body, the short, light breathing and gently accelerated heartbeat move him resolutely toward his coronary next year, and the angry gastric acids are already rampant and will ruin his dinner tonight and the muscular strain around his anus is bulging forth the hemorrhoids which have begun to bother him. In such ways, an American nation or a Western culture can produce so many disappointed infants that the subsequent swarms of suffering and unhealthy aggressive business leaders create the deadly myth of "American manliness," as they rush blindly toward early death with their eyes steely, their jaws taut, their shoulders wrenched back and their thoracic and pelvic cavities uptight with the muscular contractions of repression.

Wilhelm Reich did not discover these bodily devices of repression and leave it at that; he isolated the areas of the body where these counter-reactions had their effective domain. He saw the human body as a soma which had evolved into seven segments of muscular bands: the pelvic, abdominal, diaphragmatic, thoracic, cervical, mouth and eye segments, in each of which the complex of musculature had developed to dilate or contract in various combinations according to the energy movements within that segment. These segments do, of course, overlap and work together; and, taken together from crotch to crown, they constitute for Reich the central body of a human being. Arms and legs are secondary appendages evolved for the grasping and locomotive needs of the central soma.

So erase from your thoughts the image of a human being with arms and legs; visualize that long, rounded bodily shape, extended along a vertebral column which extends its lines of communication to internal organs, various senses and bands of musculature and unites these functions all along its length as well as through the complex relay and stimulus centrum of the brain stem. Or visualize, if it seems simpler, an amoeba, a paramecium or—better still—a segmented worm, and you have the simple, thoroughly biological vision which Reich had of the human creature. In fine, visualize an *organism,* just as Freud did—an organism, whose structure and pre-programmed functions testify to an immense history of somatic adaptation to the demands of the world's environment.

Thus, the soma "man": fundamentally similar to all other animal somas but specifically different in the adaptations made by his species. This soma, now grown tall and complex with its many refinements and its reaching arms and moving legs, must be seen *first of all,* insists Reich, as an organism: Reich, like Freud, was clearly focusing upon the primordial "primary processes" at the origin and core of man's evolutionary history as an organism.

Place some particle of food near an amoeba, and this one-celled organism moves toward it, then opens itself around it expansively and engulfs it. But place the point of a needle against this amoeba and its surface contracts, retreating inward, away from the danger which has appeared within its environment. Man, at the core of his organic being, is like this one-celled organism: the primary movements of his nervous energy and of his tissues are those of *outward, dilating expansion* and *inward, constricting contraction*. Reich saw this pulse of life—the diastolic and systolic movements—as both basic "physiological" functions and basic "psychological" functions, i.e., to speak of the former was, automatically, to include the latter, inasmuch as, being a somatic scientist, Reich knew one could not make such categorical distinctions concerning somas.

The human soma is, then, an organism which has, through incalculable generations, gradually molded and grouped the tissues of its body into membrane, nerve fiber, tendon, muscle and bone as the effective avenues along which the impulses of dilation and contraction could travel in their task of moving the organism into adaptation and survival in its environment. And this evolved, complex soma, which is you and I, now exists with this same primordial pulsing rhythm coursing back and forth through the evolved organs of beating hearts, breathing diaphragms, peristaltic squeezing-and-relaxing along the alimentary canal and in myriad other far-from-obvious functions. Many of these evolved processes and structures— the primitive and essential life functions—are autonomic and are embedded within the evolutionary depths of the central nervous system. And Reich rounds out this description by indicating that the two basic and opposed systems of the autonomic nervous system—the parasympathetic (craniosacral) and the sympathetic (thoracolumbar) motor systems—are, respectively, the two primitive somatic avenues along which flow the energy movements of dilation and contraction.

With this brief outline of Reich's somatic view of man, we can drop back into the clinic of Wilhelm Reich and watch him as he treats a patient, trying to understand why he sees the patient as he does and handles him as he does. For one thing, Reich did not, unlike Freud, need a couch, because—unlike his older colleague—he came to the conclusion that *looking* at the patient was more important than *listening* to him. To look at a patient is to observe his body in expressive action, and, thus, Reich's therapy was radically somatic.

Here is a man speaking to Reich. The man is unhappy; he doesn't know how much longer he can go on this way. Everybody and everything seems to be pressing *in* on him; it is as if he were a constant prisoner: he wants to escape, but the insufferable constricting pressure of the world that he sees around him will not allow him to escape. He is helpless. He is unable to free himself from the tight confinement that binds him. He has tried this means or that, but somehow no matter what he attempts, he always ends up feeling pressed in and imprisoned by the world. Even things in his childhood which Reich had asked him to remember are not there: he searches his memory to find them, and it is as if they are off somewhere, blocked away from the effort to find them.

And Reich watches the man. The eyes seem fairly bright, even moist. The mouth area shows certain patterns of exaggerated disdain or feigned surprise or quick tight smiles. Minor symptoms that may not say very much. But, below that head which bobs about and expresses the man's thoughts, there are quieter events which have nothing to do with these words. The shoulders primly pulled downward and slightly backward into a kind of self-contained posture that looks rather stylish and "upper-class" beneath the tailored lines of his suit. Self-contained, indeed, as if he were holding something in. And, at the level of the thoracic cavity, there is more quiet testimony: as the man talks, the chest seems rigid and the folds of his shirt do not show any deep movements of the diaphragm when he breathes. The breathing is invisible—light, short little puffs of air, quick sips that do not even make the nostrils flair. The diaphragm also seems contracted, over-controlled, making the man's breathing shallow. And down farther, in the pelvic segment, there is a light backward thrust of the lower stomach into the cavity of the pelvis as the man sits with his legs crossed: muscles in the buttocks and in the lower abdomen would have to be held in tension in order to maintain that "well-bred" posture.

Having looked, Reich asks the gentleman to be silent for a moment and breathe deeply. The man uncrosses his legs and inhales then exhales for the doctor. Reich listens to the forced air of the exhalation and sees the pressure upward of the diaphragm. He places his hand on the diaphragm while the patient continues the deep breathing: on exhaling, rather than becoming loose and letting the air pressure out of the lungs, the diaphragm remains spastic—holding and controlling even the exhalation of air. The patient is asked to relax the diaphragm when he exhales. He says he will and tries to relax it completely; the diaphragm musculature remains spastic. It is not within the control of the patient but within the control of his autonomic nervous system and its sympathetic functions, as also appears to be the case with his pelvic and shoulder posture.

The doctor then makes an extraordinary "psychoanalytic" request of the patient: "Stick your finger down your throat until you think you will throw up." Reich, anticipating this possibility, had asked the gentleman not to have breakfast before his appointment. The man puts his finger down his throat, pauses and—encouraged by the doctor—puts it down as far as he can, and abruptly lurches forward with a dry heave, sucking in breath, heaving again and exhaling, gasping deeply, and heaving again. And what happens is not simply the "dry heaves," but is stronger and more prolonged: it is more clearly a convulsion—a sudden, off-and-on flooding of the spastic diaphragm with energy impulses which wrench the musculature into a knot and then dilate it outward into full expansion. The diaphragm constricts and dilates, the patient draws in and breathes out deep draughts of air, with his face flushed, his eyes bright with pupils dilated slightly, his shoulders and chest and pelvic areas restlessly moving into unexpected, experimental postures.

An extraordinary somatic transformation has suffused the patient: the man did not know what it felt like to have a relaxed diaphragm; he could not know, and so Reich had had him elicit another autonomically controlled motor action (the gag reflex) which had overridden the other autonomic event of a spastic diaphragm. And the patient sits before Reich breathing deeply and loosely, a surprised expression on his face, a new-found relaxation in his posture, and he comes forth with the statement that he has never felt quite so good. He feels different, and—oddly enough—those things which Reich had asked him about his family life were now remembered with utter clarity—indeed, he had always known them, always clearly remembered certain things that happened, but only now did they seem to flash into his grasp.

This purely fictional and—for pedagogical reasons—ca-

ricatured account of Reich's way of seeing, understanding
and treating a patient is an attempt to make dramatically
clear how somatic seeing, somatic understanding and somatic therapy may operate.

The picture which Reich draws for us of ourselves is
that of a creature whose life energies alternate between dilation and contraction of its bodily apparatus. Dilation is
a streaming outward of somatic energy that is pleasurable:
it is sensual, open and relaxed. Contraction is a tensing inward of somatic energy that is unpleasant: it is anxious,
blocked and constricted. The bodily feeling of dilation is
that of welcoming openness to the environing world; the
feeling of contraction is that of being defensively tensed
against a world which is feared. To the degree that the
human creature lives in a world of actual or only presumed dangers to be feared, he will necessarily protect
himself through the neuromotor response of contraction;
depending upon the length of time or the intensity of this
contraction, it may eventually become spastic and unconscious. This is repression, the functional genesis of neurotic and psychotic conditions. But to the degree that the
human creature lives in a world without actual or presumed dangers, then to that degree will he respond to that
environment openly and fluidly, with the outwardly-
streaming, sensual happiness of dilation.

The notion of constricted "muscular armor" is a brilliant and revelatory insight into the nature of the repressed
person and of how he can be anxious and suffering but unable to help himself by his own "voluntary" efforts. And,
through Reich's description of the various patterns of muscular armor, we gain an understanding of the multiple
ways in which the human soma fights against the kinds of
energy patterns which are evoked by feared ideas of feared
situations, whether actual or only presumed. Different pat-

terns of counter-contraction take place in varying segments of the body, according to the kind of feeling that is to be controlled and repressed. And the knowledge of these varied patterns is the stuff of practical Reichean therapy.

Reich, as has been noted, placed central emphasis on sexuality and the bodily tensions and the attainment of a relaxed, dilated and healthy somatic state. In genital sexuality the complementary male and female organs mutually stroke one another, building up and centering by their friction a mounting concentration of somatic energy, which radiates gradually outward from the genitals and the other erogenous zones until the entire body is suffused with this charged energy. At a given moment in coition, the movements of the lovers are no longer voluntary but are taken over by the orgastic reflex, which then grasps them in its somatic embrace and drives the accrued energy in convulsive movements throughout the entire musculature of the body and releases it downward and forward through the genitals. Afterward the body is totally relaxed, loose, blood vessels dilated, and heart and breathing easy and slow.

But this is the ideal orgasm, the normal orgasm programmed into the ancient, animal soma of man. Not all humans attain this full orgasm and thus a full, healthy release—very few Western men at all, Reich seems to believe. But without this central energy release of the full orgasm, he feels that humans are deprived of full health and will be automatically plagued by tension, anxiety and illness—whether to the sharp degree of neurotic anxiety or merely the fretful restlessness of the middle-class citizen who knows that something is wrong but cannot put his finger on it.

Wilhelm Reich is, without question, a bit frightening.

His willingness to risk bringing on convulsions in the emo-
tionally ill bothers many psychiatrists because no one is
sure of all that can happen when convulsions are evoked.
His strong emphasis on the necessity of the orgasm for
health seems to leave out the many ways in which a gentle
everyday sensuality may slowly expel these same energy
tensions and achieve a continuing homeostasis without
having to save up such tension uniquely for the electrify-
ing blast of the orgasm.

There is much that we do not know; but Wilhelm Reich
has shattered our timidity by building a structure from the
known out into the not-quite-known. It is a structure for
the not-quite-known which *feels* right and is waiting for
the presently rising generations to brick it in and, perhaps,
modify its structural lines. It is an uncompleted structure,
standing mockingly and offensively before the eyes of our
traditional culture: but it was not built for them; it was deliberately built for the unseen, unborn children who now
lie dreaming and waiting in the patient, ancient egg.

Once hatched, they will feel, I suspect, that Reich's somatic structure looks very much like home.

6

SUMMING IT UP:
A SUB-TOTAL

The revolutionary insights of the somatic scientists are of exactly equal importance to the revolutionary insights of the natural scientists. Both types of science go hand in hand in a complementary fashion. The natural sciences have focused on the environment of man and have moved to understand and to control it; the somatic sciences have focused on man in his environment and have moved to understand him and give him control. Both sciences have made possible man's liberation from the tyranny of the past—in one instance, the tyranny of the old earth, in the other instance, the tyranny of the old man.

Without the achievements of the natural sciences, which culminate with a technological society, there would not be the relevance of somatic science and the human transformation it promises. At the same time, without the possibility of a liberated society of men, by men and for men, opened by the somatic sciences, there would not be any final justification or human relevance for the understanding and control of man's environment by natural science. Historically, the natural sciences have created the groundwork and possibility for the liberation of the human soma within the next century.

Darwin, Freud, Lorenz, Piaget and Reich: these are not all of the somatic scientists; but they are the men whose insights have provided the essential evolutionary-revolutionary stepping-stones to an understanding of how we, as men, came to be what we are, and how we, as men, are now becoming something different from what we have been up until now. Because of their various focal points of interest, all of the many views of these five men cannot be compressed into a single picture; however, the main lines of their findings and ideas are roughly identical, and the richly complementary nature of each man's work to the other's provides a composite view of the nature of the human soma. Pending a more comprehensive summing up at the end of Part Two of this section, it will—I hope—be enough if we content ourselves with a brief sketching-out of these general findings of the somatic scientists.

At the foundation of somatic science is the insight that if we are to understand what we are as men, then we must take as much account of our environment as of men themselves. It is not a matter of focusing on either one or the other but of focusing on the constant interaction and interchange between men and their environment: whatever man is, is a common achievement of himself and his world in interchange. The millions of generations of adaptive interchange mean that man has slowly come to resemble the world as much as he resembles himself.

And, at the same time, to speak of the interchange within this dialectic is to speak of the changes and mutations that are going on now and the changes and mutations that have already gone on during the somatic history of our species. Men are the living product of an immensely long period of never-ending adaptation with their environment; and, as living products, you and I are continuing this adaptation at the present moment.

Hand-in-glove with the above two insights is the understanding that, as a living product of a history of soma-environment interchange, men are immensely ancient somas; they are complex creatures whose bodies are genetic reincarnations of the countless adaptations of their foresomas to this earthly environment. The long interchange of soma-environment is borne within each of us as a mute "unconscious memory" of how all the somas before ourselves had successfully managed to adapt and survive and to make our entrance into this environment possible. When we are born, we are born *already* in relation with our earthly world, *already* "knowing" and anticipating what it is, what it can do and what it cannot do for us. We are born into this world with a somatic pre-program of expectations, which means that we are *already* involved in interchange with this world, that we are *already* a part of this organic-like mechanism of soma-environmental interchange, that we are *already* ready for the world and do not wait for it to come *to* us. As the contemporary representatives of the species man, you and I were, from our inception, already suffused with an ancient somatic wisdom concerning this world, a wisdom which is the genetic heritage of past success, of former survival-giving adaptations; a wisdom which embodies a skein of somatic triumphs whose active but unspoken presence is a reflection mirroring the lengthy corridors of biological time.

The three insights put forth in these three paragraphs are the fundamental and interlaced insights which these men bring to their study not only of human somas but also—quite obviously—of all living creatures. At this quite fundamental level, we do not need to speak of the imagistic-verbal consciousness of man, inasmuch as man and all other living somas have survived up until their present species status without the use of consciousness: squirrels and mice and worms and elephants have the same basic adaptational abilities and wisdom as we have. Somas have "intelligently" adapted and survived for millions of years, not because they were conscious, but because they were adaptive somas. The conscious abilities of man are simply one more adaptational device developed by one species of somas in order to survive. It is not necessary for survival; it is, rather a clever means of survival. And this consciousness is in no wise completed in its evolution and adaptation but, in terms of biological history, is only beginning to develop.

And so, when the somatic scientists address themselves to the soma called man, they simply extend their fundamental understanding of all somas to the nature of this one species. And, like all other creatures, men are born into this environing world with the genetic inheritance of a specific bodily and neurophysiological structure and with a specific set of sensory-motor and neuromuscular behavior patterns. Men are also born into a human society that itself has physical structures and patterns as well as verbal structures and patterns which—rather than being a pre-program of somatic wisdom—are a pre-program of human "wisdom." The prime problem then, is to adjust one's somatic programming to an environment not only of earthly contrivance but also of human contrivance. Squirrels are fortunate: they only have to adapt to the former.

Whereas the work of Darwin was intended to show that men—and all other species—are a product of previous adaptations to their environment, the other four somatic scientists have filled in the nature of this picture with a good deal more clarity in respect to the somatic nature of men and of how their bodily energies are programmed to cope with their environment.

Freud saw the energies of man primarily channeled through the impractical mechanism of pleasure needs and secondarily channeled through the unpleasant but practical mechanism of aggressive conscious thought which focused on the environment and which could at least bring man a "delayed satisfaction."

Lorenz and the ethologists see the "big four" drives of men (and all animals) as nutrition, mating, flight and aggression.

Piaget views human adaptation as, simply, accommodation *to* the environment or assimilation *of* the environment.

Reich has a number of ways of speaking of the basic alternation between dilation and constriction, such as pleasure/anxiety, diastole/systole.

The resulting composite view of the somatic scientists is the following:

FREUD: *Pleasure* *Displeasure*
(Impractical, au- *(Practical, aggressive*
tonomic physio- *consciousness: the work*
logical process: *necessary for attaining*
the play that *delayed pleasure.)*
brings direct sen-
sual satisfaction.)

LORENZ: *Nutrition/Mating* *Flight/Aggression*
Hunger/Lust *Fear/Anger*

PIAGET:	Accommoda-tion	Assimilation
REICH:	Dilation	Constriction
	Pleasure	Anxiety
	Diastole	Systole
	Parasympathetic Nervous System	Sympathetic Nervous System
	Craniosacral System	Thorocolumbar System

This composite view of the human soma sees the dilational, pleasure-giving energy drives of hunger and lust as motor patterns which have their channeling through one division of the human central nervous system. The constricted, unpleasant energy drives of fear and aggression involve motor patterns which are channeled through a different and opposing division of the central nervous system.

It is the extraordinary similarity of their views which makes this composite picture of the soma man so striking. Working with varying concerns and various research methods, each of these men has ended by speaking of the human creature in fundamentally the same manner. All of them see man as functioning essentially according to two ancient patterns of energy drives, and whether our point of reference is psychoanalysis, comparative behavior, developmental biology, neurophysiology or simply our own subjective experiences—all points of reference confirm and support one another with an enormous variety of scientifically obtained data.

From this composite view of the somatic scientists, we see that man is not quite the mystery we take ourselves to be; that the way we are constructed and the way in which each of us functions has an underlying simplicity which is translucently displayed through the complexity of our behavior. The pulse of life, the diastole and systole of energy expressing itself outward and energy protectively constricting itself inward, is mutually confirmed in the work of these men and of all their many colleagues.

That we aggress upon things which are fearful and that the tense, constricted searching of the attentive consciousness is the practical, evolved instrument of this protective need to control a dangerous environment—these complementary insights describe a creature which has slowly developed neurophysiological structures which have allowed it to survive in an untamed, fearsome earthly environment. And it is this same systolic, fear-aggression drive of human consciousness which has adaptationally led the human race to the achievement of a technological society in which the earth has become tamed, controlled and manipulated by men.

That all men have throughout their history sought for and cherished every moment of what they have vaguely called happiness or peace is the continuing testimony of that under-drive toward open, dilational sensuality, which, rather than being a tense assimilation of things in the world, is instead a pleasurable accommodation and giving of oneself to one's world, with the relaxed, outward-pouring abandonment of all restraints and fearfulness.

During the first period in the history of mankind, the needs of adaptation to a hostile, threatening earth have made it necessary that the fear-aggression drives of assimilation and attack upon the environment should become dominant; and the neurophysiological structure and external sensing abilities of the attentive consciousness have slowly evolved to support these adaptational needs.

And, in the wake of these paramount early needs of mankind for its survival, the other and less-needed channels of the dilational drives of pleasant, relaxed accommodation *to* the world have necessarily been repressed, controlled, discouraged and held back—lest we not survive at all. One prime function of the human soma has had to take precedence over the other prime function of the soma. And the eventual, long-suffered-for consequence was the gradual creation of an environment which was benign, while simultaneously suffering an unbalanced, deviated human soma which paid the price for what we are now finally achieving.

In order to survive, we have been required to become oblivous to the other prime aspect of our being, a part of our being which became hidden, inscrutable and forbidden. One half of man had to be accused of danger—the dark, unconscious part of the soma which was viewed as the source "immorality," irrationality and corruption. It has been an extended and difficult price for the human soma to pay: to deny half of its being so the whole of it—although suffering the unwholeness of sick imbalance—could at least survive. And it is those men who suffered most and, thus, sacrificed most for the conquest of a fearsome earth—namely, those of us within the technological societies—who are also the first to be able to discover what it communally means to live in and adapt with a world around us that has been tamed and robbed of all its dangers, excepting only those which we humans have traditionally contrived: namely maiming of somas through war or maiming of the environment through pollution.

We have come to the time of our reward. At long last—after so many generations that we had come to believe that it would never end and that this sick, unbalanced life was the given and eternal life of man—at long last, we are just yawning and awakening from a protracted, restless nightmare into another kind of light. And it is a light of our *own* creation: the tamed world now reflects back to us the fierceness of our desire to survive.

And we *have* survived. That part of the battle is over. The only question now is, How, then, shall we live? The new light that now shines back at us from our environment permits us to see ourselves in a new way and also gives us the answer: We need no longer be sick; we shall now become whole and balanced, and we shall walk the earth at last like the full men we have earned the right to become.

PART II

SOMATIC PHILOSOPHERS

1

KANT, OR FIRST LESSONS IN TURNING THE WORLD INSIDE-OUT

When historians describe Immanuel Kant, they invariably depict a conservative, methodical little stay-at-home who did his duties at the University of Königsberg, then locked himself in his chambers like a recluse, except for his regular daily constitutional which was precisely at the hour of four o'clock. By doting on such details, they depict Kant as cute and cuddly; without realizing it, what they are actually attempting is to clip the wings of a great and soaring human being. Historians, like all Johnny-come-latelys in the critical professions, often find it difficult to stomach the raw presence of human greatness, and so they trim a little here, add a little there and balance things into the "proper human perspective": after all a man is, finally, like all other men, and his virtues balance out with his vices.

This is tripe. No man is like any other man, and no great man is like a clod. Kant, like his younger contemporary, Goethe, represents a milestone in human achievement; and both men stand above the bombast and drivel of German *Kultur* as two of that small group of men who have made it possible to even speak of an authentic German culture.

This "little man" ladled out to us by historians was not simply a giant, he was an audacious revolutionary. Nothing modest about Immanuel Kant: he told his contemporaries that he was creating a second "Copernican Revolution," and he did just that. "Little" Kant reached inside the grab bag of philosophy, took hold of the bottom of the sack and yanked it inside-out, spilling out many precious old relics and games and leaving us to look at the sack in an entirely different way.

The work done by Freud, Lorenz and Piaget is the confirmation, correction and fulfillment of the revolution begun by Kant late in the eighteenth century. What Kant did—guided only by his own tenacious argumentation and a passion to unriddle a seemingly insoluble puzzle about human knowledge—was to show us that what we see in our environing world is not entirely given to us through our senses; but, rather, much of what we perceive to be "out there" does not actually have its source "out there": instead, its source is within the *way* in which we naturally see and understand our sense experience. As Kant described it, sense experience gives us the raw *content* of what we see in the "world" and our very human way of experiencing this sense data gives the *form* and organization which we "see" in this world.

Before Kant's *Critique of Pure Reason,* men had believed that the natural world which greeted them as they awoke each morning was something totally outside themselves, that it was what it was whether they or anyone else looked at it. Before Kant's Copernican explosion, men believed that this separate natural world came *into* men's experience like light pouring through a camera lens into the empty darkness within; men, like cameras, only *received* the picture, and this world which all of us experienced was lock, stock and barrel a non-human product which was *given* to men, who were merely passive recipients.

And, certainly, this is the way it seems to be to all of us: it seems obvious that this world which we see is "out there," solidly and sovereignly being its independent self— whether we like it or not, whether we see it or not, whether we exist or not. This, from the beginning of time, has been the "natural" way in which we think about it, the obvious and naive manner of thinking about our experience of the world. The English, who, philosophically, have always had a vigorous interest in the obvious, summed up this naïve viewpoint in consummate fashion: Thomas Hobbes set the pace for this in the seventeenth century, and later the marvelously careful minds of John Locke and then David Hume elaborated the "natural" view of perception to its zenith. In the course of these three successive elaborations, there was no significant transformation philosophically (reflecting English cuisine, it remained bland and practical), but there was, with Hume, a significant change in attitude. In effect Hume concluded that a philosophy of meat-and-potatoes may be the only philosophy of perception, but, nonetheless, it seemed a futile and pointless way of satisfying the human appetite for truth.

Hume took the naïve view of perception and refined it to the point of boredom and skepticism, thus preparing the way for a radically new attempt to understand human perception of the world. That, despite Kant, many philosophers continued and still continue to plod the pathways of Hume is surprising testimony to the capacity which many philosophers have for issueless boredom.

So then, Hume set the stage for the Kantian revolution, a revolution in our understanding of how we perceive our world. Kant's laboriously wrought arguments were designed to show that the basic structural laws which we see in operation in our world and which we can scientifically observe, formulate and predict are not "given" to us in sense perception but are the lawful ways in which we necessarily *must* see and lawfully structure sense experience which is "given" to us. What we experience as "our world" is, then, the result of an accommodation between sensory input and the way in which human beings are innately programmed to receive and structure this input.

From our present perspective, informed as we are of somatic science—and particularly the work of Jean Piaget—what Kant pointed out now seems obvious. But there was not then—and, for the somatically uninformed, now—anything obvious about the notion that human beings are active participants in unconsciously and automatically structuring the world which "naturally seems to be out there, separate from us." The Copernicus of Königsberg wrenched our thinking into a categorically new mold: no longer could we think of our worldly environment as "the world out there apart from me"; instead, it was inescapably and undeniably "my world," a "human world." Kant took the skeptical puzzles which Hume had lucidly pointed out, and made sense of the skeptical impasse into which Hume resolutely drove English philosophy.

It all seems too perfect, this transformation: Hume terminated his philosophy in a *cul-du-sac* and Kant had only to turn the sack inside out for new light to be shed on the dark puzzles concerning human perception of the world. And Kant did this without the somatic confirmations which were to come during the twentieth century. He did it without the concept of organic evolution, according to which sensory-motor structures gradually develop within human neurophysiology and thereby guide, limit and control what we see and understand in our world. Because he philosophized without this later evidence and this later concept, many of his surmises about the *a priori* structures of human sensing and understanding were in error. Jean Piaget, for example, has made it clear that—among other things—the human apprehension of space and time is not something inherited in toto by the human child but is only gradually developed as the child actively handles and interacts with objects in his environment. It is the same with the much debated concept of causality.

But the several specific failings of Kant are as nothing in light of the revelation and revolution which he brought to our understanding of ourselves and the environing world which we experience. Before Kant there was only the *world:* sovereign, omnipotent and magnificent as it poured its light into insignificant little human cameras, so dependent and so empty inside. After Kant, the little black box was no longer empty and no longer in helpless dependency: the box was full, living and teeming with yet-to-be-explored structures, processes and possibilities. Immanuel Kant had discovered the *human soma.*

Who cannot help but smile at the justice of it: the first Copernicus took away man's belief that he and his earth were the center of all creation and left him feeling insignificant amongst the far-flung gyrations of suns and planets; the second Copernicus rescued man from the oppressive tyranny of a blind cosmos and gave him a new centrum: himself. No longer would the adventures of men's hearts be the challenge of sovereign gods beyond the cosmos or the challenge of sovereign laws within the cosmos; the new adventure of men was man.

2

KIERKEGAARD, OR HOW TO LEAD YOUR PEOPLE TO THE PROMISED LAND WITHOUT BEING ABLE TO GET THERE YOURSELF

A number of people believe that, as he grew older, Soren Kierkegaard progressively showed evidence of insanity. Amusingly enough, there is a contrary-minded number of Catholic scholars who believe that Kierkegaard progressively showed evidence of becoming converted to Roman Catholicism. It would be of great interest to me to see the two groups come together and compare their lines of reasoning.

True it is that late in his life Kierkegaard's contempt for the institutional Christian establishment of Denmark broke out in a plethora of pamphleteering attacks on

"Christendom," which seem to show a loss of restraint; but this was the case with Nietzsche as well. Both men appeared to overstep the boundaries of normalcy when they attacked—among so many other things—the Christian culture of the Western world. But if an uncompromising indictment of the Christian establishment once seemed a symptom of madness, now—a century later—an uncompromising affirmation of this same establishment would appear to be a similar sign of insanity.

But if we are to face the issue squarely, that wondrous, gray-eyed sage of Copenhagen *was* a bit insane, just as Nietzsche was clearly so during his last decade. And what is so very ironical is that the madness of both men was due to the same cause: love. Karl Jaspers has gone to great pains to diagnose Nietzsche's malady and has concluded that in the winter of 1889 when Nietzsche fell weeping upon the streets of Torino, he was stricken by paresis: the genial little venereal spirochetes had finally destroyed one of the keenest minds in human history. It was Venus who destroyed Nietzsche. But not so with Kierkegaard: he was not destroyed by love but only made to suffer; and it is in this venereal suffering of Kierkegaard that we come closest to the secret strength of this otherwise inscrutable human being.

Nietzsche—as always—had a *bon mot* for it: What doesn't destroy me, makes me stronger. Therein lies the ironical comparison of their two fates.

The similarities between the anti-Christian Nietzsche and the Christian Kierkegaard are almost incredibly numerous, and I have discussed these in an earlier work, *The Lyrical Existentialists.* Both were "abnormal" and were totally aware of it. Both were, as Nietzsche aptly phrased it, *unzeitgemässig:* they were out of step with, out of tune with their times—they knew it, accepted it, suffered it and wrote for a species of human beings who were not yet born but who they knew would soon appear. Again, using Nietzsche's expression, they were condemned to be born posthumously.

Put simply, Kierkegaard and Nietzsche were the two great proto-mutants of the nineteenth century. Both were accidents. Both lucidly knew that they were biologically condemned to be out of step with their times and could only write for the future. Kierkegaard said it over and again: he was not a normal man destined for a normal life but was an "exception." Nietzsche also said it repeatedly: he was a "free spirit" and the precursor of the "Overman." And it is because both men were proto-mutants that their extraordinary lives have remained as compellingly important as their extraordinary literary production.

Both men loved. Nietzsche would have gladly cut off an ear to have had either Cosima Wagner or Lou Salomé (I, myself, would have cut off two ears for Lou, who was one of the most fascinating women of the turn of the century). For Kierkegaard it was Regina Olsen, a delectable, utterly feminine, middle-class girl. Regina was the kind of lass all males dream of when they read pastoral idylls of lonely shepherds suddenly coming upon a docile and blushing beauty gathering flowers in a secluded dale. Kierkegaard found Regina in the narrow streets of Copenhagen; he loved her, courted her, proposed to her, was engaged to her and dropped her. Why? Because he was an "exception" to the normal life of marrying comely middle-class girls and becoming a *pater familias*.

That was the central reason. Contributing reasons were that Kierkegaard had something less than an ideal family background. It was difficult enough to have a dour father who, as an amateur theologian, worked out his brooding guilt feelings through endless religious dialogues with his son. But the difficulties were infinitely compounded when the son learned that his father's Old Testamental concerns with guilt were not simply theoretical but were practical: by a hair's breadth, Kierkegaard escaped being a bastard, and the woman who birthed him was the housemaid, and subsequently his legal mother. Such matters do not predispose any man to felicitous feelings about marriage and family. Nor, finally, did it help matters that his father had drilled into him that he was destined to die before middle age.

All of these oddities need to be mentioned so that we can understand why Kierkegaard came to understand himself as fated to be an exception to the normal life of men and to draw from this exceptionality the unique character and strength which he had as a philosopher.

For reasons, then, of his peculiar family history and of his own fated *Unzeitgemässheit,* Kierkegaard recognized that the idyll of bourgeois marriage with the nubile Regina was an impossibility for him—and yet, to the end of his days, it was this that he never ceased yearning for. And the suffering which underscored all his writings was simply this: a bachelor by choice, he was an exquisite sensualist by biological fate. And the literary consequence of this sensual celibacy was a series of stunning explorations of somatic experience from Don Juan to Christ, both of them ideal possibilities which Kierkegaard embraced within one single vision of human existence.

What I am suggesting is that Soren Kierkegaard was a proto-mutant who knew within his own body that a balanced, totally fulfilled somatic existence was possible, but that within the Christian society of the first half of the nineteenth century, his environment would not allow this possibility to be realized. And so he became a most exceptional exception by living out these possibilities in the only way possible: by an incredibly complex literary career where he became, alternately, many different persons and explored the whole gamut of somatic possibilities. All of the pseudonyms, all of the roles, all of the myriad situations and experiences played with by Kierkegaard are the rich evidence of what he had determined as his fate: to be the greatest somatic actor of all times—to play all the roles out within himself with a studied exactitude until he knew and could describe in minute detail every mood, motivation and behavioral detail of a certain personality role. That fate, family and an unfavorable environment constrained him to suffer through such an extraordinary life career is to our benefit, for not only did he play out these roles within himself but he also experienced the difficult transitions whereby one role is given up and metamorphoses into a new personality role: the dialectics of change and mutation and human development. That he experienced and studied all the somatic possibilities of man and then that he proceeded to describe them to us in such vivid detail established Soren Kierkegaard as the first humanistic psychologist in the history of man.

Or as the first existential philosopher and phenomenologist. In the 1840's and 50's, the distinction between somatic scientist and somatic philosopher was not significant. But now that we are in an historical position where we can appraise what has been developing during the past century and more, it is clear that the movements of existentialism, phenomenology and humanistic psychology can only be understood as crucial confluents of a single movement: namely, the development of somatology—as both a theoretical and a technical discipline. And, because of this clearer historical picture which we now have, we can appreciate why it is that Kierkegaard, as well as his compeer, Nietzsche, have not been classifiable as either "philosophers" or "psychologists," even though their revolutionary contributions to both these disciplines have been incalculable.

As I have suggested already, both the man Kierkegaard and his corpus of literature are complex and unique; and with the initial understanding which we have of the extraordinary and "exceptional" career he plotted for himself, I do not wish to plunge the reader into the labyrinth of Kierkegaard's literature, but rather to indicate as best I can the particular contribution which it made to somatic thought. The scores of specific works of this Danish genius are a magic theater of many, many chambers through whose varied demonstrations the reader can wander at his own pleasure. The task here is to describe as succinctly as possible what the theater itself was all about.

The theater was a theater of man: man as he lived intensely, exultantly, slovenly or tragically within an environing world which he could never escape or overcome. This was the stuff of the existential dramas re-enacted for us by Kierkegaard, complete with next morning's critical reviews and comments. The plays and the characters were both happy and unhappy; the total repertory was finally neither comedic nor tragic. Rather, it was existential: the way it is and the way it can be for human beings. And all human beings were seen by this consummate dramaturgist as caught within a man-environmental dialectic where the relentless and remorseless tug of time twisted, transmuted and remolded this dialectic into first this transfiguration and then another, with sometimes most of the action taking place in the environment and at other times the action centering in the human soma. Nothing really new, said Kierkegaard about his dramas: just the old story of man, told once again and perhaps in a more heartfelt way.

Soren Kierkegaard's modesty was patently false: it was

not only perhaps a better telling of the old story of man but a unique telling, inasmuch as he saw in these dialectical dramas something other than a ceaseless tug-of-war between ourselves and our world: he espied a hidden, crucial theme which had to do with a subtle kind of sickness and health which no one had ever noted in the drama of human life.

As a brief theatrical comparison, it should be noted that there was, at that time, another and most famous kind of dramatist whose concerns were with historical dramas. His name was Georg Wilhelm Hegel, the only human ever—in terms of expressive style—to succeed in dancing classical ballet while wearing clodhoppers. Hegel, also, was an extraordinary dramaturge, but he saw his human characters in much more classical terms: as largely unwitting pawns in an historical drama which controlled their movements and destiny. Like the tragic figures of Sophoclean drama or the comic figures of Molière's farces, his dramatis personae were oddly empty and helpless figures which were quite incidental to the real historical situation which swirled about them and swept them along to a *dénouement*. Hegel was all the rage.

But Kierkegaard, like his contemporary, Karl Marx, saw a blatant falsity in the way Hegel saw the drama of human history. They, neither of them, denied the central importance of an on-going historical dialectic between man and his environment, but they were perceptive enough to see that man was neither empty nor passive in this tug-of-war.

What Kierkegaard described in the human drama—and this is the hidden, crucial theme just mentioned—was that human beings had untold possibilities of growth, change and development within themselves and, moreover, that these hidden, inner possibilities could become more richly and fully realized to the extent that the individual learned to free himself from the tyranny of his environment.

The ways in which a man could live with his environment were, as described by Kierkegaard, three: a man could live in "aesthetic" (i.e., sensory) dependence upon his environment, letting the events of the world call the turns of his life; or, secondly, one could live in an "ethical" adaptation to one's environment, a stance in which one still remains dependent upon the environment but only on one's *own* terms as one judges the world and aggressively changes it to a more acceptable world; or, thirdly, one could live in a "religious" adaptation to the world, a stance in which a man no longer feels that his environment is something to be in the least anxious or fearful about. In this last stage, a human being has, by dint of gradually ceasing to be anxiously attentive to his environment, achieved the possibility of being attentive to himself. He has learned to affirm himself and, thus, to stand authentically and radically autonomous before the events of his environment. Within each of these three "stages" or "spheres of existence," there are various sub-stages and directions, but it is obvious enough that the three stages themselves are a phased movement away from sickness and imbalance toward health and balance.

Now when one encounters such terms as aesthetic, ethical and religious, when one recalls that Kierkegaard's prime concern was with Christianity, and when one realizes that most of the writers interested in Kierkegaard have seen Kierkegaard as a theologian, then one may wonder how he qualifies as a somatic thinker. But what we must realize is that the very vocabulary, culture and age within which Kierkegaard thought and wrote were the given limitations with which he had to contend in the impossibly

difficult task of describing something that no one had ever
clearly comprehended.

For anyone who, more than a century later, has famil-
iarized himself with somatic thought, it is a simple matter
of translation; and once this translation is made, one
stands amazed at what Kierkegaard was able to discover
within his own somatic laboratory.

As Kierkegaard saw it, all men are born "aesthetically"
dependent, and, thereby, all men are sick; their authentic
selves are asleep and latent, and they are controlled unwit-
tingly by the pressures of the world on their most obvious
sensory needs. But this is, by and large, what Nietzsche
also saw to be the case. And, jumping a bit farther, this is
precisely what Freud saw to be the case. And still later,
this is what Reich saw to be the state of man in the traditional environmental culture of the West. All of these somatologists are saying the same thing: that the normal run
of men in Western society are imbalanced half-men whose
anxiety over what the world and people may do or say has
caused them to repress the central core of their somatic
being.

And the stages which Kierkegaard saw as the movement
toward self-discovery were the processes by which a man
could cease to be anxious and fearful of his world and—to
that exact measure—begin to discover, feel and express
the latent, repressed aspects of one's being that had always
been there as a haunting, unconscious possibility.

What I am saying is that one must come to understand
Kierkegaard as a somatic thinker or else one cannot understand him at all. And, of course, for generations no one
understood him: at first he was unread, then he was seen
as an eccentric theologian and literary dilettante, then as
an existentialist theologian, then as a strange contributor
to psychology. But at present, through a somatic perspec-

tive, anyone can read Kierkegaard and savor the brilliance of his insights and the magnificence of his achievement.

Even the theology. Perhaps *especially* the theology may disclose to the somatic reader some of the most penetrating evidence of biological introspection. For example, Freud and Reich, in their straining reach into the living body to discover the very essence and foundation of organic life, were not the first to do so. It was, ultimately, this very pulsing heart of structured, living matter that was the God which Kierkegaard believed that one approached to as one died away from the immediacy of the environment and allowed one's consciousness to expand and embed itself within the secret core of one's somatic being. His formula for this was that the final direction and terminus of this movement away from the world and into one's self was to become one with that *power* in which one's being is transparently grounded. Whether one terms this theology or meta-biology matters not a whit; what matters is that such a statement renders testimony to a simultaneous recognition of man, his body and the ultimate reality of all existence as, essentially, one.

I believe that Kierkegaard's existential dramaturgy and its recorded Magic Theater will likely offer more for readers of the next century than even now. The present-day concern with "expansion of consciousness," "sensitivity training" and the multitudinous explorations of humanistic psychologists and neurophysiologists is only now beginning to take some shape and theoretical direction. As the new mutants in a new neo-technological society begin in earnest to relax into an exploration of the new world of their somas, they will discover paths, niches and mammoth rooms which show the footprints of an infinitely gentle and suffering Dane.

Kierkegaard died a man reviled, feared and hated by

the masses of his fellow men. This did not matter: he had forgiven them far, far in advance—he knew that they did not know what they were doing. And he forgave with a smile, not a sad smile but with the same fun-making, Olympus smile he had throughout his life. Toward those last days he was constantly ill and in pain. At a small party of intimates he was chatting away, brilliantly and wittily as always, and suddenly his thin legs gave way and he collapsed on the floor. His friends flustered about and then bent down to pick him up. Soren waved them away and said, "Oh, don't bother: the maid will sweep it up tomorrow morning."

I have saved the worst for the last. Soren Kierkegaard was not a proto-mutant; he was a mutant. He knew it, accepted it, suffered it and lived and died for those human beings who one day would be like him but would not need to suffer for it. In the end, he was more of a Christ than the Christ about whom he had written so beautifully and so despairingly.

3

MARX, OR THE COMMUNITY OF BODIES

If economics were a science, there would be no question but that Karl Marx should be ranked along with the five other somatic scientists. But economics is not a science: it is a difficult, rough-and-tumble amalgam of philosophy with its helpmates of history, mathematics, statistics and the kitchen sink. Nor was Marx himself an economist; he was a philosopher—a somatic thinker *par excellence,* who saw the business of philosophizing to be not merely speculation or analysis but basically a way of changing the world. The effective success of his point of view is, at this stage of our history, beyond argument.

The reason why economics has not been able to become a science (and will not yet become so for many more generations) is that it has been playing a catch-up game with the unheralded, uncharted technological explosion that has been mutating Western society right out of its own shoes. The economic shoes which were left sitting on the ground less than 300 years ago were heavy clogs made for the earth and bound to its tyranny. But the technological transformation that has brought man to a new evolutionary stage of human possibilities is the transformation of society *from* an economy of static wealth *to* an economy of dynamic wealth. This is to say that in less than 300 years we have come to realize that the wealth of a society is not in its possession of static extrahuman commodities such as precious stones and metals but rather that the wealth of a human society is in the ability of humans to produce and consume commodities.

Activities: the human activities of producing, consuming, producing, consuming—this was the spiral of mutually reinforcing activities which became the powerful, ever growing vortex that has swept Western civilization away from the bondage of the earth and into an open, undreamed of future in which men have become confident not of the earth but of themselves and their capacity to change their history.

Inherent in the nature of somatic evolution is, as we now know, the primary problem of survival in the face of an environment which is indifferent to human survival: for somatic science, the ancient, primary needs for survival are economic—enough food, water, warmth and protective sheltering from the world so that, at least, the existence of the species might continue. Unfortunately for man or any other soma, an indifferent and untamed earth does not "naturally" yield up *enough* of these material necessities for all to survive. The "natural" state of *man*—and all somas—in his dependency and bondage to the heedless earth is a state of scarcity, an economy of scarcity wherein only the luckiest and most adaptable will survive. This has been the environmental history of all organic life, and it has been the situation which has maintained the fear-aggression drives as foremost in the history of the species man.

For thousands of years neolithic man had distinguished himself from all other animals by his development of the basic talents of civilization; in pottery, weaving, agriculture, shelter-building, domestication of animals, and in art, he had already achieved a basic technological science. And, this being the case, why was it only a few centuries ago that man's burst into modern technological science took place? The great French anthropologist Claude Lévi-Strauss calls this the Neolithic Paradox. And he suggests (as Ernst Cassirer also does) that this extraordinary transformation, which has led us to the present watershed in the evolution of man, took place because of a transformation in men's thinking: they began to perceive themselves and their world differently and, thus, began to conceive of their situation differently. And, as Marx has suggested, new human conceptions about the human situation can become the prelude to new human actions.

The answer to the Neolithic Paradox is, undoubtedly, that by the eighteenth century, man's complex history caught up with him and began to coalesce. There is no single "cause" that we need look for: the long chain of human intellectual, artistic, political, religious and technical achievements reached a stage of fermentation and transformation in which neither man nor his environment were the same. The environing earth was no longer a feared opponent whose unexpected thrusts could, by men, only be parried; instead, the attentive eye of fear had come to see openings and patterns of weakness in the old terrestrial opponent, and suddenly an aggressive upsurge brought men into a full attack upon the ancient enemy. Men espied a brave, new world of men who need not be in fear of and in bondage to their earth. Confidence and self-affirmation were the result, and, just as abruptly, the very human sense of time and history were metamorphosed as the future opened up in its full range of possibilities. Men could, of themselves, understand and control the ancient enemy; and, with this realization, as yet untapped sources of aggressive human energy were unleashed into the world.

So then, the unriddling of the Neolithic Paradox is not a matter of pointing only to the material environment (as do so many dogmatic Marxists) or of pointing only to an emerging inner spirit of man (as do so many idealists) as the causative area of this human transformation but of comprehending both environment and man simultaneously within a single vision of soma-environmental evolution. For this event to have occurred, *everything* was necessary. This, by the way, is what Nietzsche means when he looks at all events in a cosmic manner and speaks of the "fatality" of becoming and, consequently, the "innocence of becoming."

Man and his environment shifted gears and fears, and a new energy was released, whereby men began to devise ways in which they could actively consume as much as they produced. Science and technology are the progeny of this shift in environment; and economics is the grandchild.

For the human energy of aggression to be effectively released, there had to be a philosophical understanding and apology for it, inasmuch as no human emotional expression can be directly vented if it is blocked at its periphery by moral-intellectual reservations. The energies for this technological aggression found their champion and apologist in a Scottish moral philosopher named Adam Smith.

No one need be surprised that the great apologia for the capitalistic system came from a Scot: the highlands and lake country had already been well prepared with a generous fertilization of the theology of Jean Calvin. The tough and canny Scots had taken solidly to the Presbyterian tenet that God's elect must justify their preordained salvation by a serious devotion to the business of labor—to relax and behave as if one *knew* his salvation was certain would appear to be a sinful presumption that one knew as much about the future as did the Sovereign God. And so the only option was work: the more one labored, the more one thereby displayed a humble incertitude concerning the Will of God. What Calvin gave with one hand, he took back with the other; and the *Eglise réformée* blessed its converts with one certitude: incertitude. And, thus, work became a prime virtue; idleness a prime vice. A specter was haunting Scotland—the specter of sloth. And not only Scotland: the fearful shadow of this same wraith had long since been cast over all of Britain and the American colonies. The ground was ready for Adam Smith. Calvinism had performed the somatic trick of driving men to anxious labor because of the fear of relaxation. All that Smith needed to do was to tap fully another and intimately related organic drive: the drive of aggression.

Every Young Republican must be aware of the wondrous fact that the *Wealth of Nations* was published in 1776; it seems most likely that Calvin's Sovereign God foresaw, preordained and blessed this union of nation and economic system. Adam Smith's treatise was ingenious, confusing, simple and complex; and through the maze of the *Wealth of Nations* there shone the sharp outlines of a system which, almost magically, gave order to what had till then seemed the chaos of economic life.

Smith tapped the explosive reservoir of aggressive

human energy by pointing out the necessity for society to *allow* men to follow their own self-interest; then they would be placed in competition with *all other* men, and this fact of competition would have a uniquely salutary effect on society. Unbridled self-interest and competition would balance off against one another in a self-regulatory manner, as every individual scrambled for his share of the market. If one man sold his goods too dearly, he would not finally profit, inasmuch as others would come along and undersell him, driving him out of business. And so, competition guaranteed the lowest possible prices for consumers. And this was not all: the plentitude of goods was also guaranteed to consumers. If the quantity of one type of product was scarce, then the consumer demand for it would edge the price upward until it was expensive; and this would attract other producers into manufacturing the same item, thus putting many producers in competition and making that product not only more plentiful but cheaper.

Moreover, if profits or wages in one line of business were low, both capital and labor would flow toward more lucrative businesses. If, however, another area's profits and wages were high, the flow of investment and labor would expand it until its higher-than-average profits and wages would level out within the competitive market.

This is the magic of philosophy: suddenly, through the cloudiness of events, everything comes together and makes sense. And Adam Smith had the sense of economic events within the grasp of one hand: unimpeded self-interest in competition for the same market would create a self-regulating system that was for the benefit of all—there is his insight in a nutshell. And not only was Smith's apologia intellectually satisfying but it managed also to be satisfyingly Christian: if one is *truly* concerned with the welfare of others, then one must have a society in which self-concern is paramount.

The *Wealth of Nations* was—and still is—a stunning intellectual achievement, and it ranks Adam Smith alongside Karl Marx—these thinkers being the two major economic philosophers of the modern period. The two men are intimately complementary and necessary for one another: in much the same way that Hume's clarifications made possible Kant's revolution in epistemological thought, so did the results of the remarkable analysis of Smith make possible Marx's revolution in economic thought. The greatness of Smith and Marx is unquestionable not because of the ultimate "truth" of what they have said, but—more importantly—because of the fantastic *effect* that their writings subsequently had upon the development of economic institutions. Without the effect which Adam Smith's ideas had on the development of Western technology, Karl Marx would not have had the ruthlessly productive factory system which he saw to be the essence of Smith's capitalism and which he saw to be headed for inevitable, self-inflicted ruin.

Both Smith and Marx wrestled with the explosive, absolutely extraordinary event of scientific technology, and both men came to see these evolving events in terms of a system: Smith saw it as an ever expanding and beneficial system; Marx, at a later stage, saw it as a doomed and vicious system. That both of them were right in their analyses but wrong in their predictions is not an indication of their mutual lack of genius but is simply testimony to the fact that economics is not a science but is a series of philosophical perspectives which are trying to keep up with a rapidly mutating technological history that has not yet reached the maturity of homeostasis. What Smith saw in 1776 and what Marx saw in 1848 were as penetrating visions of what-is-the-case as is possible. But if capitalism was *not* forever self-regulating and if, also, capitalism was *not* to destroy itself, this is because the very technological evolution of the past few centuries has constantly created new elements in the economic picture which neither Marx nor Smith would ever have deemed possible. Similarly, the unhappy predictions of Thomas Malthus and David Ricardo have suffered the same kind of half-falsification.

Once he had pointed it out, there was nothing more obvious than Malthus' pessimistic equation concerning population and poverty: land for agricultural production is limited, but the multiplication of the human race is unlimited; therefore, it is inevitable that there will eventually be more mouths than there is food to feed them. Ergo, necessary poverty, famine and death by starvation for the excess mouths.

Or Ricardo's exquisitely drawn picture of how capital and labor will expand and produce more commodities just as Adam Smith had foreseen. But, observed Ricardo, the one thing that does not expand is the land which produces the food to be sold to these busy capitalists and workers; thus, inevitably, as profits and wages rise, they will be accompanied by an equal rise in the price of agricultural products, thus eating up the gain of the capitalists and workers and redounding to the profit of the landlords who control the fixed commodity of agriculture. Ricardo explained to manufacturer and laborer alike that they were literally going nowhere economically; they were, rather, caught in a system where their efforts enriched only the land-holders and not themselves.

Like the economic prognostications of Smith and Marx, the predictions of Malthus and Ricardo looked like airtight cases of inevitability. But the very economic process they were describing was not standing still, suddenly mummified into a rigid system; rather, the economic process was undergoing "impossible" mutations. Population in the West has *not* shown its "inevitable" doubling growth but has declined, remaining in rough balance to economic production. And agricultural production has *not* remained fixed and enriching for land-holders but, instead, has become over-productive and thus impoverishing to farmers who have watched, horrified, as agricultural prices dropped ever lower on the free market.

Nor could Adam Smith have envisioned within his system the inflationary and depressive cycles that later were to become the constant dragons within advanced capitalistic societies. And Karl Marx, given what he saw of the European economy in the mid-nineteenth century, would never, never have believed that the proletarian unions would some day be in league *with* the bourgeois industrialists against the interest of lower prices for the consumer. Nor would it have made sense that when a capitalistic system got in trouble, the federal government ("bourgeois state") would intervene into the free system, either regulating its inflationary expansion or investing public money into a depressed economy when private investment had fallen flat.

What I am saying is that economics is a rough game to play, inasmuch as it is not, as yet, a predictive science. Rather, economics has, from the beginning, been a somatic game, whose mutational dialectics have been hidden within the interchange between changing human somas and their changed environment.

The continuing significance of Karl Marx is that, as a social philosopher, he was the first man to see penetratingly into the primitive biological processes which underlay not simply "economic" history but all of human history. As his elegant alter ego, Friedrich Engels, said in

1888, Marx's theory was to do for history exactly what Darwin did for biology. And Engels was correct. A full generation before the publication of Darwin's revolutionary *Origin,* Karl Marx—in his youthful reactions against and his permutations of Hegelianism—had discovered the evolutionary process of somatic-environmental interchange.

Marx's discovery was the following: the kind of political and intellectual structures characteristic of *any* stage in human history have *always* been a direct reflection of the more basic situation of how the necessities of life are produced, who produces them and how society sets up the distribution of these necessities; the class divisions in any society are simply the divisions of function in terms of which some have more rights to what is produced and some have fewer rights to what is produced.

Now if ants and bees could talk or if Marx had had all the biological data which Darwin had, ants, bees and Marx would have pronounced this as not simply a generalization about the human species but about *all* species of animals. In an economic situation of scarcity—which has been the lot of all living creatures up until the past few centuries—there is an unavoidable struggle for survival, and the result of this struggle is always a pecking-order ("ruling and oppressed classes") where some get the short end of the stick and some get the long end. Whether we call this a biologically motivated "pecking order" or an environmentally ordained "class structure" is a matter of academics, so long as we understand that, somatologically, by saying either we are saying both. For anyone to take Marx as purely an environmentalist is to see Marx falsely as just another dreary and unimaginative determinist (and this is the wretched pitfall of most dogmatic Marxists). In the same fashion, if any ethologically oriented person takes a pecking-order to be a purely non-adaptive and automatic programmed organic event, then he ceases to have any understanding of either evolution or ethology and has reduced matters to an equally absurd biological determinism.

But this is only one part of Marx's original discovery. Not only did he see that we must understand all *past* societies as essentially expressions of their own gutty problems and solutions of how to subsist in a scarcity situation, but we now must see *present* societies as operating under radically changed conditions. At this point, Marx takes the ball from Adam Smith and romps right out of the ballpark and into a new one. Marx saw that the scientific-technological developments which had taken place under the capitalistic system (which, otherwise, would merely be one more in a long series of oppressor-oppressed systems of typical *scarcity* economies)—that these developments had produced a new event of epochal importance in human history: our technology *now* was producing surplus value and we were, for the first time in history, no longer in scarcity. Technological developments had brought us to the stage of social history where the ancient business of economic pecking-orders and class structures of oppressors and oppressed are no longer the necessary ways in which human society must *inevitably* be ordered.

All previous societies had *necessarily* been have and have-not societies, and so there was no help for it: it wasn't Marx's concern to condemn such past societies—rather, he knew that they *had* to be class societies. But the radical, the decisive event which had (incredibly) taken place was that a typical scarcity economy such as capitalism had had the very grounds for its scarcity system evolved right out from under it: the "system" operated as if there "was not enough to go around," but the surplus production was demonstrating that there was "more than enough to go around."

Nothing at all complicated or sinister in all this: Marx simply saw the truth. The system of economy was no longer in accord with the facts of the economy; and, thus, the technological environment would bring about a mutation in the human system of economic organization. That Marx (like all great economists) fell into the trap of "predicting" that this mutation "had to" take place through socio-economic revolution rather than evolution is, at the present time, only a matter of pointless dispute between academics or fanatics on either side of the East-West Curtain. The fundamental point is that Marx saw what was happening in this confrontation between a surplus-producing *actual environment* and a scarcity-organized *human environment,* and he predicted that the actual environment would finally compel the human order to mutate and adapt.

And, in its explosive way, that is what the twentieth century has been all about: the triumph, finally, of human technology and the nightmarish problem of adjusting human society *in all of its modes* to this event which no one (and precious little in our traditional culture) ever conceived of as possible. The "age of *anxiety*"? No, the "age of *adaptation*"—an age which, in the West, is now nearing its completion. The adaptation is afoot, the proto-mutants are confusedly but pointedly changing the old, irrelevant systems on *both* sides of the East-West Curtain, and the life of the next century is being painfully constructed.

As the present century fades, the lies will also fade. In all of the information-dispensing and educational institutions of both the capitalist and communist countries, the habitual pastime of the cultural traditionalists is to lie about both Karl Marx and Adam Smith. For the traditionalists, their remaining task is not to think, examine and readjust but simply to plod on with the same trite falsehoods about each other's system, while—at the same time —fewer and fewer people listen. When either American or Soviet leaders claim that their economic philosophies are responsible for their respective achievements, they are, thereby, either lying or babbling like madmen. No knowledgeable American capitalist even *believes* in Adam Smith, and for American political spokesmen to give the credit for American productivity to a rejected Scottish philosopher and not to the scientists, technologists and engineers who have been responsible for it is to show a lack of somatic adaptation to the real environment that is tantamount to political insanity.

And the Soviets are no cleaner: they need not credit Marx with what they have achieved over such an incredibly short period of time. Marx has been betrayed and the man who made it all possible—the "satanical" little Stalin —has been officially repressed from the social consciousness of the Soviet bloc: Stalin coldly took a backward people and—"for their own benefit"—murderously compelled them to fit the cookie-cutter of a technological reorganization of society: either you fitted the mold or you got crushed. The Chinese feel that it is precisely just such cold-blooded regimentation that they, too, must follow if they are to rapidly industrialize. But "regimentation for technology" is a totalitarian engineering project and is neither a Marxist nor communist project. So it again approaches political insanity for Russian leaders to give Marx and communism the credit for what technology has done and to give Stalin no credit at all for the fact that he did it so quickly and effectively. But the younger intellects in the Soviet bloc know very well what the facts of life are, and they know that official pronouncements are habitual lies poured out by a traditionalist, blind machinery which is politically inadaptable.

The proto-mutants in the industrialized societies all over the East and West are rapidly adapting to the facts of a technological environment and are struggling to get rid of the traditional trap of ideological thinking. To the extent that they do, they will discover that Marx was *not behind* them but *ahead* of them. Marx wasn't an ideologist. Even as Christ was not a Christian, Marx was not a Marxist; rather, he was the greatest social philosopher of the last century and a half, who saw that the mutation of man with his technological environment would take men beyond economic classes and beyond the political ideologies which are their expressions. Ethologists have a technical expression for what Marx (and Adam Smith) have done: they have been "releasors" of somatic energy. Just as a certain species coloring or a certain undulation of hips will bring forth aggressive energies in a fish or sensual energies in a man, in the same way, the great economists have been the "verbal releasors" of types of human energy. Adam Smith helped us up to the near-present through aggressive release; Karl Marx helps us toward the future with a final drive toward non-aggression, relaxation and a relaxed community of human bodies—bodies which will have other projects to pursue than aggressive ones motivated by fear.

Marx had already seized this soma-environmental vision of man's past and future by the time he was in his late 20's. In *The German Ideology,* he saw all science to be historical and evolutionary in focus, and he saw that the historical science of man and of nature could not be treated separately but only conjointly, inasmuch as the evolving influence of man on nature and then of nature on man was reciprocal. And at a near moment in this reciprocal historical process there would come a time when we would no longer see man as a worker or capitalist struggling to survive, but we would simply "assume *man* to be *man,* and his relation to the world a human one. Then love can only be exchanged for love, trust for trust," etc.—these human verities no longer being exchangeable for money. Then human evolution will have shaken off the leaden weight of the past and will move toward further adaptive adventures.

There is no end to it, this soma-environment, dialectical process. It keeps moving and weaving what we call history, and it is a hard game to keep up with: if you're not alert, you will lose track and get left behind. The name of the game is life; and it is always worthwhile reminding ourselves that it is only for the living.

4

CASSIRER, OR HOW TO SPOT A MUTANT BY HIS SYMBOLIC SPOTS

Perhaps one should be wary of Greeks bearing gifts but not of Germans; they have been the great gift-givers of the twentieth century, not giving their second best to other countries but their best. Behind this generosity is the fact that the German people have, amongst the Western nations, been pre-eminent in the special manner in which their fear-aggression drives are triggered by their own culture.

It is not only that the Germans have had the usual ancient somatic fear of their environment, which has driven them to attack environmental problems, but particularly that they have a unique fear: fear of themselves as being somehow weak and inferior. And to the fear of inadequacy has come the answering response of anger with oneself, of a punishing aggression and control of oneself as well as one's environment. Caught in a special somatic imbalance —their only traditional outlet for sensual expression being the alimentary sensuality of gluttony—they have driven themselves to extraordinary achievements in science, scholarship and technology: never merely *enough* achievement in these areas but always *far more than enough* has been the characteristic German drive—as if, having responded to the challenge of the earthly environment, they then had to respond to the challenge of themselves.

This is why, in both philosophy and the sciences, Germans have been the great over-achievers, the great systematizers, completers, perfectionists. The Mediterranean peoples, in contrast, are not driven by this obsession with *Vollkommenheit:* of *having to* work things out to completion, to a system. They are the environmental realists, who do just enough and then leave it at that.

So then, our debts to the Germans are considerable. Out of this over-achieving culture have arisen great philosophers, scholars and scientists who were not simply the "great men" of their particular culture but—given the obsessive over-education through which they had passed— were truly astounding men. But, ironically, for a German to achieve greatness he invariably becomes a cosmopolitan and loses his German-ness: he stands apart from his culture and is alienated from it and it from him. Heinrich Heine's *Heimkehr* is a wicked and witty description of this typical inability to "come home again" to the German culture that was one's nurture.

But the Germans finally and triumphantly drew together all the strands of their national being and achieved the coherent *Deutsche Kultur* for which they had so long panted, and this solidified national culture was precisely what the cosmopolitans had always sensed might happen once they had achieved a full understanding of themselves and their people; and it was this suspicion which estranged them. The cultural tendency finally became coherent in Nazism, and the German people exultantly found themselves. With startling precision they directed their self-loathing at their somatic opposites: their repressed other-beings were the Jews, a unique people whose normal social avenues for aggressive expression had been denied them by the Christian West and, therefore, like all oppressed minorities (women, blacks, gypsies), had become a sensual and more somatically balanced people.

And then the gifts poured in: the German Jews and the friends of German Jews—all exiles, all impure and un-needed for the crystallized German culture. All through the 1930's there flowed into the rest of Europe and, especially, into the United States an undreamed of boon of some of the most accomplished and sensitive intellects in the Western world. That we now have great universities throughout the United States—not simply within a few centers—is due to the simple fact that as the Germans emptied their universities and research institutes, ours began to fill up.

One of those gifts from the German nation was Ernst Cassirer (gifted first to Columbia and, later, Yale). Cassirer was a scholar, a man whose breadth of knowledge, in its variety and in its intimate detail, is but rarely encountered. This in itself would have been sufficient to rank Ernst Cassirer among the great cosmopolitan scholars of the past two centuries. But Cassirer was not only a "scholar"; the colossal scholarship he had attained was a tool for something else: philosophy. And the match between the breadth of his knowledge and the breadth of his philosophical concerns was, under the circumstances, appropriate: Cassirer's philosophical project was no less than to understand the evolution of human culture and human consciousness from the beginning to the present. The result was the three-volume work, *The Philosophy of Symbolic Forms,* a book which only a German and a cosmopolitan German could have written.

I have wanted to devote one brief chapter to Cassirer, not merely to speak of his ideas but primarily to describe his place within the tradition of somatic thought and to underline his importance for it.

In discussing Kierkegaard and Marx, we have on both occasions made reference to their reaction to the philosophy of Hegel. With Cassirer it comes up once again. Obviously, Hegel is undeniably important to the history of somatic thought and science if for no other reason than that he served as a catalyst for somatic thought. The reason *why* Hegel was such a catalyst was that he had taken Kant's Copernican Revolution and put it on wheels— magnificent wheels. Kant's revolutionary discovery was that the human being possessed structures of perception and understanding which spring into action and interaction with sensory stimuli in such a way that *we* are as much (unconscious) participants in seeing the world the way we see it as are the sensory stimuli. What Hegel did was to take this insight and put it into time, into history. Specifically, he suggested that there is not simply one set of structures in terms of which we humans experience the world (which was Kant's theory) but that there have been many earlier, more primitive ways in which men experienced their world and that there were still to come more advanced ways in which men would come to see and understand their world. In fine, Hegel tried to show that there was an evolution in human consciousness.

But Hegel's notion of evolution was not somatic: it did not see human consciousness as evolving out of a soma-environment exchange in which each influenced the other in bringing about change and adaptation; rather, Hegel saw evolution as an idealistic process: namely, that the single, organizing power behind the evolution of human consciousness has been the transcendental Spirit of God. This Spirit has, from the beginning of time, been feeding into mankind progressively more rational ways of seeing, understanding and acting in the world; the environing world doesn't contribute to this, but, rather, only *reacts* to it in a balky, half-hearted manner. Every new idea fed into man by the Spirit gets only half-accomplished in the environment: physical matter and organic matter get in its way so that each progressive step in human history is only a half-step and a compromise. As Hegel sees it, it's a slow game; but the Spirit, being eternal, has all the time in the world to play the game, slowly and patiently, as it compels man toward that final stage of history when not only man is totally and lucidly rational but so is his environment.

Now this is pretty exciting stuff: the magnificent wheels which Hegel had put under Kant's ideas and the carriage which he erected on it had all the pomp and circumstance of a P.T. Barnum circus calliope. And, during the first half of the nineteenth century, when men began to feel the effects of technological change, Hegel's historical view was clearly the one vehicle that seemed to move with the sense of the times.

But the two men who had a much keener sense of the times were Kierkegaard and Marx, and they (unaccountably at that period) ridiculed Hegel's system: Kierkegaard laughed at it; Marx, being German, took it apart brick by brick. From our later perspective in time, we can understand precisely what Kierkegaard and Marx were up to:

the former was defending the human soma and *its* powerful structures; the latter was defending the worldly environment and *its* powerful structures. Both Kierkegaard and Marx saw that there was no need to evoke the ancient notion of a trans-personal, trans-natural Spirit to explain what was happening to man and his history; soma and environment sufficed. And each pursued his separate defense brilliantly and with effect.

By the time Cassirer began to put together his three-volume *Symbolischen Formen* during the 1920's, these reactions of Marx and Kierkegaard had been confirmed environmentally by Darwin and somatically by Freud; and Nietzsche had summed up the whole of it somatically. In the wake of this, Cassirer became a Hegelian—not in the sense of *following* Hegel's *system,* but, instead, of *approving* Hegel's *project* in philosophy: namely, to describe the evolution of human consciousness. The importance of Cassirer is that he re-did for the twentieth century what Hegel—lacking the experimental data—had initially attempted for the nineteenth century. And *The Philosophy of Symbolic Forms* has all the power and scope and scholarship that was so evident in Hegel's effort, but this time the effort has somatic relevance. Like a massive storm covering all horizons, Cassirer's great work encompasses the twentieth century with flickers and flashes of light that constantly light up the entire scene. With his searching concern for evolving types of human perception and intelligence, Cassirer is a philosophical counterpart to the scientific work of Jean Piaget; and also he is illuminating to an understanding of somatic science and thought in general.

Cassirer saw the evolution of human perception and understanding of the environing world as having been constructed each step of the way on man's ability to devise and handle *symbols* which mediated between man and his world and allowed him to interpret it, see it and understand it more effectively. As a species of animals, what is special in man is his success in inventing and using symbols. Men do not *see* any more of the sense world than do animals; the human evolutionary success has had nothing to do with seeing the environment more clearly but, rather, of *understanding* it more effectively so that one can work with the environment in order to survive. Given the constant flow of sensory stimuli into the human soma, the problem for man was to obtain something fixed and stable in his awareness of his environment; and it *was* through the medium of symbols (images, language, number, algebra) that man has succeeded in isolating and fixing this sensory flux so that he can study it, remember it, predict it and act practically upon this ever-changing environment.

What Cassirer makes undeniably certain is that, in the course of the slow cultural progress from primitive mythical mentality to modern conceptual mentality, the human race has come to *see* less and less of the sense datum and to understand its usable rules more and more. The evolution of human consciousness has been a steady movement *away* from the multitude of sensory particulars and *toward* the simplicity of abstract concepts; in a word, modern civilized humans are incapable of perceiving with the acuteness and attention to detail that is characteristic of primitive men—between ourselves and our environment there is a learned tradition of symbolical forms which compels us to perceive and understand the environment in a radically different way from that of primitive men.

And primitive peoples cannot perceive and understand the world as we do, precisely because they do not have the symbols to do so. And, through extensive analysis, Cassirer shows how the language of a primitive tribe (its symbols) is directly reflective of the consciousness which they have of their world: their language and their behavior are utterly in accord in expressing just exactly as much understanding of the world as they have symbolic structures through which they can mediate this world.

This is a somatic understanding of human consciousness, which sees man and his symbolical abilities within an evolutionary framework. And it points to the significance of language as a living, mutating, practical human event. Cassirer links together the study of language-as-living as begun by von Humboldt and as continued by Chomsky; and this is a radically different approach from that of the Oxford linguistic analysis school, which has preferred to limit itself to linguistic autopsies.

But, even though Cassirer stands in open admiration before the presently evolved conceptual abilities of modern men, he is nonetheless aware of the fact that man is continuing to evolve, and that even these present high achievements are limited and in question. In the long struggle away from a mythic consciousness and into a conceptual consciousness, men had moved from one kind of "world" into another kind of "world"; but there are still other "worlds" which we shall discover.

Like all somatic thinkers, Cassirer gives full credit to the magnificence of scientific technology and to the type of consciousness that has produced it; but scientific technology is not the final way of understanding and acting within our world. And conceptual, outward-turned consciousness is not the ultimate form of human consciousness. Because men are living, they are evolving; and because they are evolving, new forms of consciousness, understanding and behavior will appear.

And, because of Cassirer, we have a key to discovering whether such mutations may be taking place: he has told us that they take place only through the medium of new symbols and new linguistic adventures. Look at the youth within Western society and decide for yourself. Are new symbols emerging, oddities of language or appearance or adventures in behavior? If so, stop and look more carefully: they are the signs of a mutating consciousness.

5

CAMUS, OR MURDER
AND SENSUALITY

What is so interesting about Albert Camus is that not only did no one ever succeed in pinning him down and categorizing him, but no one ever seemed able to come up with a satisfying answer as to why he was so important. There is no question that he has a compelling influence on his readers, but finally, what is it? Professional philosophers read his essays and conclude that he was an interesting philosopher but not all *that* good. Literary professionals read his novels, short stories and plays and conclude that he is definitely a good writer but not necessarily great. But somehow and in some way he *was* all that good and he *was* great. And so everyone settled for an answer that was unsatisfying but vaguely right: he was a good man. Or, presumably more modestly, he was a *man*.

I'll buy that. I had sat with him during a long session in his crowded little office in the Gallimard publishing house, speaking with him about the amazing similarity between his ideas and those of Kierkegaard and Nietzsche; and Camus kept shaking his head and saying he wasn't in the least religious. Typically, he insisted, *"Je suis artiste"*—by which he meant no more than that he did a number of things artfully.

Then, on one corner of his piled-high desk, I noticed there were several black-bound volumes of Karl Barth's theological works, and I said, "See, you *are* interested in philosophy of religion." Camus said, "Perhaps so, but I keep things in balance: look at the book that's on the opposite corner." I looked: it was *Lady Chatterley's Lover.*

And that was precisely the difficult-to-pin-down secret of Camus' importance and influence: he was a man who maintained balance. He was a human soma in balance. And his work, his way of living and his thought all reflected this balance: the themes of "equilibrium," "measure," "proportion" and "balance" are the central focus of all his literary and philosophical works. Within himself he had achieved an equilibrium; outside himself he saw a world that lacked equilibrium. Camus: a student during the fermenting 30's, a *Résistance* journalist during the Occupation of the 40's and an enormously influential French moral and political figure during the turmoil of the 50's. He was nurtured on the violence of a Europe in the throes of Nazism, Stalinism, and social revolution and never ceased to be actively embroiled in this violence; but the special job he had chosen for himself was not simply that of an activist but also that of a man who could step back from the clamor of his times and reflect them. This was his "art": the ability to be a special reflector of his times, both in essays and literary pieces. And the special quality of his reflection was that it was always a balanced man reflecting an imbalanced human society. This is not only the secret of that peculiar impact of Camus' writings, but it is also the reason for the irony which is so characteristic of his style.

A balanced man in an unbalanced society, Camus was aloof and apart from the ailing Europe in which he had his way. Having grown up on the Mediterranean and identifying with North Africa and Greece rather than with France and Europe, he was self-consciously a pagan, adamantly Greek and somatically non-European. And just as his positive philosophical ideas were of ancient Greece ("not too much, not too little, but just the right balance") so was his own manner of living: a man must fight those men and situations which anger him and make him fearful, and he must fight them with every bit of aggression he possesses; and, also, a man must love those humans and situations which make him hunger and yearn for sensuality, and he must surrender to beauty and love with every bit of openness he possesses. For the pagan there is not one god, but many, and each calls to different aspects of a man's being. When the gods call you as a warrior, then go as warrior; but, just as certainly, when the gods call you as lover, go as lover. Like Nietzsche, Camus felt caught between his identification with an ancient pagan nobility, who were no more, and with the not-yet-existing noblemen who might someday walk the earth.

Now the above paragraph you have just read is simply twaddle. And it is characteristic of the romantic twaddle which scores of French philosophers and American littérateurs and religionists have written about Camus. Camus was no anachronistic pagan, alienated from the present while he bayed at the moon and yearned for the past.

Rather, he was a tough sensualist, committed to the here and now, who could give as rough a time to men who angered him as he could give a diverting time to women who attracted him. Ultimately, he didn't give a damn about the "future of man," but only the present of men. His disinterest in the future of humanity was not simply because he was not—as he said—a philosopher but because he saw the hands of systematic philosophers and religionists behind all of the murder and violence he had known since his birth in 1913—the death of his own father during the First World War being but the beginning.

Camus was absolutely not a revolutionary nor was he an ideologist: from the very beginning of his career, he saw with utter lucidity that it was men who were incapable of accepting the present for *what* it is and struggling with it *as* it is who were the architects of the suffering and destruction of mankind. He lucidly saw that it was precisely those who lived in hope for the future who were quite incapable of ever accepting any present, even a future present. In short, those men whose drives can only be motivated by not-now-existing future social or personal hopes are men who cannot accept reality as it is. They are estranged from present reality; and this is their sickness, a sickness which had spread and contaminated all of Europe.

When Camus looks at the "pathetic" creature called man and at the "indifference" of the natural world and says *yes* to these things, finding them beautiful, he is not in the least a nature-loving Greek pagan. The comparisons with the ancient past are, finally, pointless, inasmuch as the ancient past was a mythic past; and when the mythic consciousness saw the world as "beautiful" it was with totally different eyes which saw a totally different universe, whose very existence, causality and personality were categorically separate from the depersonalized universe of the modern conceptual consciousness. Camus, indeed, loved sun, women, water and a good fight, but he loved these things without the slightest illusion or sentimentality: they were exactly what they were amongst the shifting relativity of all things that are. Nothing could be absolutized, finalized or deified. There was no ultimate meaning to anything—to human life or the world.

What I am saying is that Camus had totally accepted the modern, depersonalized and relative universe without the least trace of rancor or disappointment. It is one thing for men of the twentieth century to prattle about a relativistic cosmos, but it has been a totally separate matter to be able to open oneself somatically in total behavioral acceptance of this. Camus could do this. He did not *need* gods, absolutes, final authorities and ultimate meanings—all of which are symptoms of men's inability to accept and live fruitfully with the immediate and shifting realities of *this* human being *here* and *those* streets and doorways *there*.

It was not, then, the "present" that Camus was a stranger to, it was the traditional culture which drove men to deny the relative but all-sufficing reality of the present in favor of a non-existent future. To deny the present and affirm the future is, as Camus saw it, the religiousness of the twentieth century—a religiousness especially obvious in those who were fanatically anti-religious (such as militant atheists, Fascists, Communists, positivists, et al.). The technical achievements of their self-conscious "minds" were far in advance of their frightened and insecure somas. And this is why German or Soviet scientists could be utterly matter of fact in their professional view of the world, and yet be led about like dependent, starry-eyed children by the man who exuded authority or was spokesman for the ideological truth. And this is also why Camus referred to the wars of this century as "religious wars."

Camus simply lived through and documented what Nietzsche saw looming up in the twentieth century: namely, the nihilism which would result while the technological world adapted to its horrifying discovery that God was very, very dead, and that there was no ultimate and absolute meaning to either human life or the universe: they simply *were.* Nietzsche knew that the traditional Western culture would continue to produce frightened somas which were unable to accept and live with the discoveries of the scientific explosion. And, as Camus so saliently documents in *L'Homme Révolté,* as soon as God was pulled down from the heavens, men rushed to create substitute gods and religions to fill that aching void in the old firmament.

Like all somatic thinkers, Camus saw that men had finally achieved dominion over the physical world, and that further aggression was not needed. There was *enough* —enough for men now to relax and accept themselves and their world for what they actually were—even though such admissions about both self and world would be painfully difficult at first for those whose bodies were entrapped in the yearning illusions of the traditional culture. A Marxist to the core but completely antipathetic to all utopian revolutions, Camus understood how, by forever destroying "scarcity economies," technology had not only undercut the need for further aggression on physical nature but had obviated the need for struggle over possession, which is what had always been the primary division of man from man. In a technological society, not only could men for the first time accept each other without the fearful and angry flicker of aggression but they could, also for the first time, accept themselves for what they were without either fear or anger for being pathetically human.

Camus already existed with this acceptance. He had already adapted to the new earthly environment. But during his brief, forty-odd years, it seemed to him that precious few other men had so adapted. And so, professionally, he could be considered lucky: all he had to do was be himself and, mysteriously, this was enough to compel people to stop, listen and become entranced—especially young people, who have a keener eye for a mutant. When people saw themselves and their times refracted through the confident and relaxed balance of this mutant human being, they caught a glimpse of what they could be—and without even trying. Camus help up a mirror in which they saw the juxtaposed images of a balanced human and a tensely distorted unbalanced human, and the specific feeling that resulted was: "I, too, have the possibility of that balance but I haven't quite given in to it yet."

It almost goes without saying that Camus' extraordinary modesty was not a guise: he was, indeed, just "doing his job" and trying to reflect his times. I think he himself was always amazed at the effect of his writings. They were unusual to everyone but himself—to him they seemed obvious: he was just being himself as he had always been.

As he had been in his early twenties. There in a little café in the Algerian coastal town of Tipasa, glorying in the sun, the lights, the colors, faces, movements and smells that swirled about him—he, biting into a ripe peach as if gnawing at love itself, and the juices running down his chin and neck, as he looks upward at the hill where he has just finished walking through the remains of a Roman town. Earlier, having arrived on the hill, he had walked about among the columns and friezes, the cornices and shattered archstones: proud remnants of an empire that was to last forever but which now lay covered with the exuberant presence of field flowers, whose colors and odors simmered throughout the ruins. The works of man, like man himself, finally absorbed back into the tender indifference of the earth. The sun rocketed down over the flowers, the ruins, the surrounding mountains, the restless glistening sea and over the young mutant himself; and he was happy—happy with this remorseless and beautiful world and happy that his whole being was so finely attuned to it. And in this, *Noces,* one of the first and most beautiful things ever written by Camus, he celebrated his "nuptials" with the world. He knew then, as he always knew, that there was nothing wrong with life except that it did not last forever.

Years later—after the war, the Occupation, the post-war struggles and the endless controversies—he came back to Tipasa, wondering if that same love, that same sensual surrender to the world was still there; and wondering if a man could play the rough games of life and still be able to play the tender ones. He found that Tipasa was different; but different in that its preciousness balanced into the whole of things. He found that a man *could* be many things and yet remain whole. He found that one didn't need the blessings of the Greek gods in order to be a man, but one only needed, finally, to be a man in order to know the blessings of the gods.

6

MERLEAU-PONTY, OR PERCEPTION LEASHED AND PERCEPTION UNLEASHED

One of the curious things about Maurice Merleau-Ponty is that he could be French and yet write badly. The same goes for his pal at the Collège de France, Claude Lévi-Strauss, the phenomenological anthropologist: in a most un-Gallic manner, Lévi-Strauss handles words like each one weighed twenty pounds. The symptoms are obvious: when a man begins to write paragraphs in which the words do not fly but, instead, are shifted around like leaden weights—then it is sign that he has been reading too much German.

But the French have been generally immune to this stylistic Teutonic plague. A little south of the Collège, up on the hill, Jean Hyppolite had for years been interpreting and translating Hegel at the Ecole Normale Supérieure de l'Enseignement Technique; and, without question, if you want to read Hegel, don't learn German but learn French and read Hyppolite—through Hyppolite, Hegel finally says what he could not say in German. And so, it is an anomaly to find two French intellectuals who write so laboriously and yet who have spent their years strolling down the same halls of the Collège de France that the elegant Bergson had made famous.

But even though Merleau-Ponty writes as if language is a jungle out of which one has to fight his way, his safaris are highly rewarding if you can bear up; for the great French phenomenologist is not simply fighting a language, he is also fighting the most deeply entrenched convictions of our cultural tradition concerning the psychology of man.

To say that Merleau-Ponty is a phenomenologist means, of course, that his focus of interest is the nature and structure of consciousness, the arena itself of human experience. The very possibility of presuming that one *could* study the structures of human consciousness was—as we have seen already—opened by Kant during the late eighteenth century. Once opened, the field for phenomenological studies was hectically explored through the nineteenth century but only found itself during the *fin de siècle*. Edmund Husserl gave phenomenology its characteristic form, Jean-Paul Sartre took a bath in it, leaving two rings around the tub, and Maurice Merleau-Ponty drew phenomenology out to its final limits and was about to complete and, thus, kill the movement when he, himself, died.

If phenomenology seeks to understand human consciousness then it finds its most emphatic spokesman in Merleau-Ponty: he jumps on the matter with both feet with his unequivocal announcement that *consciousness is perception* and *perception is consciousness.*

Now, although a little surprising and disconcerting to philosophers, this statement has no shock value for neurophysiologists or for those men in the traditions of psychoanalysis and humanistic psychology. For them it is obvious. What else *could* consciousness be but perception? And to look for the "structures of consciousness" is a vague way of saying that a man is trying to understand the neurophysiology of his perception in the way *he* perceives.

To say that Merleau-Ponty was a somatic thinker is a bit obvious; indeed, he was immersed in the study of physiology, neurophysiology and the history of psychology. And he brought all of these foci together in two labored but marvelous treatises, *The Structure of Behavior* and *The Phenomenology of Perception.* Both books are thoroughly somatic and treat, respectively, the somatic structure of bodily activities and the somatic structure of consciousness.

Once Merleau-Ponty has equated consciousness with perception we are abruptly within the somatic world of authentic human experience as each of us actually experiences himself and his world. Left behind are the notions of a "mind" superimposed somehow on a "body"; instead, "mind" and "body" are part of the same function in relating man constantly to his environment: the function of perception.

Of course this was the fundamental view which Freud also had reached about human consciousness: namely, that it had evolved somatically as a practical sense instrument for surveying and searching the environment; and by virtue of this practical, evolved function, consciousness was an instrument turned *toward* the environment and incapable of being turned back to perceive the somatic centrum from which it originated. To anyone who has achieved a somatic appreciation of Freud's work, much of Merleau-Ponty's own work will seem an extension and clarification of Freud's initial insights. And, after one has noted the similarities of the two men's viewpoints, one suddenly encounters the quite different and surprising insight which carries Merleau-Ponty a long jump beyond Freud.

The surprising suggestion is this: not only is consciousness perception, but, moreover, there are *two* forms of perception and, thus, of consciousness. He has several ways of speaking of these two forms of perception, the most exact being *analytical consciousness* and *phenomenological consciousness.*

When we are "analytically" conscious, we are perceiving our environment in the manner which Freud and all of us usually refer to as "consciousness." This is to say that what we have always called "consciousness" is only *one* way of perceiving—the analytical way. And this analytical consciousness is simply a practical searching out of the environment, a scanning whereby we are *looking for something.* Using his own observations as well as those of the Gestalt psychologists, Merleau-Ponty makes it indubitable that when we perceive our world in this searching, attentive, analytical manner, we have adjusted our somatic controls so that the resultant experience we have will have a basic shape: the shape of figure/ground. This simply means that when we are looking *for* something we trim our sails in such a way that our perception is focused to pick up *one* thing, *one* entity, *one* "figure" from out of all the many things that our senses are picking up. And when you are programmed to pick up *one* configuration, this means that you are sharply focused on *one thing* to the exclusion of *all other things* which are pouring into your sensing apparatus—*all other things,* consequently, are out of focus; they fade into the background in quite the same way that all the other dancers fade into an anonymous background when the spotlight is focused upon the prima ballerina. It's not that the other dancers aren't *there;* they're there, all right, but you're not conscious of them. Figure/ground: the prima is the "figure"; the rest fades back into the "ground" which anonymously provides the backdrop against which the "figure" can stand out sharply.

What Merleau-Ponty is saying is that this figure/ground perception is not the whole story about consciousness; rather, it is merely half the story. It is merely one way of perceiving our world. It is a most practical way: it finds things and isolates them, so that we can study them, reach for them, work on them. And this analytical manner of perceiving is, indeed, "analytical" in the way that it breaks up our experience into parts, into the units or subdivisions which are called "figures."

If you want to play a simple game with yourself to demonstrate how your analytical consciousness always has this underlying structure of figure/ground, do the following. Stretch out in front of you the fingers of your left hand, all five digits spread out and evenly spaced. Now look at the middle finger; concentrate your attention on its centrality as opposed to the double digits which flank it on either side. Now when you've done that much, try a switch: *without moving your eyes in the slightest,* focus your attention on a new configuration, namely, the three middle fingers. Notice how they suddenly become a unit, and separate off from the lonely fingers which now flank them. A moment ago those two fingers (your ring and index fingers) were not part of the figure, they were part of the ground; now, without having moved your eyes, you are perceiving the same sense data in quite a different way. The sense data is not what has changed; rather, the way in which you have perceived the sense data has changed. You are playing the figure/ground game, which is the way our practical "analytical consciousness" can sift through and regroup what we perceive. Having seen a unit of "one finger" and a unit of "three fingers," now see a unit of "five fingers." Keep breaking it up and regrouping. And if you have a window in your room with lots of panes, you can have a fine game of figure/ground grouping.

So far, this is fairly obvious. But what is not "obvious" is precisely what Merleau-Ponty now pounces on. We have for so long meant "analytical consciousness" when we have spoken of human consciousness that we have been blind to the fact that we also perceive in a quite different manner, a manner so different that it simply never occurred to us to think of it as perception at all, much less consciousness. This other way of perceiving is *not* practical, it does *not* look for something and it does *not* break up experience into units such as we see operating in the figure/ground setup.

Merleau-Ponty calls this other way of perceiving, "phenomenological consciousness." And the reason why we have not noticed this other way in which we perceive is that there is nothing to notice: it is a way of perceiving whereby we are not noticing *any*thing, not looking for *any* figure, and therefore we never notice anything that we specifically remember.

If we recall Freud's original description of the way consciousness relates to memory, this, again, may appear fairly obvious. When consciousness focuses its attention on *one* thing, it gleans a specific memory-trace of one thing; memory is the aide-de-camp of this practical business of analytical consciousness, and most likely it uses fairly restricted and specialized areas of the brain. But when we are no longer *focusing* our perceptive apparatus, and when we thus allow perceptions to tumble in upon us without their being broken up and organized by our effort, then we don't have any specific memory of *any* particular thing or, certainly, of our *absence* of perceptive effort.

Even so, we were perceiving; you and I were idly and effortlessly perceiving the phenomena of our world just as they tumbled into our perceptive basket—raw, unorganized, undifferentiated and flowingly unified. You were not only unaware of any particular *thing* in your perceptive world, you also were unaware of your "self": you were perceiving in an unself-conscious manner. And then suddenly a voice says, "What are you thinking about, Tom?" And immediately you are "back in the world," you are self-conscious and your figure/ground perception springs into action, seeing that there is someone *there* in the doorway asking a practical question of you. "What are you thinking about, Tom?" And you or I answer, "Oh, nothing. I wasn't thinking about anything." Which is precisely correct: you and I *were* thinking and we *were* perceiving, but we weren't thinking about or perceiving any*thing.* We were perceiving without the figure/ground device whereby we intervene in and fragment our world for the practical purposes of getting along with people or with our physical environment.

So if we reflect on it, Merleau-Ponty's insight is, after all, obvious—but obvious in a curious way, because his insistence on it suggests that there is much more involved in our being "phenomenologically conscious." He is insisting that, notwithstanding its impracticality and its elusive non-noticeability, phenomenological consciousness is just as much perception as is analytical consciousness. It is just as significant as is analytical perception.

Just *how* significant is an open question; and it is ultimately a question to be answered by evolution and mutation. Obviously, Merleau-Ponty felt that phenomenological perception is *more* significant than analytical perception, for it is the manner in which we experience our world *as it is* and ourselves *as we are.* It is not practical, but it has a different virtue: it is true.

Throw them all together: whether we are talking about artists, little children, lucid philosophers, Saint Francis of Assisi or Zen meditation—in all instances we are referring to those who have the perceptive ability to see things *as they present themselves to us,* and not as we reorder their presentation for our own ends. Obviously, phenomenological consciousness is letting-it-be and letting-yourself-go. It is effortless, for the simple reason that it is in the flow of things, not trying to break up or change or resist the flow of things. And, in the course of this flow, there is no "you" and no "world," no differentiation of any kind beyond the differentiations of shape and pattern that are part of the whole of things. Marshall McLuhan understands this perfectly without having read a line of Merleau-Ponty: for him it is the emerging contemporary perception of the young, namely, "pattern recognition" as opposed to the fragmented, breaking-up-into-parts perception that is the mark of mechanical-mindedness.

As long as you still have your left hand lying around, we might try another experiment in perception: this time in "phenomenological perception." Put your left hand face-down on your knee or the table top, then take your right hand and feel for something: namely, look for the knuckle of your left hand that has the highest ridge. Move the fingers of your right hand along the row of knuckles of the other hand and search for the biggest knuckle bone.

Now, while you are engaged in this process, please notice something: your right hand is a "searching hand" and your left is a "searched hand." Have you noticed how all your attention is flowing through the right hand while it is engaged in the task of "looking for something," of searching for the most prominent knuckle? But if all your perceptive attention is pouring through your right hand, what has been happening with your left hand—the inert, "searched hand"? Is it "dead"? No, of course not. Well, then, what is it doing? Is it perceiving at all? Yes, it is perceiving passively; it is perceiving phenomenologically. In terms of your tactile sensing, to perceive (or sense) phenomenologically means *to be felt, to surrender one's self to being felt.*

Please bear in mind that to "perceive passively," to let oneself *be* felt, does not in the least mean that we are not perceiving (far to the contrary), but rather that we are *not making any effort* to perceive any particular thing. The left hand was perceiving just as busily as was the right hand but in quite a different manner. Verily, our right hand didn't *know* what the left hand was doing.

But this has to do only with the tactile perception of our skin surface. If consciousness, however, is nothing but perception, then *all* of our senses have this capacity to be used in either of two ways of perceiving: there are two ways of seeing, two ways of hearing, two ways of tasting and sniffing. We can look *for* something, listen *to* something or, simply, we can see and hear. This is to say that we can make the effort to subject the perceived environment to *our* structuring powers, or we can relax and surrender ourselves to the structuring powers of our environment.

Because of the cardinal importance of this distinction of two ways of being conscious, I hope I shall be excused for making very explicit what Merleau-Ponty only suggests implicitly. I would like to state explicitly that the movements of existentialism and phenomenology have largely been the effort to vindicate and explore this other way of perceiving, namely, the surrendering of effort and *allowing the environing world to perceive you.*

The learning of "despair" and the action of "dying away from immediacy" counseled by Kierkegaard is precisely the task of ceasing to be in fearful thralldom to the environment, always anxious in one's concern to cope with it; Kierkegaard would have us forget about trying to overcome the world—we don't *have to* try in order to overcome our anxious analytical consciousness. A reverse strategy is all that is called for.

Heidegger, especially in his later works, is directly concerned with the possibility of men being conscious of their world in this other fashion. There is no other way of understanding what Martin Buber means when he speaks of becoming aware of the Thou-ness of other persons, of animals or of things; as he says, it involves a different way of seeing, a different way of perceiving. Nietzsche, his body ringing with music and poetry, was constantly abandoning himself joyfully to the is-ness of the cosmos and its "innocence of becoming." And Camus, peach juice sticky on his face, moves through the fertile ruins of Tipasa, loving it all, despite the impermanence and death; like Meursault, he opens himself and accepts the "tender indifference of the world."

It is this phenomenological perception of surrender to the potent ordering of the environment which is described biologically by Piaget as "accommodation," whereby the organism adapts to the environment by letting the environment mold it. It is this same human experience which the ethologists see driven by the sensual drives of hunger and mating, under whose impulses the organism opens up and gives itself to a bodily merging with something within the environment. Freud calls it pleasure or Eros, and

Reich sees this same perceptive relation with the world as a dilational streaming outward in somatic relaxation.

And, still again, it is exactly this kind of perception, this kind of somatic stance and relation with the world which draws the concern of humanistic psychologists: what they are trying to do is to understand this other mode of perception, describe its direct relevance to emotional health and develop techniques by which we can induce this other mode of consciousness. Humanistic psychologists are nothing less than modern Hindu and Zen gurus who are going over the same ground as the Indians and Japanese but this time with a knowledge of neuro-physiology and with far more sophisticated techniques. "Peak experiences" are just such moments of giving way to healthy adaptation to one's immediate environment. And the therapy of "self-disclosure" is, similarly, the human action of fearlessly surrendering oneself *to* the environment, of allowing oneself to be *perceived by* and *disclosed to* the human environment.

That this is sensuality is, of course, obvious. That this can also be termed honesty is also obvious. And whether we approach this human experience of phenomenological perception through this or that pathway, we are still using varying words, varying disciplines and varying methodologies to get at the *same somatic event,* a type of human experience which is becoming increasingly common within the mutating bodies of our species.

And so, when we suggested that it was an open question as to just *how* significant this other way of perceiving may be for Merleau-Ponty or any of us, we are placing the question about this alternate mode of perceiving into the evolutionary context out of which it is emerging. There is, finally, nothing new about what Merleau-Ponty calls "phenomenological consciousness"; men have always had it, and a few exceptional men have centered their lives in the cultivation of it. The only difference is that now the exception seems to be becoming the rule; we are propelled by our evolving bodies into a balanced, less anxious adaptation and stance toward our environment. We seem forced to become healthier, more serene and more balanced.

It is not an easy transition. After spending thousands of years learning to hop around on one leg, it feels awkward and unnatural to walk on two.

7

SUMMING IT UP WITH NIETZSCHE: MAN UNDER AND MAN OVER: A TOTAL

The somatic scientists have told us about the basic structure and functioning of the human soma and of how the human soma has evolved this structure and functioning. The somatic philosophers—implicitly assuming this basic somatic structure and functioning—have ranged wider and told us about the way in which human somas experience themselves and the world, and the way in which they behave within themselves and within the world; and not only the way they *have* experienced and behaved but, particularly, different *possible* ways of human experiencing and behaving.

During the course of our examination of the somatic

viewpoint, there has been a liberal scattering of references to that extraordinary man, Friedrich Nietzsche. This is no mere happenstance: Nietzsche is the oracle of somatic thought. It is inevitable that his observations should haunt these pages inasmuch as his presence has subtly guided the development of all subsequent somatic thought. He could be such a guide because he had, far in advance, sensed what was happening and had summed it up in his oracular manner. "Oracular" because, like an oracle, his pronouncements were puzzles, astounding and momentously important puzzles which men sensed to be oracles of the future but not oracles which could at that time be unriddled and interpreted.

Fated to be "born posthumously," Nietzsche was a square peg in the round hole of history; and human history had to evolve and change its shape before men could realize how precisely Nietzsche had anticipated the present historical shape of the Western technological world.

The peg now fits, and the oracles are no longer puzzles. Nietzsche, who was as much cultural historian as he was philosopher, saw human history on a broadly stretched canvas. He saw the history of Western culture as the gradual construction of social, moral, and religious institutions which succeeded in binding men together into strong communities in which the rule was a practical, military-like conformity in their defense against and attacks upon the threat of their environment. In order to bind men together in such conformity, these institutions had to repress the savage non-social instincts of men which, if allowed to run unhindered, would threaten the practical cohesion of the community—a cohesion needed for the survival of the human community.

Well and good: in order to survive, men had to become efficiently herded together, their somas tamed by a herd morality. And Nietzsche saw the anti-natural, anti-somatic institutions of Judaeo-Christianity and Hellenic idealism as the ingeniously effective behavioral controls which guaranteed somatic repression or redirection and behavioral conformity—an "opium of the people" as one somatic thinker expressed it. But the opium was necessary for community survival, and it effectively served its purpose.

However, like all drugs it had a side-effect: by taming the savage drives of men into civilized docility, it didn't destroy the drives; rather, it held them down. The animal energy and the original animal circuits for venting that energy were still there within the human somas, exerting their pressures and seeking other avenues of expression: with the blockage of their evolved (and, thus, normal) somatic avenues of energy expression, these energies found other (and, thus, abnormal) avenues of expression.

It was obvious what these abnormal avenues of somatic expression would be: inasmuch as they would have to conform to the practical survival needs of the human herd, the "allowed" avenues of behavioral expression were the needed labors of aggressing upon the fearful environment *outside* the community or of spreading the balm of sweet conformity and altruism *within* the community. In this way the allowed avenues of behavior reinforced the speculative concerns of the Hellenic institutions even as they reinforced the anti-somatic concerns of the Judaeo-Christian institutions. In this way Western society poured its energy into the theoretical and technical work of understanding and taming the hostile environment of the world; or other energies were poured into the priestly and moral-political work of understanding and keeping tamed the repressed normal circuits of the human soma. Not only do we have the "opium" mentioned by one somatic philosopher but we have also the "repressed" somas of an aggressively "conscious" society described by a somatic scientist.

Nietzsche had sketched all this on the broad canvas of cultural history which he bequeathed us. He saw the benefits of the techniques of social control and of the growing theoretical and engineering capabilities of environmental control: these contributed to community survival and community advancement. He also saw the deficits of these social controls and scientific achievements: they contributed to individual sickness and to the repressive limitation of human capacity.

In order to appreciate the full importance of Nietzsche's insight into our present and our near future, a comparison with Marx will be helpful. The genius of Marx is that he saw how an original situation of scarcity had inevitably produced the human exploitation of class-structured societies; but he further saw that class societies had finally evolved to the stage where there was no longer a situation of actual scarcity and that, therefore, the exploitative society—which had been necessary to create a situation of surplus economic value—would now disappear, leaving men united rather than divided by their economic situation. And there is no denying that Marx is right. But the scope of Nietzsche's vision has the breadth and depth of an evolutionary and somatic viewpoint, and we must learn to see the ingenious and irrefutable insights of Marx as part of the broader canvas stretched before us by Nietzsche. Nietzsche's picture is the following: in order to survive as a species, men have had to gather into communities where *all* individuals of all classes have been repressively exploited so that the human community could concentrate its unified efforts in the aggressive work of taming and controlling a non-human environment; but Nietzsche further saw that these very efforts to understand and control our earthly environment have now borne fruit: men have now guaranteed their survival, and therefore there will no longer be a need for the repressively exploitative social *and* cultural traditions which have maimed individual human somas and prevented the free and normal expression of their energies.

This is the evolution-revolution about which we have spoken since the beginning of the book. In order to survive the evolutionary requirements imposed upon all organic life, all men have, up until now, had to make individual somatic sacrifices so that the human community might survive and prevail. Now that we not only have survived but have shown that we can prevail over our environment in an almost effortless manner, these individual somatic sacrifices are no longer called for by our environmental situation. The new, technological environment is steadily liberating the formerly repressed and maimed somas, despite the forces of the obsolescent cultural tradition which vainly attempt to combat every evidence of this liberation.

There is no possible manner for somatic liberation to be prevented within a technological society. It cannot be prevented for the precise reason that the motor forces of history are not cultural but are somatic-environmental. Human culture is the secondary expression of the primary constructors of human history: namely, the actual human somas and the actual environment in constant adaptive interchange—man adapting to the exigencies of his environment and man forcing the environment to adapt to the exigencies of his own somatic being. Having forced the earth to be an environment in which it is certain that men *can live,* the technologized earth has now made it certain that we, in response, finally *must* live as men.

If the motto for the present is "Adaptation" and that of the next century "Anything is possible," then we must expect that the years ahead will reveal a resolute and exploding disinterest in our traditional culture and an equally resolute and exploding interest in the matter-of-fact recognition of our world nakedly seen as it is and our somas nakedly admitted for what they are. During much of the past century, for a man to see himself and his world nakedly for what they are, stripped of their cultural tradition —such a lucid vision was the "absurd" and "dreadful" experience of realizing how ultimately "meaningless" is the fact of *this* soma and *this* world. But such a lucid vision is no longer unsettling to the growing number of proto-mutants; it is simply the business of seeing it and saying it as it is. Honesty and lack of repression are no longer goals toward which men must vainly strive; they are somatic conditions to which our children are destined and which the cultural traditionalists can but vainly strive to prevent. Lucid and naked recognition of what you and the world actually are is not an anxious experience for anyone—except for the cultural traditionalist who has had to see reality refracted through so many lenses of religious and idealistic repression that a naked vision of reality is absolutely indecent. He would rather see it with its clothes on; he is more accustomed to it that way.

Seeing; recognizing; admitting and expressing what is seen and recognized: this, fundamentally, is what is involved in the adaptation currently taking place. And if the new mutants resolutely turn their interest away from an ancient cultural tradition which cannot aid them in adapting, they will just as certainly drain every drop from the revolutionary somatic tradition which *can* guide them, for the simple reason that it has been guiding and conditioning our society toward just these mutational events which are now upon us.

The somatic scientists have let us know about our

bodies and about *all* living bodies: gathering and dispensing energy, growing and changing, in tension with the world and in loving surrender to it, and here we stand, human somas with one very practical and very overworked system of fear-aggression drives and another suddenly very practical and very under-worked system of sensual-accommodative drives. Those who are somatically lucid recognize that the environment calls strongly to their sensual-accommodative drives and but faintly and failingly calls to their fear-aggression complex. And the lucid mutant responds accordingly: in an "untraditional" manner.

It is this kind of understanding which the somatic scientists have brought us so that we can grasp what has happened to our environment, what is happening to our somas and why the young proto-mutants are responding in the way they are.

And not only have the somatic *scientists* given us an incalculably rich understanding of basic somatics to guide us, but the somatic *philosophers* have opened the door to that future where anything is possible. What the somatic philosophers have done is to take these nudist activities of "seeing, recognizing, admitting and expressing" and have experimentally speculated on all the possibilities which they offer.

The themes of somatic philosophy are, quite simply, perception and behavior; and, to be even more precise, *mutational perception and mutational behavior.*

I have heard it said, and you will hear it repeated *ad nauseum* during the next decades by desperate cultural traditionalists, that what somatology is up to and what the existentialists, phenomenologists and humanistic psychologists are up to is "playing with perception and experimenting with behavior for the fun of it, and thus they are not seriously facing up to reality." In piously asserting such a scathing opinion (their fangs may literally drip through a Presbyterian snarl as they say it), the traditionalists haven't the foggiest awareness of two horrifying facts: they are absolutely wrong, without at all knowing why; and they are also absolutely right, without at all knowing why.

The traditionalists are wrong in that the somatologists are not exploring alternate perceptual and behavioral possibilities because these are pointless, idle pursuits without relevance to reality; rather, from this stage on, men who are lucidly responsive to their environment are driven into these explorations because only through *new* modes of perceptive experience and behavior can we begin to relate ourselves responsibly and relevantly to our transformed environment. In a word, our traditional cultural prescriptions for "normal" perceptions and behavior cannot help us in relating ourselves and adapting ourselves to the extraordinary challenge of a technological environment. From this point onward, the perceptual and behavioral directives of our tradition can only destroy us and make us sicker. There is no responsible option other than to experiment with new ways in which somas can relate to the reality of their environment; in this case, "responsible" literally means "inevitable somatic adaptation to the needs of environmental survival."

The traditionalists are right—again without understanding why they are right—in claiming that such experimentation is fun, that the somatologists are "playing" at life. What needs to be understood is that when one lives in the midst of a technological world which is the end-product and goal of an aeon of work and seriousness, there is no manner for a healthy human soma to respond to this end-product of work other than through an adaptation which entails learning to play and experiencing enjoyment for the pure fun of it. I am saying that the only responsible adaptation to the sovereign realities of a technological environment is the cultivation of the experience of rich enjoyment and the learning of playful behavior. And, in saying this, I am acutely aware of how repugnant, how incredible and how naïve such a statement sounds to the ears of a cultural traditionalist: "It just *couldn't* be true; it is so wrong and blind to reality and so irresponsible!" Nonetheless, it is horrifyingly true, and I shall state it again in another fashion: If we do not create a culture which positively approves sensual-accommodative drives and positively educates its populace in the artful enjoyment of its technological environment, the human race will literally destroy itself; it will destroy itself because a serious-minded, fear-oriented, aggressive cultural tradition has only one function and *raison d'être,* namely, the achievement of a technological society for the conquest of man's environment; and, once this environment is achieved, if the fear-aggression drives engendered by a work-oriented cultural tradition *continue* to be engendered, then the massive energies of human technology will cease to be directed upon the non-human environment and will be extended to the human environment in a fearful-aggressive manner. The unparalleled destructiveness of the twentieth century is the black symptom of this achievement of a technological society within a culture which is still frightened and serious-minded. In such a not-yet-adapted situation, we see how a technology developed for the benefit *of* man is murderously turned *against* man without reason. Ideology and national honor are not "reasons"—they are the cultural habits of stupid and fearful men who are so deeply trained in their senescent culture that they cannot see and respond to the new environment which now stands nakedly before them.

Nietzsche foresaw the coming of this awful, dislocated period of "nihilism" in the twentieth century—a terrible and anxious period when science and technology had completed their basic job of construction and then waited for a stunned humanity to overcome the initial blindness which its dazzling, incredible technology had caused. And when the gaudy brilliance of "modern science" had ceased to blind, and when men began to see again, Nietzsche knew that they would see the effects of their technological triumph, understand it and adapt to it. And with this momentous adaptation, they would no longer be men caught under a repressive culture which drove them to defend themselves; rather, they would transcend this ancient culture and develop cultural traditions which would elevate men and enhance them. They would be Overmen (*Uebermenschen*), who stood over and above a culture which now undergirded and supported them because it was *for* them. No longer would men need to be gnarled and suffering instruments for the conquest of their environment; now they could be the healthy ends toward which thousands of generations had worked by being the instrumental *means* for the attainment of this human goal.

What Nietzsche is speaking of and what somatology is pointing toward is the adjusted human mutant who, because he has become adapted to his environment, is no longer a mutant but is a normal man. Such a man is an intact human being, a balanced human being who is no longer distracted *from* the business of living with his fellows and with himself by the frightening presence of a non-human environment which threatens the non-survival of him and his fellows. Such a balanced human being is now possible; and by "balanced" we mean a human soma whose energies can be expressed directly through those avenues of somatic behavior which seem appropriate to the environmental situation which evokes these energies. Such a man adapts smoothly and efficiently with the contingencies of his environment, even as he adapts his environmental situation smoothly and efficiently to his somatic needs.

Fear is a most practical somatic talent: when an environmental situation is threatening, a healthy man is fearful and removes himself from the danger. Aggression, also, is a most practical talent: triggered by its early-warning system of fear, anger will flare out at the intruding, unwanted person or situation and it will act to remove the threat and intimidation. Both fear and anger are somatic possessions which have allowed us to survive, and they will continue to do so. They are the constrictive drives, which protect, consolidate and preserve the individual and his possessions. They are the drives of isolation and pride and loneliness.

Hunger, too, is a most practical drive. It has many forms because we have many hungers: for food and drink and orgasm, of course, but, in hungering, we hunger through *all* of our senses. As every good Frenchman knows, there is a universe of taste and a universe of smells; and one can just as yearningly seek to envelop oneself in the bouquet of a Châteauneuf-du-Pape with just the right body as one could yearn to fill one's hungering belly with beef and potatoes. And even as hunger for food or for drink is not simply a matter of the belly but of sensual experience, our hungers—actual and potential—are immensely complex.

The middle class American generally hasn't the least conception of what hunger is. Which is difficult to believe when one notes that we are the most obsessively acquisitive society on earth. Enormously acquisitive, but yet not motivated by any somatic hunger, gross or refined. And because Americans have bodies whose hungers are stifled, they are deemed by other nations of the earth to be wealthy and insensitive clods who are easy prey for the world's con men. Lacking authentic hungers, Americans spend their days eating symbols, looking at symbols, courting symbols, fighting symbols and making love to symbols. They are so sealed off from sensual interchange with their environment by their fear-aggression myth that they are capable of going to the ends of the earth and making any effort, any sacrifice, just so long as it is for a symbol and is not tainted with somatic openness and honesty.

But the American middle class, the major bearers of the cultural tradition, are mutating out, so we need not grieve for them or prescribe remedies. With the new mutants no remedies will be needed; only training and guidance. And Nietzsche set the somatic tone for this guidance when he remarked that the problem for a man is not *what* he should want, but rather to discover *that* he wants.

Those reared in our traditional culture do not know that they, as individuals, can be an authentic source of wants: very specific wants that arise from a most ancient and beautifully structured system of desires: their somatic inheritance. And this structured and sophisticated soma has developed with a certain family environment, a certain language and a certain community, all of which have modified the specific way in which that individual soma can express his needs and satisfy them. Every human being has his own individual treasure-house of needs and his own individual style of satisfying these needs—*if* he can be taught that he is allowed and expected to express this individual style of wanting, *if* he can be told from birth that he is uniquely himself and he doesn't *have to* be someone else, seeking to satisfy needs which are someone else's and not his. Once an individual lucidly sees that he is, indeed, the source of his own desires and proceeds to affirm himself as such, then desiring is automatic, spontaneous and easy. He knows *that* he wants and thus knows *what* he wants; then, at this point, his intelligence swings into action seeking a behavioral route within his environment through which his desire can be realized in his world as he sees it.

How one realizes a somatic drive is a technical task for the educated intelligence which is trained to judge the environment. But *letting* the specific somatic drive grow and express itself as a specific desire is another problem. And it is this problem with which the first mutants must tangle: namely, cultivating and educating oneself somatically in the experience of one's sensual-accommodative drives.

The soma's hungers are sensual-accommodative drives. Unlike the fear-aggression drives, they do not preserve and isolate the individual from his environment; to the contrary, they impel him toward it, inasmuch as there is something in the environment which he must participate in, merge with or be a part of. In hunger one leaves off from constricted isolation and relaxes outward toward the environment in open invitation to its impact. *All* desires are sensual; but traditional Western culture has struggled to restrict recognition of sensuality only to those drives which have had practical survival value. Thus, we would expect that, in its purest expression, our traditional culture would say that "eating and drinking are good *for* health, strength and labor but not for any reason in *itself.*" In this case, a "reason in itself" would be somatic satisfaction. Or, "sex is good *for* procreating new human beings but not for any reason in itself."

But if the frightful environment is no longer there and if the serious and practical social needs no longer exist, then the restricting of sensual drives to those drives which can be justified as "good *for*" some survival need is a restriction without purpose or relevance. The "good for . . ." disappears, and the sensual drives that move within us are neither "good for anything" nor "good for nothing"—they simply are. They exist, and they exist as part of that total complex which is myself as a man or of yourself as the embodied man or woman you are. These desires are *me*, and I do not need to justify them, anymore than I need to justify my own self and the fact that I exist. I was made to exist by the innocent fatality of the cosmos; and in the same way that I do not and cannot justify the existence of the universe, I also do not and cannot justify *my* existence and the pulsing, structured soma which is the home of my existence.

Not only is the "innocence of becoming" the mutant's discovery; just as significant is the innocence of being. To recognize the somatic fact of being what one is may, for a person of the present time, require an enormous psychotherapeutic struggle toward honesty; but in the near future it will be as inevitably necessary as saying "A rock is a rock" or "All men have two legs."

The somatic philosophers—from Kant and Kierkegaard's early insights right up to Merleau-Ponty and the experimental present—are our first guides for discovering the richness of our sensual-accommodative drives through whose structures we are able to adapt and mold ourselves and our experience to the structures of our human and physical environment. This "phenomenological consciousness" has been mapped but is, as yet, largely unexplored by men in our own culture; and it is we who must do the exploring in our own way—even though the techniques developed long ago out of the Hindu and Buddhist traditions have made trails through the same somatic experience. We can profit from these earlier explorations, but to take them as a final report on the somatic experience of sensual-accommodative drive patterns would be pointless. We have gone too far, learned too much, sacrificed too long for a technological society to let our evolving need for sensual-accommodative experience be satisfied by the groping explorations of men whose minds were largely governed by a mythical reality which is quite alien to us. Compared with what we shall discover about somatic experience during the next few generations, the Yogic science may be but a drop in the bucket.

From the point of view of our present unbalanced somatic state of fear-aggression, what will take place during the next few decades will appear an "unbalanced" exploration and immersion in sensuality. That man's final achievement of somatic balance and health should seem, at present, so "unbalanced" is the ultimate symptom of how unhealthy, suffering and deprived have been men and their traditional culture for all these ages.

SECTION THREE

HERE WE GO
ROUND
THE MULBERRY
BUSH
SO EARLY

O'HANNAHAN: Anything is possible.
BONES (*cunningly*): Even the *im*possible?
O'HANNAHAN: Possibly.

1

THE THIRD EYE

"But if anything is possible and nothing is impossible, then life and the cosmos aren't going anywhere in particular: existence couldn't have a final goal or meaning."

A few years ago George Schrader of Yale University was writing a review of a book of mine on existential philosophy, and toward the end he made the sagacious observation that if what I had written about existentialism was true, then existentialism was not at all a morose exercise in anxiety and misery but was, instead, a very happy philosophy. I thoroughly enjoyed Schrader's comment, inasmuch as during my first years of teaching and writing I had always thought of myself as a happy existentialist; and Schrader was the first to notice the presumed anomaly of this.

Like millions of other Americans, I had spent half my energies during my early university years doing a bit of study and the other half groaning and aghast over my discovery that "everything is meaningless." This was all to the good: the only positive attainment that I could put my finger on after four academic years was not the B.A. which I acquired but the God and virginity which I lost. Even though my particular college would never have dreamed of programming such a result, it inadvertently succeeded in the basic task of an ideal four-year college program: decorrupting the young student of all the corruptions of ignorance, fear and prejudice he had sopped up from the cultural environment during his first seventeen years. I was cleansed of the traditional corruptions of theology and morality, and, although this reprogramming of my youngish soma led me, suffering, through many a dark night of the soul, I emerged a somewhat more balanced and efficient soma: and a rather happy man.

The twentieth century has been a period when growing throngs of men and women have incurred these dark nights of the soul, during which they experience an uncanny dislocation and out-of-jointness which they can only sum up as an awful feeling that life is pointless and meaningless. This is, indeed, an awful experience—losing one's traditional mind—for it involves the profound disappointment and frustration that comes when one discovers that one's cultural training, which has centered on conscious attention and rational attack on all adaptational problems, is not, finally, the most effective way of coping with one's environment.

That life in this world is discovered to be "absurd," "irrational" and "ultimately meaningless" doesn't say one blessed thing about life in this world. What it *does say* is that the complex panorama of man and his environment cannot be totally grasped by or reduced to the mechanism of the conscious intelligence. It is not a commentary on the world; it is a commentary on conscious intelligence. After all, how could there in the least be anything ultimately wrong about the world: it simply *is,* and since it is in no way responsible for its being as it is, there isn't any point in accusing the is-ness of our cosmos. On the contrary, the experience of "meaninglessness" is a living accusation of that hypertrophy of one aspect of our somas: namely, conscious attention and rational effort.

What is ludicrous about this anguished and frustrated search for ultimate meaning is that it is totally needless; before we even began looking for it, we had the meaning we were seeking, and as soon as we began seeking it we lost it. Like the absent-minded ninny who searches all over the house for the spectacles which are on his nose, our frustrated seekers are doomed to their frustration by the very nature of their situation: it requires no effort, no conscious search, no rational operation to discover the meaning of life, inasmuch as the meaning of life cannot, by the nature of things, *be discovered.* It cannot be "discovered" like something that is separated from you and lost, because the meaning of your life is not "out there," separated from you: the meaning of life already *is* you, the living soma. And it is not possible to seek something which you already are but, rather, it is the different question of *letting yourself be.* The fundamental problems of human life are not even approachable by intellectual effort; they can be solved only by somatic enlightenment.

So then, what we are saying is that if life is found to "have no meaning," this is a clear symptom of the inability of conscious intelligence to deal with the most immediate and fundamental human problems. But, beyond this, it is also a symptom of the way in which reliance upon the efforts of conscious intelligence creates the very problem which human beings then try to solve by an even more frantic reliance on conscious intelligence. In brief, somatic science and thought have demonstrated to us that conscious intelligence and its aggressive tradition of technological science are designed for an attack on man's environment but are not designed for an attack upon man himself. To aim at such an attack is to apply the wrong tool and the incorrect method for a pathetically mistaken motive.

But if the post-adolescent dark night of the soul and its "discovery of meaninglessness" have been the experience of myself and millions of others, this is but the preface to the first act of a mutation which is now in evidence: the proto-mutational young Americans know that life in this world has no ultimate rational meaning; and they have known this from the beginning, and have not had to suffer through and overcome a somatic education which a traditional culture had imposed upon them as claiming to be truth. These young Americans—either through deliberate parental permissiveness or through parental indifference— were, if you will, educated "in the technological streets of America": they have seen their environment and used its facilities and come to understand it without the benefit of having it interpreted by our traditional culture. And, lacking this "benefit," the earlier generation's problem of "Does life have a meaning?" never even occurs to them. They are already beyond that point. If you were to pose the question to them, their telling reply would be, "But where did you ever get the idea that life *should* have some ultimate meaning?"

To realize that life need *not* "have a meaning" in order to be livable is the first step in acceptance of life as it is; it is the beginning not only of acceptance but of relaxation and growing trust in your somatic being and in the world's being as they are given to be. It is the moment when one no longer fears the is-ness which surrounds him but begins to open to it and love it for what it is. To love and accept the somatic-environmental universe even though it is devoid of any "ultimate meaning" is the sign that one is ceasing to rely strictly upon conscious intelligence as one's medium for relating to one's environment. It is the sign that one is beginning to slip out of his mind and to adventure into his entire somatic being in order to relate to his environment.

The marvelous Marshall McLuhan has gaily recognized this change within increasing numbers of the young: namely, that they do not see things in the same way as their traditionalized elders. And even though McLuhan's focus is on the technological media which have been the teething ring against which these youngsters have gnawed their way into adulthood, still this focus is sharply on the central event of a change in human perception; and his description of this mutation in human perception is totally immersed in somatic terminology. The key words which sound through McLuhan's writings like a passacaglia are such terms as instant, organic, information, electric, form and pattern, media, communication. And McLuhan is quite aware that when one describes the cybernetical organization of electronic communication systems, one is describing the neurophysiological system of the human body. As he sees it, the technological triumph of the twentieth-century West is an extension of our somas, so that our communicational technology is like an extension of our own nervous systems: the earth is like a village because our communications are just as immediate as our own nervous system, and thus we perceive things immediately. To have been reared within this recent technological environment (and to have been reared without the distortions wrought by our traditional culture) is, without a doubt, to perceive the environment in a radically different manner.

But McLuhan might carry his analogy even farther: not only is our communicational technology patterned after our central nervous system, it is an *objectification* of it. In the cybernetical organization of computer processing and electronic communication systems, what we have achieved is a *getting rid of the human function of rational-intelligent labor*. We have, within the twentieth century, literally objectified what for centuries had been considered a mysterious and inviolable possession of the human "spirit." The ghost of the intellect is not only incarnate, but he is presently sitting in the basement of every large industry purring and clicking away inside of shining steel cabinets.

Philosophers have frequently engaged in vigorously boring debates over whether there are any significant differences between a man and a computer. The similarity between a man and a computer is unquestionable, inasmuch as a computer is a material reproduction of that function of the sympathetic nervous system which is called conscious intelligence. Not only *is* a computer consciously intelligent but it is *more* so than any human being. That is the similarity between man and computer. But the dissimilarity is much more significant: the dissimilarity is that a computer (or any cybernetic electronic system) is a cast-off homunculus; it is a human function which man is abandoning so that he can do something else. The difference is, then, that man mutates while the computer takes over an abandoned human function.

A major part of what psychologists, philosophers and other scientists and religionists have called the "human spirit" is now being manufactured by I.B.M. This I find to be very funny, for it throws into clear relief the comic nonsense that has threaded its way through our traditional culture. As soon as men get over their amazement at this surprising turn of events which computers represent, they will quickly settle into a profound indifference to computers and their functions: they will take these functions for granted, inasmuch as they will, as human beings, be engaged in other activities in which they are not called upon to be consciously rational.

Since we no longer spend a great deal of time climbing trees in our bare feet, no one seems particularly disturbed by the speculation that our little toes seem to be mutating out of existence. And once the expansion of cybernetical systems becomes general, no one should be disturbed to realize that—in a similar fashion—our concern for a highly rational and self-conscious intelligence will become considerably diminished. It will be diminished simply because it will no longer be a function which we, alone, can do: since machines can do it, we no longer *need* to do it. The law behind this is potent: a somatic function which ceases to serve a practical need in environmental adaptation will not survive but will mutate out or, at the least, will diminish to whatever functional level is still needed. And so, the instrument of aggressive rational intelligence, which we once needed to conquer a recalcitrant environment, is now being successfully objectified; now we can turn our concerns toward other matters.

What other matters? Well, for one thing, becoming acquainted with oneself. For decades there has been growing concern about discovering oneself, discovering one's being, developing, experiencing, disclosing, actualizing, fulfilling one's being, self, etc. And this steadily intensified concern has circled about, narrowing its point of focus to the point that now we can finally speak more clearly about the nature of this mysterious "self" and "being" which we have for so long spoken about. It is, of course, the soma. Your "self" and your "being" is simply your immediately embodied presence in this world: you, the soma.

And the reason that there has been increasing concern about revealing this soma is precisely because the development of a technologized environment has increasingly allowed more and more human beings the freedom to be concerned about it. But, as was already pointed out, this somatic meaning which one seeks to discover and bring to the fore is not approachable through any direct technical effort such as would be found among the stock-in-trade of our cultural tradition; a radically different approach will be needed. And, for many persons, when they finally get a clear notion of what a "radically different approach" actually entails and feels like, their somas will be flooded with the constrictive explosions of fear and anger to such a degree that this mutant approach will be loathed and reviled in the most vigorous manner.

If one's conditioning is in the traditional kind of perception and behavior typical of the Western fear-aggression approach of constrictive conscious control, then an attempt to cultivate the somatic experience of accommodative, sensual behavior will be somatically repulsive if not literally convulsive. It will be so because the avenues of a parasympathetic energy expression have been so long atrophied and constricted that the musculature is incapable of relaxing and becoming a medium for sensual-accommodative energy expression.

For those few persons who happen to have been fighting the cultural tradition all their lives, such avenues of sensual expression can be broken through. And the many institutes, burgeoning all over the country, devoted to sensitivity training and expansion of consciousness are the

initial attempts to give aid to these refugees from our traditional culture. But such refugee aid is obviously only a
transient phase in what will be developed. Wounded refugees from a moribund culture are a minor and insignificant phenomenon, presently important only to the extent
that their wealth makes the development of this experimental therapy possible.

But such institutes and the maimed middle class which
they have been serving have no future at all, except as a
stepping stone toward developing positive guide lines and
training techniques for the flood of proto-mutants who will
not be maimed refugees but will simply be relatively balanced somas whose explosive energies have no clear way
of engaging their environment. Certainly, all but a few colleges are only of the slightest aid to the proto-mutants; the
administrators haven't the foggiest notion of what is taking place—all they know is that something is scary and
wrong, and they'll keep steering the ship resolutely toward
the shoals, hoping they can get their retirement before the
whole idiotic vessel runs aground and sinks. The growing
number of private institutes for sensual-accommodative
training are, thus, almost the only centers of any mutational value; but, even at the moment of their first blush of
success and excitement, these institutes must realize that
their eventual and proper function is not with the refugees
from the past but with the orphans of the present and future. The sign of this is written plainly on the walls of their
bath-houses and massage rooms: the Hippies don't need
such institutes and the new-leftists scorn them as middle-
class first-aid stations.

The question of what positive, institutionalized means
may be put at the disposal of proto-mutants and mutants
is, rather, a separate strand of discussion that will be pursued in the final chapter. For the moment, it is quite

sufficient for us to speak first about this "radically different approach" and all that it seems to mean.

Somatic scientists and philosophers have taught us that, as somas descended from an immense evolutionary past, each of us is *already* "meaningfully" (read: adaptationally) structured in relation to our environing world. This meaningfully related structure is, quite literally, *ourselves:* it doesn't need to be searched for or thought about, inasmuch as it already exists beneath all our searching and rational thinking. Searching and thinking are the very successful instruments used *by* our somatic selves to control and manipulate the environment so that we may survive and prevail. But now that we have survived and are, indeed, prevailing, our somas no longer need to relate to this changed environment primarily in terms of these defensive-aggressive activities of searching and rational analysis. An environment which has been forced to adapt *to* the survival needs of men has now been so transformed that men in a technological society are surrounded by an environment which forces them to adapt *to* this environment. Formerly a malign environment, evoking fear and aggression on the part of men, now it is a benign environment, evoking the somatic movements of accommodation and surrender—movements little practiced and little encouraged during the perilous early career of the species.

During the course of the twentieth century, to the measure that the environment has been rendered more benign, so has there been an answering response of human beings who have awakened to an anxious desire to feel meaningfully related to this technological universe but who have discovered that this meaningful relationship is somehow unattainable. What is crucial here is just this *awakening* of the human soma to a new task of relating to the environment; and what is equally important is the discovery that the resources of one's cultural training are not capable of fulfilling this task.

The twentieth-century awakening to a quest for "meaning" is the awakening of the repressed and sleeping portion of our somas to the task of adaptation. The "dark," "irrational" sensual-accommodative drives have begun to lurch and deploy their forces and, in consequence, men have been uncannily disturbed, not really being able to consciously pinpoint or understand the nature of this strange malaise. And these troubled souls were incapable of locating and making sense of this malaise, not because what was happening *surpassed* the understanding but, rather, because it *subpassed* the conscious understanding, lying inscrutably and powerfully beneath the device of consciousness. The so-called existential anguish was the first clear somatic symptom of the mutation toward which our technological environment was ineluctably pulling us.

This is why existential philosophy is, after all, a happy philosophy: because it deals with the happiest of all human experiences—growth and adaptation. It is the kind of philosophy which Nietzsche so aptly called "The Gay Science." And if it has seemed grim and morose to many persons, this is because all rites of passage seem forbidding to the initiate *before* he goes through them; but after he has gone through them and has attained his identity and adulthood, he laughs at his former dread and sees this dread within the perspective of necessary growth. From Kierkegaard onward, an unquenchable wit and laughter has echoed through all of existential philosophy beneath its dreadful somatic analyses. In fine, existential thought has been the philosophical description of the rite of passage of the human species from childhood into young manhood.

As anthropologists have indicated, a rite of passage in-

volves the acquisition of a radically different approach to
experiencing and behaving in one's world. This rite of passage is what Heidegger has called "crossing over the line,"
and the radically different approach to one's environment
is what Nietzsche termed a "new consciousness" for mankind.

All of this indicates that a radically new "conscious" approach to one's environment means a new way of *experiencing* one's environment—a kind of experience which is
not that of a constrictive, conscious rationality but a kind
of experience which subpasses this old and limited adaptational device. As I have already suggested, every bit of somatic evidence points to this new way of experiencing as
being that of expressive love—the experience of "giving
up," of surrendering oneself in loving trust to some aspect
of one's environment. The sensual-accommodative experience will be the most obvious thing to come to the fore
when this surrender takes place; and it will come to the
fore in terms of somatic relaxation—a streaming, unfocused sensuality which allows one's somatic being to be
felt by, perceived by and molded by some aspect of one's
environment. Sensual-accommodative experience is the
experience of being adapted *to* some person or some situation that is near you, and in order to be molded and
adapted *to* other beings and other situations, the soma
must be loose, in happy surrender and relaxation down to
the last synapse and muscular fiber. Such an experience is,
obviously, unafraid; it is unashamed, honest, blatantly expressive of the motor drives that have been evoked by that
given environmental presence.

Let me repeat again what I felt necessary to stress at the
end of *Section Two:* that our mutation into balanced
human somas does *not* mean the disappearance of fear-
aggression expressions; what it *does* mean is the appear-

ance of sensual-accommodative expressions within somatic-environmental interchange to a degree never before conceived of by men. The key adaptational term is *somatic balance in relationship to the given environment.* Honest anger and honest fear are as necessary adaptational expressions as are honestly expressed hungers for the merging of one's soma with the given shape, flavor or texture of some alluring environmental situation. In either case, we have the event of adaptation. But, because human somas have for so long—and particularly during the past three centuries within the West—maintained an unbalanced emphasis upon a fear-aggression, assimilative adaptation with their environment, the energizing of the sensual-accommodative avenues of expression will become such a dominant adaptational priority during the coming generations that this development will initially *seem* to be a total mutation into sensual accommodation. There is no somatic basis for believing that such an event is even possible. Without a doubt, the parasympathetic functions of the autonomic nervous system are beginning to undergo an intensive period of development and application, but this in no wise means that the sympathetic branch of the autonomic nervous system will cease to exist.

The ineluctable mutation toward this more balanced and homeostatic human soma is a change which will open up more avenues of somatic adaptability. The raw biological term adaptability may not sufficiently suggest just how extraordinary this somatic balance is. So it will be best if we string together a few salient words which describe what takes place during adaptation. *To learn* is to adapt to something. *To communicate* is equally an adaptational interchange. *To give or receive information* is adaptation. To learn, to communicate, to exchange information are of the very essence of adaptation, and such adaptation is an exchange between soma and environment in which the soma impresses its structures on the environment (assimilation) or the environment impresses its structures on the soma (accommodation). In either of these two events we have the adaptational event of learning, communicating and interchanging of information which is an adaptational necessity if a soma is to survive in its environing world.

Up until the present period, the experience which human somas have had of their environment has been resolutely centered in the function of assimilation, i.e., we have learned and communicated with our environment primarily to the extent that this information allows us aggressively to control and manipulate that environment. Assuredly, there have been men and women who were exceptions to this fear-aggression attitude toward their world—and these are some of history's great visionaries, poets, artists and dreamers—but such humans were exceptions to their cultural tradition; and this tradition, by forcing men into a crippled, hunched up, all-out assault on their environment, made possible the technological environment which will now evoke visionaries, poets, dreamers and much more than this, not as exceptions but as the rule.

What we must understand is this: *the accommodative manner of adaptation is another form of learning, of communicating and of receiving information.* It is another mode of human experience. As Nietzsche says, it is a new consciousness for man. As Merleau-Ponty describes it, it is a radically different manner of perceiving—a perception which is relaxed, unfocused and which takes in the whole field of sensation rather than the figure-ground facet of sensation. What we are beginning to do and what we shall continue to do into the next century is to develop this relaxed, more expansive and inclusive mode of receiving information from our environment. We don't know *how* as yet and are just beginning to learn: like a man who has spent his life looking directly at a dim object in order to "see" it and is stunned to discover that if he looks away from it he can see it even better. Training ourselves to perceive *everything* within the horizon of our vision—and not simply "one thing" to the exclusion of all else—this is the adaptational task which has opened up for the sensual-accommodative drives.

No one should be shocked or even surprised to learn of the advent of another kind of science: for two-thirds of our century, we have heard it repeated over and over again that "what we need is for our morality to catch up with our scientific progress." This is precisely what is now beginning to take place. But the cultural traditionalists who have been monotonously reiterating this hope are, predictably, the last persons capable of either understanding or accepting this fulfillment of their pious plea, inasmuch as they equate "morality" with a specific form of behavior; and the heart of the problem is that the human race does not need "more" of this morality (whatever that might mean) but rather that it is precisely this traditional morality which will necessarily diminish and disappear in the course of man's adaptation to the environment created by the technological sciences. Funny but sad; and the moral would seem to be: Don't wish for miracles, because in order for them to become possible the world will change to such a degree that you may be horrified by the fulfilled wish.

With the eternal risk of appearing impious, I can state the traditionalists' injunction in a less colorful way: already we "know" enough about our environment in terms of its causative handles and knobs in order to grab hold of it and manipulate it; the achievements of technological science are *already* sufficient (this is, with certainty, the last thing which the cultural traditionalist—capitalist or communist—could believe or accept, inasmuch as he believes down to his bones that all problems are ultimately solvable only by the increased application of rational, aggressive power—either that of scientific technology or, piously, the power of the traditional God: the heavenly, providential Technologist). We already have *enough* technological knowledge of environmental control for the demonstrable reasons that (1) our American environment is sufficiently technologized to the point that it is now producing proto-mutants and (2) technological science is becoming more and more boring to more and more people and arouses their interest only when it is a question of using technological skills in order to restore the ecological balance caused by the needless *mis*use of technological skills: both reasons have equally significant weight. But what we do *not* know enough about is *how to live in this benign, technologized environment.* And we don't know how to live in this environment because we have not yet obtained enough experience of this environment—expansive and inclusive experience which can only be obtained through sensual-accommodative perception. And *this* mode of experience, *this* kind of learning is, in itself, the very adaptation we are seeking, i.e., to learn about your environment accommodatively is, by definition, the very act of learning to live in this environment—the perception, the experience and the expressive behavior are identical.

Let us now dawdle a moment on the point just made; it is a crucial observation and, at first sight, it may seem incomprehensible. The statement is that sensual-accommodative perception is *also* sensual-accommodative behavior. If this assertion seems odd, then bear with me for a moment, inasmuch as in the clarification of this crucial point, we shall have turned an important corner in our understanding of contemporary human evolution.

It is a commonplace in existential philosophy to point out that "doing" is dependent on "being." This is a verbally cute manner of saying that behavior is conditioned by perception: according to the way in which we perceive reality, so will we behave in that reality. It is this direct linkage between perception and resultant behavior which moves Sartre, for example, to say that everyone makes the right choice.

Well and good; but the relationship between perception and behavior when dominated by accommodative drives is radically different from the relationship which pertains when human perception and behavior are dominated by assimilative drives. In the human creature, constrained as he is by his attainment of rational-verbal consciousness, there is a *hiatus* between the perception of an environmental situation and his behavioral response to it. This is very human, of course; other animal somas function autonomically in their fear or anger responses: given a perilous situation, flight is immediate or, given a threatening territorial encroachment, attack is immediate. But not so with human beings: their assimilative expressions of fear-aggression are channeled through the monitoring device of a rational consciousness, complete with memory banks and scanning devices. Because our rational consciousness is a late veneer on the surface of our ancient somas, it serves as an intermediate operation between situation and response. This is to say that, without our achievement of rational consciousness, human response to threatening situations would be automatic and immediate aggression or flight, i.e., autonomic nervous responses of fixed motor patterns.

But, as it is, when we perceive a situation, we rarely

reply to it immediately but instead deliberate and make judgments concerning it. This computerlike activity of deliberation and judgment is the hiatus between perception and behavior; and, moreover, it is a highly erratic activity, inasmuch as the behavioral response to the perceived situation may, on the face of it, appear highly inappropriate to the situation. In other words the human "mind" is a very devious and dubious device in its computations of gain, pleasure and survival.

The point, then, is this: for the assimilative activity of human consciousness there is a sharp difference between perception and behavior. But accommodative experience is radically different from this: because it is more ancient than consciousness and because its concerns are antipathetic to the assimilative concerns of consciousness, it interacts with the environment in an immediate, confident, organic manner. *Accommodative perception is accommodative behavior:* it is unconscious, unfocused, unafraid and autonomic. It is, for a fact, the manner in which we may exist in organic relationship, organic interchange, organic identity with our environment.

In sensual-accommodative experience, we *perceive* in a radically different manner because it involves *behaving* in this same manner; it involves immediate, unself-conscious somatic surrender to drive patterns which were evoked by the situation. And it is, itself, pure expression: a letting-the-soma-loose in its mimetic response to its environment. In its purity, it is what Nietzsche called the Dionysian expression; in its disciplined, fulfilled form which will come during the next century, it is what Nietzsche called Dionysian-Apollonian expression.

What is frightening to the cultural traditionalists is just this autonomic, unself-conscious nature of sensual-accommodative experience: it is *unashamedly* there for all others to see. How scandalous for a man to stand there, eyes closed, moving his hips and shoulders in total abandonment to the music. How peculiar for that girl to sit on the same spot of grass or pavement, gazing for hours at the same nest of clover or the same urban blight.

Indeed, such experience, which is simultaneously perception and behavior (which is to say, autonomic expression), is shameless, untroubled and unself-conscious. Or to put it in another way, it is a liberation from shame, anxiety and consciousness. That it is "animal-like" is without question. That it is a somatic exploration that is utterly healthy because it leads toward adaptive balance is also without question.

What clearer sign could there be of the inadaptability and decadence of our traditional culture than the sudden interest that has arisen among younger Americans in hallucinogens—particularly marijuana? Well, there *is* a clearer sign: and this is the furtive horror felt by the cultural traditionalists in their reaction to this event. They know that something "revulsive and filthy and animal" is going on when human beings smoke marijuana, and they throw the whole weight of their social controls against those who enjoy hallucinogens. Millions of young Americans know that the smoking of pot is a delightful experience, and they are far more aware of the biochemistry of it than are their elders. And so when the police, the politicians, the ministers, the journalists and other spokesmen for the cultural tradition raise their many voices against the evils and terrors of marijuana, the so-called generation gap becomes sharply delineated: for it is not merely the case that the young people think their elders are lying, but more damning is the fact that the powers-that-be are condemning, prosecuting and persecuting these same young people for doing something which the elders know nothing about because they've never tried it.

How can one explain such extraordinary conduct on the part of the cultural traditionalists? Younger Americans know very well what the explanation is: the traditionalists —as usual—are afraid; and what they are afraid of is a radically different mode of experiencing. They are afraid of a mode of experience where, in terms of self-conscious constriction, they have "lost control." They are deathly afraid of "losing their minds."

The young people, for their part, are quite happy to lose their minds, occasionally, inasmuch as they know that human beings obviously have more than one mind. The uptight experience of conscious rationality is undeniably one kind of "mind," but the mentality of somatic experience lying just beneath this conscious mind is also a "mind." And the smoking of an anti-inhibitory, "consciousness-expanding" herb is an easy way for young human beings to become acquainted with that richness of their soma, about which the cultural tradition has little to say other than in a negative, fearful vein.

The use of such drugs is a minor crutch for young Americans to employ as they probe their way into a somatic-environmental future for which there is no positive cultural support. Even the use of this crutch is a passing event; proto-mutants are essentially a radically different breed in terms of health and independent somatic functioning. The traditional culture, in order to endure its repressive tensions, has become the drug culture *par excellence;* the pharmaceutical industry owes its extensive development more to traditional Western culture than it does to the motivations of chemical research. And the aggressive work-symbol of tobacco puffing is as much Western as is the profound need for alcoholic depressants to recover from the effects of that same tense anxiety over work.

Proto-mutants do not need these drugs which either repair or dull somatic experience; rather, they want more somatic experience, and they want it *now*. In this respect, the interest in the new-found hallucinogenics (which, significantly, no one in the West formerly had any interest in, even though the fields of marijuana existed) is of a pair with the concern for social revolution: the proto-mutants sense the future of which they are the harbingers, and they want to have the somatic experience of it *now* (through pot) and they want to have the environmental presence of it now (through revolution).

To say that what is now taking place is a "discovery of self" is to say that the newer human beings are learning a new form both of experience and of behavior. It is not that there is anything "there" to be discovered; it is not something that one looks for, finds, takes a picture of, then files away under the rubric "SELF: Discovered." To the contrary, the radically different mode of experience entailed means that "discovery of self" is a constant, unrelenting event of somatic expression and adaptation to one's immediate environment. One "discovers," "knows" and "is" a self only to the extent that one's somatic being is constantly revealing itself and growing in endless adaptation to an environment which itself never ceases changing. In fine, there is no such thing as "discovering" one's self— this is traditional talk which conceives of "self" as a mounted trophy, such as soul, spirit, et al.—instead, there is only *being one's self:* which means letting one's full somatic being function in living, fluid adaptation to the immediate environment.

This is not an easy thing to learn, especially when there is little cultural background to guide you other than the writings of some Western mystics and heretics and the treatises of Indian and Japanese mystics. But the mutational task of developing a sensual-accommodative interchange with the world is precisely what the environment not only invites but, more exactly, compels of us if we are to adapt and survive within a technological environment.

The legend that man once had a third eye for perception, now covered over but which can become uncovered again, is as much a legend for the recent Western tradition of somatic science and thought as it is for Indian thought. The powerful and perceptive eye of the soma is there, hidden and overlaid with all manner of late-developed assimilative paraphernalia, and this somatic eye will become able to see only to the extent that the fear-aggression paraphernalia diminishes and becomes more translucent.

A sensual-accommodative mode of experiencing is the attainment of what I would call "translucent egoism," which is to suggest a way of existing whereby the individual is in immediate and fluid interchange with the evocations of his environment. An individual who is translucently egoistical is one whose soma gives the immediately appropriate response (whether fear, aggression, sensuality, accommodation or some combination) to what the environment demands in terms of adaptation. It is easy and fluid adaptation with the least time lost and the most openness. To train the third eye is, moreover, not merely the opening up of the sensual-accommodative drives to fluid expression but is also, by effect, the retraining of the fear-aggressive drives in the same kind of fluid responsiveness.

What I am suggesting is, admittedly, a fearful prospect for the traditionalist: the possibility that not only sensual-accommodative drives will be released but that the same will occur with the now highly disciplined fear-aggressive drives, has the explosive portent of terror for any thoughtful traditionalist. This is because the keystone of traditionalist culture has been restraint and repression—or, as Nietzsche rather bluntly puts it, "castration": it is better to kill the soma than to let it be free. Consequently, the behavioral and experiential ideal which has arisen is that of altruism: namely, self-restraint, self-denial, attention to the needs of *every* other human being *other than* one's own self. This, of course, is a community-oriented ideal, designed to demean and restrain every individual human soma while at the same time focusing experience and behavior on "every other" soma: i.e., the community.

Altruism is a social contrivance whereby the individual suppresses his own perceptions and somatic responses to a situation in favor of the responses of all others, namely, individual suppression in favor of community standards. This contrivance has a short-range effectiveness in maintaining apparent community stability, no matter how erringly and ill-fated may be the direction in which the community is headed. The effect of altruism over the long haul, however, is to create communities which are so out of adaptation both with their environment and with somas in that community that the community finally collapses or is conquered and absorbed by another or undergoes revolution. This is to say that altruism is a contrivance for the benefit of a community *per se* and is not related to either environmental or somatic structures. To the contrary, it is the leaders of the community who decide what kind of community behavior is environmentally or somatically proper; individual altruism supports this leadership collectively by bringing about conformity and regimentation.

It is a tribute to the rational intelligence and good fortune of the human race that it has been able to survive and prevail with such a self-defeating and unadaptive community system which, via altruism, throws away 99 percent of its somatic sensitivities, leaving adaptational policy to a few leaders who may themselves be afflicted with altruism. But it was not only intelligence and good fortune, it was also violation of the altruistic ideal which kept our species steadfastly headed away from the primeval muck—violations by random charismatic fools, saints, prophets and dark-horses who, as Bergson so beautifully argued, broke the rings of a closed and inadaptive society and opened it to wider somatic and environmental adjustments.

In any case, the suppression of one's immediate perceptions and responses to environmental problems is the last way imaginable of reacting effectively to one's own situation. The first and basic guide that human beings or any other soma has for adaptation is the immediate response of one's somatic being; to by-pass this basic guide is to by-pass adaptability. It may seem altruistically polite not to tell Maud that her breath smells like that of a dyspeptic sea lion; it may seem better not to tell Harvey that he is so near-sighted that his driving is a menace; it may not (as will be explored in the next chapter) seem socially proper to go against community hebetude and shout out to the emperor that he has no clothes on or to shout out to a president that he is a murderer: none of these immediate reactions of the soma would be altruistic, inasmuch as they would momentarily upset the community balance. But, of course, an upsetting of the community balance (namely, an *adaptivity to the situation*) is precisely what is called for, and the suppression of that somatic reaction is eventually damaging to both that individual and the community.

But if men have heretofore felt compelled by their fear of the environment to lay such stress upon community conformity, the basis for that fear has now faded into the past. The compulsion toward non-adaptive somatic suppression has had its grounds stripped from beneath it, and the community of men now stands free and clear of the overarching menace of an untamed earth.

We may now begin to be truly adaptive, truly efficient, truly helpful to the community process, and we shall do so by being fully human and fully happy. The third eye and its translucent egoism are beginning to shine through, perceiving more openly and responding more fluidly and exactly to what is perceived.

It is disappointing that we have not yet realized that the very essence of human courtesy and human love is translucent egoism. In human relations, it is such open perceptiveness and flowing response which startles you into the remark "Why how courteous of you to have thought of doing that!": the courtesy which caused that remark was not due to any effort on the egoist's part; he saw the situation and could not help but respond to the adaptational invitation of that situation. He didn't even "think"; he didn't need to: he simply perceived the situation and fluidly responded in terms of immediate, uninhibited (unrepressed) behavior.

In the same manner, in the long run no human love endures without constant adaptation: either you adapt the situation or person to yourself (transformation or teaching) or you adapt to the situation or person (giving in and letting *your*self be molded). Without this ability no two human beings can live and love together long; which may be another way of saying that the great lovers are translucent egoists—artists at adaptation and at getting the most out of *any* situation ("Dearest, the roof just collapsed and the rain is pouring in on us!" "Good! It gives us our first chance to make love in the rain.").

Because it is immediate adaptiveness, translucent

egoism is another name for honesty. It is honesty in its purest expression: naïve honesty such as one only encounters in a child.

As in a child. As in one's primordial being. As in one's "Primary Process." How suggestive. The quotation was made earlier, "Except ye be converted and become as little children, ye shall not enter into the kingdom of heaven."

Maybe, just maybe, He was a somatologist after all. Unfortunately, we shall never know: He, too, became drowned in the community and its altruism and its transcendent deities. So then, we'll just have to do it on our own.

2

Por mucho madrugar,

no amanece más temprano

One cannot speak either too well or too ill of the year 1968: it was a year of enlightenment and hebetude, triumph and humiliation; it was both an alpha and an omega, depending on which side of the alphabet you stood. Even though some Americans were exultant and others were bitter, all Americans knew that the election year of 1968 was the year of the serpent: a great serpent slid across that dividing line in American history, and it was plain to see that half of him was past and far in advance of the events of that year, just as it was plain to see that the other half was still trailing in the rear, not even aware that the head of the serpent had not only reached that moment in political history but had far surpassed it.

The watershed year in twentieth-century American political life is now behind us. In 1968 the cultural tradition won its last inglorious political battle against mutation; and the proto-mutants lost their first inglorious battle for the sake of mutation. Nothing can be the same since that date: the lines were drawn, the issues clarified, the illusions dispelled and the lies exposed. What took place during that fateful year was not a confrontation of political parties nor even of political ideologies: it was a confrontation between two modes of perception and two forms of human culture. Spurred by the quick-growth process that is created by a technological society, the young proto-mutants had suddenly, surprisingly arrived on the political scene as a vocal, intelligent, insistent and energetic presence in American political life. In the short span of one generation since the Second World War, there had popped up from under the cabbage leaf a throng of young Americans whose first interest was not in making a buck, getting married and settling down to the stable, leech-like existence which the middle class world almost gratuitously offered them; instead, they were interested in their society. Like aliens from outer space, they had suddenly appeared, taken one serious and long look at the political and economic patterns of the United States, and had seen it to be rotten.

To see sharply and lucidly the corruption of a society is, in itself, only an act of perception; but to learn, in addition, that those who sponsor this corruption and participate in it not only do not see this corruption but are totally incapable of seeing it—this is an act of revelation. And it was this revelation of 1968 which made it obvious to millions of young Americans that our society exists in an evolutionary-revolutionary situation.

To the proto-mutants it was lucidly clear that the war in Viet Nam was not only senseless to the point of absurdity but that it was also a monstrous and insane policy of murder, destruction and waste. What, however, the proto-mutants saw as lucidly clear was not at all clear to the political representatives of the traditional culture: they simply didn't *see* it that way. Like another race, speaking another language and describing another situation, the political traditionalists described a quite different war in a quite different world situation with quite different reasons for it and motivations behind it. Both groups—whichever end of the serpent they were on—had access to roughly the same information and were looking at the same war, but they saw and described two different events. The perceptions were different: one was lucid and flat, the other was abstracted, historically conditioned and somatically gnarled. It is easily understandable to all of us how foolish men can show themselves to be, when the child sees the naked emperor and naïvely calls out, "The emperor has no clothes on!" even when neither emperor nor adult crowd can *see* that this is obviously the case. How much more easily understandable should it be to all of us when young proto-mutants look at what is before them and call out, "This is wanton, senseless murder!" and the president and a docile adult crowd reply, "No, it is not wanton murder; it is something else: something necessary and almost glorious!" A declothed emperor and his admirers are merely fools, but a murderous president and his followers are a menace to humanity.

The proto-mutants, after having taken one serious and long look at the society they were inheriting, perceived that American society was a racist society. Nothing could be more obvious than that the social, economic and political patterns of this country were a subtle patchwork of racial fear and anger: it is obvious to the proto-mutant in the same way that it is obvious to any foreigner who visits this country. But, unquestionably, it is not obvious to those who control our major institutions and are the official spokesmen for our country. They say, "Why certainly, of course we have our inherited racial problems, problems brought on by the inexcusable introduction of slavery into our country. But that's over now, and we are steadily making progress in integrating all people into the mainstream of American life. It's only a matter of time." This last sentence, of course, is quite correct, but for reasons that would disturb the man who uttered it. Racism is not a social pattern sponsored by intellectual error—this is where the liberals err. It is a pattern of social repression, control and punishment, sponsored by profound somatic drives of fear and anger. It is very easy to talk about racial progress through the veneer of conscious rational discourse, but it is a radically different cup of tea to feel this so-called racial progress as a somatic event of inter-racial acceptance, trust and love. The cultural traditionalists of America are generally incapable of acceptance, trust and love of men of sharply different racial backgrounds. They are capable of intellectualizing about it and of devising "programs" which technically seem to do something without dirtying anyone's hands. Somatically, the difference between the Democratic and Republican parties is instructive in this respect: the former prefer to keep what they've got—including their fear and hatred—but at the same time devise ways of doing something about it; the latter are more honest, in that they prefer to keep what they've got—including their fear and hatred—and do absolutely nothing about it. Both, then, are incompetent to deal with the problem and are, consequently, in for some rude shocks of enlightenment.

The suddenly emergent proto-mutants looked at their society and saw its war and its racism for what they were;

and they pointed out how the policies supporting these situations were inconsistent with their own knowledge of the world situation and of the internal economic situation of their own technological society. They saw a resolute madman, relentlessly expanding a war that was unconscionable and unwinnable: to "win" it would be to obliterate all of Viet Nam and likely create a Third World War which, of course, is not "winnable" by anyone. And so they became a political force against madness; so effective a force that the incumbent president—who had dipped heavily into the ranks of these same proto-mutants for his cannon fodder—was moved to retire from the political scene, and the way toward sanity seemed clear. And if the incumbent president left the presidential race because of one issue, Viet Nam, and if the proto-mutants' own chosen candidate entered the race with only one issue, Viet Nam, then it might have seemed obvious that the political party which both men represented would respond positively to this crucial issue and the man who represented that issue.

But neither sanity nor lucid perception emerged from the Democratic Convention at Chicago. What did emerge was an inglorious reaffirmation of the illusions, deceptions and lies of a political establishment which seemed committed not only to its own destruction but also to the social destruction of its own country, if it were voted the chance. It was not granted that opportunity; instead, a man named Richard Nixon got his heart's delight: the chance to play president.

But the experience of 1968, with its attendant assassinations of even the least revolutionary of evolutionary-revolutionary politicians, was the end of traditional party politics in the United States; its insensate inadaptability to the environing world and to its own technological system is too obvious and too costly to be endured. Our traditional politics, with its identical parties, is mutating out of American life because it embodies commitments which render its programs inefficacious and irrelevant. The proto-mutants, having been firmly told in 1968 that they have no voice within the traditional parties, have, by this rejection, become the designated political executioners of the Democratic and Republican parties.

Cultural traditionalists are the last to understand what time, evolution and mutation mean, and, typically, they have not understood that within, perhaps, little more than one generation, the proto-mutants will represent a majority viewpoint. And the radically different perception which they have of their radically different environment will express itself in a radically different political behavior. There is no way of halting this mutation short of—as I have said already—the deliberate destruction of our technological society, a destruction whose hidden motivation would be: it is better to destroy the final fruit of what the traditional culture has achieved, than to see it mutate into something radically different from what the traditionalists dreamed. There is, perhaps, a chance of this happening; but, at the same time, I think that by the very act of saying this and taking cognizance of this chance, it is all but ruled out.

Inasmuch as one can speak about the future only by reference to that in the present which shows adaptability and, therefore, duration, if we are to think of the future political life of the United States, we cannot do so in terms of the present, senescent traditional parties but only in terms of the political inclinations of the proto-mutants who will from now on be calling the shots. I have used the term proto-mutant throughout this book, always without definition; now it is appropriate to speak directly about these frightening creatures in whose hands the future seems to lie.

The first mutants—or proto-mutants—of the post-technological age are those who are adapting to their environment without the guide of any established culture which reflects and mediates that environment. Devoid of a culture, these mutants have only two compass points with which they can orient themselves: (1) their own somatic drive-systems which offer a general adaptation to their environment and (2) the traditional culture which offers a sharp negative example of where the proto-mutant does *not* want to go.

In possession only of these two points of orientation, the proto-mutant is necessarily embroiled in an experimental situation of trial-and-error. His only recourse is to rebel and improvise until he hits upon some pattern and rhythm of experience which feels both satisfying and effective. Without the benefit of a positive culture, such improvisations are, but seldom, positive adaptations. Instead, the initial tendency of proto-mutants is to seek one another out and join together for survival. When proto-mutants form into groups they create patterns of adaptation which have a certain simplicity, inasmuch as they are largely determined by the two compass points just mentioned: this is to say that they undergo a somatic reaction against the traditional culture. Such somatic reactions—even though they are a movement away from the imbalance of the traditional culture—are, predictably, over-reactions which settle into a new imbalance that is an inverse reflection of the cultural tradition. Typically, the proto-mutant over-reacts simply because his basic somatic guide is the culture from which he is estranged.

The proto-mutants, then, are not mutants; they are unbalanced improvisers who, initially, have little choice but to be unbalanced—but, at the least, this is the first step toward the creation of a mutant culture.

In their group expressions, the proto-mutants have over-reacted and achieved a new imbalance in the following two ways: (1) either they have moved toward a totally sensual-accommodative stance and have fled their cultural environment or (2) they have moved toward a totally aggressive stance and have launched an attack on their cultural environment. In either case, the direction of movement is toward a radical somatic imbalance in respect to the cultural tradition. The first type of group expression is that characterized by the Hippies. The second type of group expression is that characterized by the Militants.

The somatic imbalance of the Hippies and the Militants means that, adaptationally, they are maimed somewhat like the very cultural traditionalists whom they are either fleeing or attacking. The short-lived destiny of these two group expressions of proto-mutation is due to the fact that they have one foot in the technological environment (a positive adaptational factor) and one foot in the moribund cultural tradition (a negative adaptational factor) upon which they must depend in order to orient themselves.

But the Western cultural tradition, because it is moribund and environmentally irrelevant, is quickly mutating out; and to the hurried pace of its disappearance, so will the orientation of the Hippies and the Militants hurriedly lose its initial compass points.

There is no question but what there are, at the present time, many mutants living successfully among us in American society. There is no question about it, at least to me, inasmuch as I know a goodly number of them. But the authentic mutants who have successfully achieved a healthy somatic balance and a viable pattern of behavior are hardly known of or noticed—certainly not by the traditionalists. Instead, the easily noticed *bêtes noires* of the traditionalists are the conformist groups of proto-mutants who insultingly ape the traditionalists by inverting the image of the traditionalists, i.e., they rub the traditionalists' noses in the very somatic experiences which the traditionalists are so desirous of, yet afraid of: to be relaxed, slovenly, hairy, dirty, unhurried, unafraid and—particularly—to appear that one is reveling in all the delights of sexuality—these are the very repressive sacrifices which the cultural traditionalists have made so that the technological society, now enjoyed by the proto-mutants, would be possible. The traditionalist stands transfixed with horror and revulsion before the spectacle of those who take the fruits of his labored sacrifice and either wallow in them voluptuously or throw them back at him savagely.

These initial group expressions of proto-mutation are, thus, passing phenomena which have only as much longevity as does the cultural tradition against which they enjoy their revenge. Both the tradition and the revenge seekers will dissipate together, leaving us with a bit more wisdom about somatic imbalance and leaving the air a bit cleaner so that other proto-mutants can be seen and appreciated for their experimentations.

The Hippie somatic ideal is not viable because all accommodation and no assimilation makes Jack a dull boy. And Jill as well. Leave sex up to the Hippies with their fumblingly sweet attempt to remove from it all fear and anger, and sex will have about the same attraction and consistency as last night's mashed potatoes. But—forgetting the Hippies as a group—even for single, non-grouped individuals, the Hippie ideal is not viable for a lifetime unless one becomes a professional Hippie (lecturer, trinket seller, eccentric artist, etc.) and thereby has the possibility of living *off* of Hippyism rather than with it.

The Militant somatic and environmental ideal is not viable because it has less environmental intelligence than does the cultural establishment which the Militant attacks. The Militant's heart is halfway in the right place—namely, in knowing that acceptance, trust, and love among men is now an historical inevitability, so why not achieve it *now;* but his heart is halfway in the wrong place by being more viciously aggressive than is the establishment he is hoping to destroy. The Militant's failing is in not realizing that aggression cannot destroy the cultural tradition; to the contrary, the techniques of aggression (and the justifications for it) are something of which the establishment is a past master. The cultural establishment can tolerate and toy with the Militant up to a point, and then suddenly squash him—sending out prompt notes of condolence and proper expressions of regret.

With his head brimming with the most irrelevant aspects of Marxism and revolution and with a soaring indifference to the profound and simple mutational truths of Marxism and the evolution-revolution, the Militant strides forth ready for Armageddon; he is prepared to organize, initiate action and perhaps even give his life so that the new culture will come about with revolutionary quickness. His blatant failure is that he is ridiculous. The new culture is *already* coming about with revolutionary quickness; we are in the midst of an evolutionary-revolutionary period that we need merely press through in a resolute, positive manner in order to see it triumph. We need only to confront and pressure the representatives of an ill-adaptive culture in a positive and unrelenting manner, always looking them directly in the eye, perhaps even smiling, as we explain what we are, what we feel, what we perceive and what we insist upon to accommodate the growing number of proto-mutants. The revolution is taking place as a stepped-up evolutionary event, and, thus, the militant's notion of going back into the cultural tradition itself and dragging out revolutionary ideologies of the past is patent nonsense. Certainly exciting nonsense for bored, middle-class young Americans of non-black skin, but nonsense nevertheless. When the mansion is burning, one can only look with stunned incredulity at the young man who runs up and angrily yells, "Let's burn this whole rotten place down to its foundations!" One may have a modicum of sympathy for his sentiment, but, nevertheless, one is a little put off both by his anger and by his limited intelligence.

Total and continual confrontation, rebellion and guerrilla tactics? Of course: this is adaptationally relevant and mutationally effective. But total, immediate revolution? Of course not: this is adaptationally irrelevant and mutationally defeatist—it can only delay the evolution-revolution by futile false starts which succeed in bringing reaction and repression from the establishment tradition. To attempt to destroy an established Gibraltar by sudden, immediate impact merely stuns the precipitate attacker; to relentlessly pressure and overcome its inertia is to move this same Gibraltar ineluctably and acceleratingly into the sea.

It is a question of acting as a revolutionary without trailing along the traditional romanticism of revolution, namely the naïveté that a revolution is not really a revolution unless it happens abruptly with maximal explosions and bloodletting. This is nonsense, inasmuch as the only viable and lasting revolution is one which dismantles and reassembles the past without destroying the positive technological achievements of that past. Revolution is not, then, "total destruction" of the past but total rearrangement of the social relationships of the past in order to create a radically new human culture which corresponds adaptively to the present technological environment.

Black Americans are, of course, the only Americans

who have good reason for suspecting that they are automatically not included within the mainstream of the evolutionary-revolutionary mutation brought on by our technological society. They understand the whites and the subtleties of racism far better than the whites themselves are able to. For this reason, they will develop their own kind of militancy and their own tactics. They are aware that the white Militants are getting a free, vicarious ride on black shoulders; and they also know that there is only one kind of man that can be totally trusted and confided in when it is a question of black power, and that is another man who, like you, is stuck with a black skin. One cannot be "intellectually black": it is an environmental impossibility and, therefore, a somatic pretense.

But black Americans cannot yet be main-line proto-mutants. Their situation is far more elemental: they are struggling for the right to become proto-mutants and to be a part of the construction of a new culture. Black Americans did *not* have any part in the construction of the traditional culture and, thus, have never found a place within it; they, therefore, have always been future-oriented, always ready to take leave of the alien land of Egypt and seek the land promised them. One must not confuse black Militants with white Militants: the blacks have *always* been in a negative relation with American culture, but the whites are only just now discovering this negative stance—not, like the blacks, because of obvious social injustice, but because the traditional culture offers them no handholds for adapting to the contemporary world.

The black revolt in America is a coordinate part of the evolution-revolution, and it is within that context that it will work itself out and achieve its success. The somatics appear obvious: American blacks are becoming more roundly human by experiencing and expressing the anger which American society has traditionally denied them; they are becoming more balanced. In response, the white traditionalist society cannot meet this explosion of group anger except with its typical reaction of fear and, subsequently, angry counter-aggression. This is to say that the "wasp" society is incapable of accommodating the black revolt. But fortunately the "wasp" society is mutating out, and, to the degree that the proto-mutants are simultaneously moving toward dominance of American society, a human environment is being created which can accept the emergence of black anger without becoming afraid of it or angered by it. As the proto-mutants increase, so will an authentic racial integration also increase its pace.

But not merely will the blacks, by expressing and learning anger, become similar to whites; reciprocally, the whites will become blacker, expressing and learning the somatic wisdom of accommodative sensuality achieved within the sub-culture of the black soul. Integration is a two-way street, and the American blacks represent a positive contribution to the development of the evolution-revolution in America. They represent both a promise and a temptation for American culture, in almost precisely the same sense that the Jews represented such possibilities for German culture in the 20's and 30's. Lacking at that time both technological maturity and a proto-mutant rebellion, Germany responded to the Jews with fear and aggression; the American response would likely be the same except for the presence of these same two factors. America is now too deeply embroiled in a mutational struggle for the future for the nation to crystallize into a self-conscious fascist affirmation of the past such as the aging traditionalists might dream. The political struggle is now radically different: the German militants wanted to crystallize the pure, unmixed Teutonic *past* "now"; the American Militants want to crystallize the impure, mixed American *future* "now."

It is a terrible thing to be living already in the future, already certain of what will inevitably, unquestionably come to be, and yet see the days drag by while the traditional culture and its functionaries blithely continue on their pointless course, ticking off the numbered days of their irrelevance. It is a terrible thing to be a proto-mutant, knowing *now* what the future will generally be, knowing *now* what are the only viable adaptational policies which will fit the environment of a technological world. And in the heart of the proto-mutant is the constant theme: If the traditional culture is already doomed, and if I already know what is the general direction that will need to be taken, then why draw it out? Why wait? Why not now? And, consequently, the proto-mutant does something *now:* he flees his society *now* for sub-cultures of openness and love, or he attacks his society *now* in order to hasten the day, or he responds more individually by seeking his own destiny *now.*

Whichever direction the proto-mutant goes and no matter how short-lived or long-lived may be his particular bent, it is the proto-mutant who is the center of significance and, ultimately, the center of constructiveness in America and Europe today. Where he is, the action is— the quick-shifting evolutionary action which, like a computer, is rapidly working out an enormous cultural problem via the responsive synapses of the proto-mutant's soma. The mutation of the cultural problem is taking place rapidly, but it is not taking place suddenly and "now." This is all to the good, inasmuch as the mutational problem is not that of growing a new tail but that of growing a new culture—a creative task that involves not only inventive wit but also considerable improvisation and invention. As the ramparts of traditionalism steadily collapse here and there during the coming decades, so, each time, will enough new space open up for the proto-mutants to fill in one more viable section in the crossword puzzle of mutant culture.

Because their manner of perceiving the world about them tends to be as much dilational as it is constrictive, the proto-mutants not only see their social environment in a more balanced, lucid manner but they also—by the same token—respond to what they see in a more direct, uninhibited manner. Lacking, by and large, the traditional somatic tendency toward repression of somatic reactions, they give immediate expression to what they see: they "tell it like it is," i.e., as *they* see it. This penchant for telling the truth (i.e., lucidly perceiving the environment and immediately expressing what is perceived) is the most potent single social-political instrument in their possession. To go around flatly and uninhibitedly describing things as they appear to you is simply not done within Western society; rather, it is a mode of conduct of which the West has always dreamt and has, accordingly, enshrined in its myths and legendary heroes. As for the traditionalist, he knew that there was never any percentage in individuals telling the truth, inasmuch as the prime requirement was for the individual to knuckle down and repress his individual perception of the environment in favor of the generally agreed upon community version of what the environment was; he had to repress his individual reports so as not to endanger the community balance which was all important and, without which he, too, might go to ruin along with a weakened and defenseless community.

But within a technological society, the community of men is not so delicate; conformity at the price of individual repression is not the rule within such a transformed environment. Quite to the contrary, for the proto-mutants within a technological environment there is no percentage in *not* telling the truth. In such a society there is, finally, nothing for him to fear about telling the truth, simply *because there is no longer anything for a technological society to fear, other than itself as an ill-adaptive human society.* And the direct effect of the proto-mutant's truth-telling is to show that any fear of any kind is environmentally inappropriate, whether of the physical or of the human environment.

The proto-mutant sees that in the final balance he simply has nothing important to lose by telling the truth and that society has everything to gain by finally being able to deal with its environment in a more positive, honest manner—rather than in a defensive, aggressive manner.

He sees, for example, that war no longer has any advantages among technological nations; the odds have radically changed and, accordingly, war is no longer a policy that is viable. It is not viable, first of all, because technological nations are by their very nature more independent in their productivity and can, in the end, improvise the products that formerly could be found only through control of other lands and of trade routes. War is no longer viable for another technological (environmental) reason: namely, because between technological nations, war automatically brings more loss to both sides than gain.

It is clear that, as of now, all wars are in some eventual sense wars between technological nations—no matter how underdeveloped the actual nations in question may be. And, this being the case, all subsequent wars of the next generation or so will show the same pattern as that made manifest in Viet Nam: the absolute fear of using our full technological resources for the prosecution of war. The contemporary goal of war (like the goal of a neo-capitalist economy) is *not* to use your technology to its fullest, lest the enemy (or, in this case, the allies of the enemy) do the same thing in return. That the American military chiefs of staff have not publicly recommended using nuclear bombs on North Viet Nam is due simply to the discomforting practical consideration that the Russians and Chinese possess these same weapons.

The development of technology, then, destroys the usefulness of war as a national policy. This development moves us into the contrary situation of seeking, at all costs, not really to wage war, because the full resources of technology have made it a losing game. This adjustment is one made by the cultural traditionalists themselves to what they intelligently see to have taken place; but the complete disappearance of war as a policy instrument awaits the disposition of the proto-mutants who, when they are numerous enough to assume power, will add a somatic balance to this perception of the new environment. Because their fear-aggression stance has been heavily diluted by the balancing somatic experience of sensual-accommodation, the political judgment of proto-mutants will deal far more positively and ingeniously with the technological environment, which is the happy briar patch in which they, like Br'er Rabbit, were born and bred.

In a technological society where conformity and fear mutate out and truth-telling enters in, it will also be the case that community pride (nationalism, patriotism) will become conditional rather than necessary; which is another way of saying that proto-mutants will be proud of that in their nation which directly inspires pride and will feel individual shame for that which is perceived as communally shameful. One cannot be proud to be part of an American community and be moved to respect its emblems, symbols and officials if that community is engaged in abominable and repugnant activities. To be proud of one's country, even when its policies are murderous and ill-advised, does honor neither to one's country nor to oneself; yet precisely this is the conformist ideal of the traditional culture: to lie because the needs of conformity require it of you. "My country, right or wrong" simply means, "I am an unconditional liar for my nation." But *un*conditional patriotism and pride are neither patriotic nor proud in the least, simply because they rest not on actuality but on a conditioned somatic response of approving of anything, just so long as it is officially designated as being for national honor or national survival. It is the one undying and salutary accomplishment of President Lyndon B. Johnson that he, in the space of a few years and almost single-handedly, destroyed the conditioning of young Americans to automatically respond to any policy as being, by definition, "in the national interest." He did, after all, achieve something lastingly important for America before retiring to his ranch.

That the American economic system must undergo a radical adaptational overhaul is also clear for the protomutants to see; and they shall not cease to tell us that they see it. And, of course, the prime economic event that towers over us, if we are able to look up and see it, is the fact that our technology is destroying our economic system. One does not need to be a Marxist to see this, nor need one be a Thorstein Veblen to perceive that our engineering and technology are running on divergent tracks from our settled patterns of economic exchange; what is already clear to observe is that the momentum of technological growth will yank the economic system right off its tracks.

In other words, an economic evolution-revolution is inevitable; it is so inevitable that we do not need to plan and plot the downfall of the American economic pattern; we can cease skulking in revolutionary cellars, come out into the sunlight and sell tickets for the spectacle. The point is just this: it is not some*body* who will bring about this economic overhaul, rather, it is some*thing,* namely a conflict within the technological economic environment. It will happen, and the American Legion will have all-night meetings throughout the country, only to emerge sleepy-eyed at dawn without having found a culprit they can blame.

Moreover, for the sake of those who still think in terms of good and bad, this revolution will be a Good Thing; it will also be a natural and inevitable thing, inasmuch as it will be an adaptation of the patterns of human life to the patterns of a technological environment, an adaptation which will release even more human energy and productivity than *heretofore* achieved by technology alone.

In our basic industries we are already at the point of evolution where our technology is an unappeasable threat to our neo-capitalistic economy. Our technology is an index of what we *can* do; our economic system is an index of what we *do* do; and the situation clearly present is that the system is now fighting its own technology so that we *do not do all that we can do.* With minimal labor we *can* now produce basic commodities and labor-saving devices of enormous endurance, extraordinary efficiency, quantity and cheapness. But we do not *do* this. We do *not* do this, because under the present neo-capitalistic system to do so would be to destroy the rising profits and wages of both corporations and labor unions: prices would lower, working-hour wages would be curtailed, and the plants would stand periodically idle. And so, the human system of economic distribution fights this technological possibility by deliberately producing defective products of short life span and with high prices. Even though this is blatantly anti-technological, it preserves the established system.

This kind of refusal to adapt to the new environment might, conceivably, be continued for an extended period, except that it is attended by other and more basic events. What I have in mind is the slow destruction of the idea and practice of one of Western culture's major pillars: work. Men are working less and less, and are hating work more and more.

And for good reason: men have begun to see through the anti-technological nature of the economic system which supports them, and they see that they are working when they do not actually need to work. What technology *could* do with dispatch is *not* done with dispatch so that they as laborers, can continue to have something to do in order to draw their pay. Jobs multiply, feather-bedding increases and slow-downs and coffee-breaks become a central concern of labor unions. And the effect of this is to demonstrate to workers *just how needless and useless they are,* by doing what they are doing within the context of a technological environment. What I am saying is that most laborers—blue or white collar—are now working at phony jobs with phony hours, knowing all the while that neither the "job" nor the hours spent at it are fully and actually required; they are required by economic custom, inasmuch as this is the only way they can draw their pay.

It is humanly demeaning for millions of men to spend their lives performing needless and meaningless tasks, simply to keep up an inadaptive economic system. But more than demeaning, this is a fantastic and extravagant waste of human energy: the energy remains bottled up, unused, as men fill up the hours with needless and boring tasks.

The event that is taking place within American society is that work is becoming both irrelevant and meaningless— meaningless in that it is not environmentally appropriate and adapted. Our society is becoming a place where there are more and more people without relevant enough tasks to do; and what they do manage to do is increasingly meaningless. Within a generation or so, the Soviet Union will also crest into this predicament, and then they will scratch their heads in bewilderment and embarrassment over being stuck with the work symbols of a hammer and sickle.

For the Western nations, whether communist, socialist or neo-capitalist, the technological situation is the same; some nations are simply more advanced along this road than are others, with the United States being the first crucible where this task of accommodation-to-technology will be tested.

As the unhappily most-advanced nation, the United States has reached that mutational point of having produced a work-oriented society whose members feel fundamentally antipathetic to working. This, in itself, is not either astounding or novel, but what is unique is that the American antipathy has a justification and solid basis in technological fact. The American ideal is to "have it made," which is to say, *not*-to-do-anything and *not*-to-have-anything-you-*have*-to-do. This means that the initial effect of a technological environment is to bring about a biological paralysis: caught between a technological capability and an organizational debility, the human soma cannot be evoked to open up its energies via an economic organization which is irrelevant to its actual environment.

The first blush of the actual mutation has already appeared, and it has done so in an absurdly obvious manner: the young proto-mutants perceive clearly that they can get along without working at all or by working only part-time, and they proceed to react according to this perception. They are, in terms of our neo-capitalistic system, shamefully unambitious; and the pious representatives of our culture's economy hurl down their abuse on these "leeches" and "parasites" like an enraged Zeus tossing thunderbolts from Olympus.

This is the first blush of economic mutation, and it flows easily into the next phase, which is to take advantage of our new technological environment and its enormous energy output, so that men may finally grasp their achieved freedom to do what *they want* to do, rather than living with the moribund economic ideal of simply *not*-doing-what-one-*doesn't*-want-to-do. As this transition begins to take place, two simultaneous energy explosions become possible: (1) the unleashing, finally, of the full powers of technology, now freed of the restraint of an anti-technological economic system; and (2) the unleashing of the full powers of the human soma, now freed of the restraint of meaningless labor.

As I have mentioned, this mutational overhaul of our economic system is a Good Thing, because it is adaptationally appropriate and is a releaser of greater energies both from human somas and from their technological environment. Our old economic systems (neo-capitalist, socialist, communist) are Bad Things in that, by being conformist and work-oriented and by being inspired by a community fear of a hostile environment, they are formally opposed to the inevitable results of their own technological progress. Each of these three economic systems, when it reaches its full technological momentum, will show—as does American neo-capitalism already—that it is an inefficient system, resulting in restraint, meaninglessness and boredom. Boredom is a sensitive thermometer of the Badness of any task or situation: i.e., without consciously thinking about it, we as somas experience the environmental irrelevance of some task or situation and, consequently, we as somas automatically "turn off" energy output through that inadaptive task or situation.

These are but a few of the political and economic perceptions which the proto-mutants will parade before the startled eyes of a fearful traditional culture. And the specific, constructive proposals which they shall make will arise unpredictably out of the situations which bring them forth; and it is *because* they will arise out of given somatic-environmental situations that these proposals will be relevant and constructive, even while only tentative, proposals for the directions we must take.

From this point onward into the twenty-first century, the overhauling and restructuring of our society will be taking place. The *Sturm und Drang* of the present will continue until the adaptive "pressures" are eased to the point that the "storms" will abate. But, pending that time, the central event of the last third of the twentieth century is the evolution-revolution which is now working itself out. And the central constructive players in this event will be the proto-mutants—Hippies, Militants, and their successors—men and women who possess the most powerful of mutational tools: the potent truth-telling which is, at once, both a perception and a form of immediate behavior—"seeing" and "saying" and "doing" within one smooth adaptational response to the environmental situation.

The rebellious proto-mutants will improvise, experiment and then let the adaptive test of historical time determine what shall become institutionalized and what shall not. The proto-mutants have no other option than to do this; they have no culture through which they can interact fruitfully with their perceived technological environment, and, thus, they must create the habits and institutions of a new culture. As Nietzsche long ago observed concerning this very transition, when men have broken the old tablets of the law, what do they do then? They must then build new tablets of law, replies Nietzsche. What is taking place at present is not a movement toward a vacuous freedom but rather a freedom from the old law, the old cultural tradition. From the viewpoint of the cultural traditionalists, this movement is simply a hurling of oneself into a void, into loss, into the empty arbitrariness and lawlessness of total freedom. But from the viewpoint of the proto-mutants—which is considerably broader historically and culturally—the movement is the resolute abandonment of a once necessary but now moribund past culture and the improvisatory construction of a necessary and adaptive culture.

Time and truth are totally on the side of the apprentice mutants: they see the environmental facts, they are developing the somatic balance to correspond to these facts, and they are thus the only ones in a position to initiate constructive experimentation for our society. During the first stages of this evolution-revolution, the ironical twist is that the young must, by and large, instruct the old. But the young do not remain young; they have a way, every ten years, of becoming thirty, then forty, then fifty years old. Some of them will cease to be proto-mutants, but, increasingly, fewer will fade back into the ranks of the traditional culture—the mutational pressures of young somas constantly pressing behind the older somas, who have constructed a modicum of adaptive culture for them, will mean that these young somas have more survival value as proto-mutants than their elders. Eventually, they shall assume a dominant position within society, and then the positive proposals for new institutions can come forth.

It is important to remember that the recent centuries which have presaged this mutational period have been centuries of revolution. The smell of mutation has been in the air a long while, and sensitive noses from the Renaissance onward sniffed this heady odor and said to themselves, "We no longer need to wait upon God in order to act, but now we know that we, as men, have the sources and guidance and power for acting out our history." This intoxicating scent in the air was the beginning of the discovery of the human soma and its ancient wisdom, which the somatic scientists and philosophers were later to confirm and clarify for us.

The humanly planned revolutions of the recent past have nothing to do with the evolution-revolution which is now transpiring. Humanly planned revolutions are inefficient and ineffective: once the deck is reshuffled, no one is honestly sure if there was more gained than there was lost in the long run. At the present time, total revolution, like total war, is, in a technological environment, as pointless as it is impossible. But guerrilla warfare and guerrilla cultural revolution are, indeed, fruitful and possible; and it is exactly this that is taking place.

We are now witnessing the beginnings of the only revolution in human history to be totally successful. It will be successful because it is not primarily motivated by men and their ideas but, rather, by the environment and its pressures. The evolution-revolution is not an attempt of men to compel human somas and the environment to adjust to human ideas (this is the old fear-aggression reflex of the traditional culture); it is the attempt of men to adjust their somas and human ideas to the compelling forces of the environment which they have already created.

The early Christian community felt their task to be that of "witnessing to the truth." This is the given task of the proto-mutants: they shall witness to the truth, seeing it and saying it and reacting accordingly. They need merely point out to the traditionalists the stupidity of inadaptivity, and to keep on pointing it out and struggling against it in every way possible. There is no need, even, to shout: time and the environment are on their side. The strongly imbalanced proto-mutant groups will gradually give way to those who are more relaxed, more perceptive, more in with their environment and, above all, more humorous. These proto-mutants will keep the lines of communication open, keep democratic process functioning while awaiting their orderly and inevitable take-over.

They will confront the cultural tradition with the truth and educate younger proto-mutants with new viewpoints and new behavioral patterns. The Spanish have a saying which is quoted as the title of this chapter: "Getting up early doesn't make the sun rise any sooner." In this anti-work dictum is the special rhythm of the evolution-revolution.

Relax and enjoy the struggle which you will win. Revolutions required work and anxiety; the evolution-revolution requires play and confidence. As soon as the proto-mutants learn to play with the revolution with all the energy that playing unleashes, then even the cultural traditionalists will become convinced that when their old sun goes down, the result will not be darkness but the arising of a new and brighter sun.

3

—

YES

—

and O that awful deepdown torrent O and the sea the sea
crimson sometimes like fire and the glorious sunsets and the
figtrees in the Alameda gardens yes and all the queer little
streets and pink and blue and yellow houses and the rosegar-
dens and the jessamine and geraniums and cactuses and Gibraltar as a girl where I was a Flower of the mountain yes
when I put the rose in my hair like the Andalusian girls used
or shall I wear a red yes and how he kissed me under the
Moorish wall and I thought well as well him as another and
then I asked him with my eyes to ask again yes and then he
asked me would I yes to say yes my mountain flower and first
I put my arms around him yes and drew him down to me so
he could feel my breasts all perfume yes and his heart was
going like mad and yes I said yes I will Yes.

JOYCE: Ulysses

Apropos of children, it is significant that the overt sucking reflex disappears about the fourth or fifth year. But

then, even though finger sucking disappears during pre-
adolescence, there still remains an obvious pleasure in
sucking or licking food, the more so when it is delicious.
But by the time that the strong new winds of puberty have
begun to blow, the sucking reflex disappears and is not to
be seen again during adulthood.

Except on certain somatic occasions. One of the most
instructive insights into the nature of sexuality is that adult
human beings do not normally have the least motivation
to suck except when they are sexually aroused.

It is known, of course, that there is a physiological con-
nection between the amygdala and septal regions, the
former linked with oral activity and the latter with genital
activity. But such marginal physiological data are not anything so revealing as is the common sight of a human infant who, while sleeping, simultaneously (1) is smiling, (2)
has rhythmic mouth and tongue movements and (3) has a
penile erection. When we contemplate human sexuality,
we should retain the image of that smiling infant who, as
he develops into adulthood, completely "forgets" this
happy linkage of three somatic events until the warm hand
of lust steals upon him.

At first blush, there are two prominent features about
human sexuality which anyone must take into account.
One is that during sexual activity, human beings are experiencing primordial childhood somatic patterns which
have continued to exist intact up into adulthood. The
other feature is that sexual experience is more needed by
man than by any other animal soma: unlike all other animals, for man sexuality is *always* in season. These are two
most remarkable somatic traits of the human species, and
they can offer us an immediate insight into human sexuality even though an ultimate "understanding" of sexuality

is, by the very nature of somatic experience and conscious experience, impossible.

So then, as I make my way around the mulberry bush, it shouldn't be of any interest to me or anyone to try to present the reader with an understanding of human sexuality (as if it were an evironmental threat to be focused upon and controlled), but it may be of interest to almost everyone to have a try at appreciating sexuality (as if it is, indeed, a somatic invitation to a fiesta which all of us hope we can attend).

It was a very interesting moment when a University of Chicago psychologist discovered that, if he held a series of photographs over his head and showed them, one by one, to his colleagues, he could tell when certain pictures appeared, simply by looking for the dilation of the iris in his colleagues' eyes. It never failed. He would flip the pictures over, one by one—snow scenes, landscapes of greenery, horses, quaint villages—and then suddenly he would see the iris dilate; and he would announce to his colleague, "Now you are looking at the fold-out of the Playboy nude." And so he was, even though he was not "consciously aware" of any change, of any effort to open his iris wider for more light. The Chicago psychologist had discovered an autonomic adaptational reflex that was quite uncontrollable, no matter how much the viewer consciously tried to prevent it. As he sat there, flipping his pictures, it was not the eye of that individual he was attentive to; rather, it was the old eye of Adam, who had given up a rib so that he might gain a dilation or two.

In such a way do our ever alert somas express themselves and have their adaptive wishes, even though we might claim both ignorance of and irresponsibility for what is going on beneath our somatic veneer of conscious, rational effort. The old eye of Adam is our self as soma, a self which few humans know on its own terms, inasmuch as they have largely been preoccupied with knowing everything on *their* own terms of fear-aggression drives and assimilative experience.

And it is not merely the old eye of Adam that peers out and betrays our most significant wishes; the old eye of Eve peers out as well in a most expressive fashion. The young miss, standing there by the shrubbery in front of the high school knows quite well that she doesn't care for or even approve of certain types of young men, such as the one who suddenly walks across the lawn, comes up to her, smiles and begins to speak to her in a most engaging fashion. Ever in self-conscious control, she responds by forcing herself not only to be polite but even to be friendly to this male, just as anyone should. But, quite unbeknownst to Mimi, old Eve is efficiently carrying out her own wishes and plans: she sends the rosy excitement of a beautiful blush coursing through the girl's face and neck, the heady flush of it making the eyelids lower and tremble. This is most becoming and attracts the young man not a little. And somehow her throat tightens, her voice rises, and when she laughs it is the silvery, shivery tinkle of giggling femininity that expresses itself to the boy, who is now even more entranced—entranced with the girl who is "doing nothing in the least" to attract him, the girl who, if she had a color film of her face and a tape of her voice, would not "think" it possible.

Nor would she believe it possible that she should yield to his entreaties and go out with him that Saturday; nor is it explicable why she and he go through innumerable repetitions of courtship patterns while in the school corridors, in the car or over the telephone; nor is it explicable that she should awake to the fact that one night she had finally allowed him to make love to her.

From meeting, through courtship to mating, she really didn't plan a thing, yet she anticipated, aided and planned for every move in the lovely game. And so, we apparently have two "she's": the post-five-year-old "she" (or, at the latest, post-puberty), who would never have *thought* it possible; and the *thoughtless* primordial "she," who not only *knew* it was possible but who *wished* for it and ingeniously brought it to fulfillment. The primordial "she" existed at infanthood and continued to exist past the waking-up changes at five years; and, even though still hidden beneath the growing up busy-ness of questions and answers, learning and training, "she" existed suddenly more potently after puberty—more alertly, more attentively looking for things and situations which the secondary "she" would never have *thought* of looking for.

Our somatic programming becomes particularly obvious when it concerns sexual experience and behavior. Functioning like a powerful "override" system, it takes over from the inefficient secondary system and searches the environment with a keen eye, knowing what it is seeking, responding when the prey is sighted, and moving in for the attack—or the surrender.

Not only is this kind of experience and behavior largely unconscious in its motivations, but the most complete fulfillment of its wishes is also largely an unconscious event: the young man or young woman is *experiencing*, certainly, but this kind of experience is not conscious experience; it is a more fundamental, earlier mode of experience which every human being knows and has known from the beginning: a non-verbal, pre-verbal experience of patterns of movement and flow and rhythm which are the ancient and familiar somatic "home" which we have never really left, even though we have lost touch with it as our verbal "understanding" grew.

Anyone who has seen a marvelous football game can, afterward, describe the basic patterns and movements of what he experienced. But anyone who has made marvelous love cannot, afterward, describe and recall the patterns and movements of that marvelous experience; unquestionably, he may have certain visual memories of patterns and movements but the wondrously unique experiencing of sexual patterns and movements are without either visual or verbal trace. The paraphernalia of the conscious memory picked up nothing of what took place in the central somatic arena; one simply knows, afterward, that it was marvelous and that one must experience it again.

Admittedly—and unfortunately—this is largely an ideal case. Most human beings still make love with an extraordinary amount of conscious effort, of playing with memory and of fantasizing. The traditionalists are rather typical in this regard, whereas the proto-mutants are atypical. The somatic mechanism of the orgasm can operate with a high degree of conscious interference; but it can also operate far more fully and fluidly without conscious interference. And it operates best when the human being is no longer experiencing in the mode of a self-conscious adult but has become a smiling infant: orally, genitally and anally excited with a power that the infant did not know.

What is obvious is that we do not leave our infanthood behind us or beneath us, dreaming, as we grow older; rather, to the degree that we develop our conscious veneer, we are to that same measure developing our primordial core into a sharply watchful perceiver of the environment as well as into a powerful source of energy explosion into that environment. The dreamy oblivion of authentic sexuality is not at all a return to the *state* of infanthood but is a recapturing of the *somatic pattern* of childhood which has been, for us, the same familiar "home feeling" all our lives but which has not remained at the same energy level; the innate sexuality of infants is like a limp windsock, awaiting the fulfilling winds of puberty.

But if sexual love is a return to primordial patterns of somatic experience (fully experienceable, "unconsciously"), this touching of the home base of infanthood is linked with the other prominent feature of human sexuality mentioned at the outset: that it is a *perennial* need of human beings, whereas with animals it is only a seasonal need. This can be marked out as a species characteristic of human somas.

The "non-seasonal" character of human sexuality is directly and symptomatically linked with another species characteristic: the evolution of rational-verbal consciousness in the human soma. The fact that we have these *two* remarkable distinctions from the remainder of the animal kingdom is no happenstance: given the latter somatic characteristic, the former was somatically required. The more the human race evolved toward a *sustained* experience of conscious, constrictive assimilation of the environment, the more it simultaneously evolved toward a sustained rather than seasonal sexual need. The ultimate witness to this is Western civilization itself: the civilization which has pushed itself to the most sustained rational attack upon the environment is, at the same time, the most erotically preoccupied of human civilizations. The latter counteracts the former. It is, in fine, a homeostatic balance attendant upon the somatic imbalance created by rational consciousness.

The Soviets—good and pious Marxists who are exceptional at understanding everything except the human soma—have attempted to train their people totally in rationally conscious effort while suppressing every trace of eroticism. But in a technological society you cannot both have your sensual cake and not eat it: you must do both. And thus, Soviet society has an enormous instability to which it seems little prepared to adjust. At the present time its "moral" climate is about thirty years behind that of the United States, and, thus, is at a level that would be given an A-1 stamp of approval by the Boy Scouts of America. It is too bad for the American Right Wing that it is as puritanistic as the Soviets, otherwise it could realize its grandiose dream of destroying the Soviet Union: all that is needed is for tons of first-rate pornographic literature and pictures to be dropped all over the Soviet Union. Within a year the country would possibly be profoundly altered.

All human somas are in continual need of the accommodative patterns of sexual experience. Caught in an unbalanced somatic stance of saying No to the environment and holding it at bay with the alert devices of conscious scrutiny and rational attack, the human soma heaves in its own manner to balance this constricted soma with the aneling balms of sexual softness and surrender.

But this somatic attempt at counter-balancing has not been more than painfully successful. And now that we have begun to crest into an achieved technological age, our obsolescent preoccupation with the constricted, fearful activities of conscious alertness and serious work have brought us to an extreme preoccupation with eroticism. But eroticism is not sexual satisfaction: it is the attempt to gain the sexual release one needs *by straining it through the assimilative function of consciousness*–as if the source of sexual accommodation was not in oneself but was out in the environment. This anguished effort to gain conscious sexual satisfaction has a name: pornography. And what I am about to say should be obvious: namely, that the somatically ordained destiny of the traditional culture of the

West is to dissipate its final days embroiled in a searing and unfulfilling obsession with pornography. Those days are now upon the cultural tradition in the United States and will shortly be the case in Western Europe.

The death rattle of the cultural tradition will be a four-letter word; but long before this final moment shall have come, a tentative culture will have formed which, rather than ignoring the technological environment created by conscious rationality, will have recognized and responded to this environment: an adaptational culture which is on its way to becoming a fruitful mutant culture.

In a proto-mutant culture, sexuality will not be a public commodity displayed directly and indirectly everywhere for the purchase and consumption of the achingly conscious customer. It will not be because this electric pretense of sexuality is somatically impossible for the proto-mutant: for him, sexuality is something that he is the source of, in the sense that it is only he who can let it happen. Ay, and therein lies a lovely secret: those who know how to surrender into sensual accommodation and let it happen are those who attract others who desire the same thing. This, however, is an "open secret" known primarily by women and kept from men.

What I am referring to is the ironically reversed situation of the cultural traditionalist and the proto-mutant: the former exerts enormous effort, finally to obtain no satisfaction; the latter exerts no effort, finally, to obtain enormous satisfaction.

Sexuality is an experience which we need not "understand" and about which we need not directly talk, inasmuch as there is nothing understandable about it and nothing to talk about. It surpasses the understanding, and its living, balancing presence gives motivation and meaningfulness to whatever we do understand in our environment. Sexual excitement centers in the orgastic reflex, yet for some lovers this reflex may never be experienced. Sexual experience seems to have its fullest expression in pure sensual-accommodative flow—utterly relaxed and surrendered—and yet for many persons it is channeled through intense and artful control and constriction. Sexual experience would seem ideally devoid of fear or aggressiveness, but, even so, the playing out of sexual passion through the enacting of such roles is deeply a part of female and male sexual roles and, in the extreme, finds clear expression in masochism and sadism, which can be enjoyed interchangeably by females or males.

Freud saw sexuality as the single human energy drive; then later he saw it as one of the two basic human instincts. Other psychoanalysts, led initially by Jung, further diluted the significance of the sexual drive. Reich further narrowed it, by centering sexuality in the orgasmic reflex and seeing it as the crucial para-sympathetic energy releasor. Ethologists see sexuality—at least in non-human animals—more squarely and functionally as one of the four basic organic drives or as mating combined with other drives to comprise a "secondary drive." Outside of these somatic scientists, the traditionalists, careening from spiritualism to pornography, see sexuality hectically as maybe nothing and as maybe everything.

It behooves us to distill some wisdom from such confusion by drawing this conclusion: It is fruitless to try to understand human sexuality, not only because it *sub*passes human understanding, but also because sexuality is itself subject to evolutionary mutation.

One day, during a stroll back from lunch, a renowned French philosopher was asked by some friends an interesting metaphysical question: "What do you think is the center of all things?" I was told that he replied, "*Le centre du monde, messieurs, c'est le con d'une femme."* He did not elaborate further, nor was he asked to do so.

Sexuality is just such a centrum for human experience. Because it is a source, a beginning, the home from which I came, it cannot be a matter of understanding this centrum, inasmuch as this centrum preceded, engendered and shaped my understanding. This centrum already is me; it *was* me before I ever began to understand, and it continued to be me after I began understanding other things. Understanding goes *out* from the center; only honest surrender to oneself goes *in* to that center.

The first questions of a human child, the very beginning of his inquisitiveness, are questions which are immediately sexual but simultaneously metaphysical: "Where did I come from?" "Where did you come from?" "Where do people come from?" In the course of somatic development, this is the first impulse to human learning and searching: the "wherefore" and "why" questions are all questions of origin, source and center— "How did I *get* here? I had to *come from* someplace." All of human civilization proceeds from that original impulse to searching and learning, and it is a question which has never been satisfactorily answered by anyone. To articulate this question is to have awakened to a mystery before which one stands in awe: the dawning revelation of the young human that, "I am I, and the world is the world. We are different, apart, separated. How did we get this way? Where did I come from, since I *do* seem to belong to the world? and where does the world come from since it *doesn't* belong to me?"

The mind of the child and the mythic mind are the same, at an early point in their maturation, in their awed discovery of individuated beings, there in a reality which is thatched with separation, estrangement and aloneness.

The primordial, childlike mind is saying No to what has shown itself to him. There is a stunned wrongness about this separation, this arrangement of things apart from one another; and what the child is asking is, "I? Why I? Why am I *here,* separated from you and from things there?" Finally, what he is asking is, "Where do we all come from? Where is our center and our source, where we were once all together before this strange separation took place?"

Thus does all human knowledge begin; and thus does all human knowledge end—unanswered. The question need not, "should" not have been asked; for, the instant it was asked we lost the answer. We lost, at that very instant, our original somatic kingdom and became, instead, conscious human beings restlessly in search of phantom empires. At least until now.

4

$$E = SA^2$$

Because this looks to be our last go round, it would not be a bad idea if we began by pulling together the many strands of this small volume so as to see what we have. In large, what we have is a kind of story or history, and—like some stories and like all history—it is incomplete.

The story is that of the human soma, a soma that lives, moves and has its being essentially like all other somas but whose special adaptive achievements have propelled it along a unique course of somatic evolution toward an unparalleled evolutionary event: it has not, like other somas, survived by virtue of having successfully adapted *to* the demands of the environment; rather, it has gone beyond this basic achievement and has succeeded in surviving by transforming and adapting the environment to his *own* demands. In order to bring about this extraordinary state of affairs, the human soma evolved an unusual formation of its somatic energy drives that was specifically adapted for an attack on its environment. Although unique in evolutionary history, this special deployment of somatic energy was, biologically, quite simple: it consisted in channeling the bulk of somatic energy through the assimilative drives of fear and anger; by the same token, the environmentally accommodative drives of sensual hunger were bypassed as thoroughly as possible.

By dint of this unbalanced channeling of somatic energy through a fear-aggression approach to the surrounding earth, the human soma gradually evolved specific neurophysiological structures for the handling of these assimilative energies. It evolved a composite way of sensing its environment, which is called consciousness. And the attack which consciousness made on the feared environment was to search it, remember it, judiciously build up a symbolic image of it from these images, fix these images with a specific auditory sound (a word), and then rearrange and think through these fixed symbols of the world in order to find ways to attack, control and manipulate this threatening world. This was an intelligent relation to the environment: the environment was seen in units which were named, and these units were organized in a measured, rational manner into larger units with names. For the conscious human soma, both perception of the environment and active behavior in it were structured intelligently and rationally.

But also, by dint of this unbalanced use of assimilative drives, the somatic avenues for the accommodative drives atrophied: the soma largely ceased to perceive the environment accommodatively and largely ceased to respond to that environment through behavior that was sensually accommodative. The accommodative drives continued to exist, but they functioned only indirectly and inefficiently. Caught in an unbalanced adaptive stance toward the environment, the human soma ceased its accommodative evolution, crystallizing its somatic core; and it vented its energies not in adapting to the world but in adapting the world to its self.

As a corollary to this crystallization of the soma, and the repression of its accommodative drive expressions, the community behavior of human somas was also frozen in a constricted attitude of defense against and attack upon the threatening environment. Individual accommodation to the environment was suppressed, and only rationally determined group accommodation was allowed, this being the prerogative of the community leadership. The consequent rational habits (i.e., moral principles), individual habits (personal moral behavior) and community habits (political-economic structures) were conformist, repressive and regimented in direct reflection of an earthly environment of scarcity, unpredictability and danger upon which the community absolutely depended in its task of surviving.

After a prolonged period of exploring the device of consciousness and of experimenting with and developing rational techniques for individual and community behavior, the human soma was ready to make its full attack on the environing earth. It poured even greater quantities of energy into assimilative, aggressive activities in a sustained communal effort to subdue and control the formerly uncontrollable but all-important environment. Simultaneously, it spent more energy in repressing the unneeded and troublesome accommodative drives.

Within the space of about three hundred years, the human soma, by virtue of this intensely conscious rational perception and behavior, had accomplished two things: it had triumphed over its environment by its knowledge and use of technological controls and it had repressed its sensual-accommodative drives to the point that it had become somatically oblivious to the accommodative techniques of adaptation. By planting itself firmly in an assimilative, aggressive stance, it had beaten its environment at the expense of having crystallized and having lost one-half of its somatic abilities. By the time the human soma had crested into its environmental conquest, it was so incapable of accommodative adaptation that it either destroyed itself, drugged itself or tried to save itself by even more intense conscious aggression.

If the conscious abilities of technological aggression had been purely phylogenetic, rather than both phylogenetic and ontogenetic (i.e., cultural), the human race would have ceased to exist as of the attainment of its technological goal—this is to say that its accommodative inadaptability would have been genetically fixed, and the human race would have destroyed itself by attempting to adapt by the fear-aggressive devices of rationality and technological power.

But, because the hypertrophy of conscious rationality and the atrophy of unconscious sensuality were culturally conditioned as well as genetically inherited, accommodative adaptation began to take place among newborn human somas; they perceived their non-threatening environment in a rational, intelligent manner and realized that it was not any longer the fearful environment against which the ancient human culture was programmed to fight. With this intelligent perception, a mutation was triggered and a cultural revolution ensued. The new environment no longer engaged the predominant interest of rational intelligence: such conscious effort became far less relevant and ceased to draw the same quantity of somatic energy through its well-oiled mechanism. Moreover, the ancient culture which guided and supported these conscious efforts of assimilation suffered, accordingly, this same irrelevance and inapplicability.

The newborn human somas could not react to their technological environment either through direct rational effort or through the guidance of their traditional culture. They had no choice but to adapt; and they had no choice but to adapt accommodatively: that is, they had to give in to their environment in a sensual, relaxed fashion and allow the environment to mold their somatic resources to its own structures. This task of accommodative adaptation was toilsome and improvisatory at the beginning because of the double problem of atrophied accommodative drives and the lack of a culture to guide one in using these drives. And thus the initial young somas were proto-mutants, who had to experiment with perception and behavior in order to lay the foundations for a new culture and a new sub-species of human somas.

In the course of this creation of a culture, the proto-mutants valued the what-is over the what-it-can-be in perception, they valued description over reconstruction in their symbolical reactions to the environment, and they valued purely individual accommodative behavior over community-imposed conformist behavior. These experimentations with perception, symbolical expression, and behavior became the foundations for a new human culture and a new type of human soma—no longer, as of its fulfillment, a "mutant" culture or a "mutant" human because it had finally become institutionalized and normalized.

The keynote of the new cultural institutions was individual adaptability, and from birth onward, every cultural device surrounding the young human was designed to invite and reward the fluid, efficient, full use and development of all the phylogenetic drive systems of the human soma. The human race, having at the climax of its first stage of development found the secret of the release of environmental energies, now spent the next period of its development discovering and developing the secret of the release of somatic energies. This secret was adaptability (formerly called honesty and sometimes sincerity or truthfulness), and it was increasingly confirmed that the more adaptability acquired by a human soma, the more energy was drawn forth. Adaptability being, of course, perception, learning, communication and interchange with the environment, the authentic, fully developed human mutant lived in such rapid and fluid communicative interchange with his environment that it was as if he had literally become an organic part of that environment, like two wheels of creation totally engaged one with the other. It was only then that true science and true human life began.

I have taken the history of the human soma and, in its recounting, allowed the story to run past the present and into the twenty-first century. This projection into the next century may not be quite correct—the plots of all stories have a way of suddenly veering and changing as new dramatic elements emerge from out of the plot's own development—but it is a fairly drawn historical index of what is portended by somatic thought and by contemporary proto-mutation.

With one eye held fast to this historical index, it is unavoidable that we should devote this last discussion of bodies in revolt to the question of what we shall do in carrying out this somatic revolt and in fulfilling this mutational task. To a large extent this has finally to do with what can best be called education, although the preparatory groundwork during the next generation will be laid, as we have mentioned, by the resolute constructive activities of revolutionary proto-mutants. With these factors in mind, let us now end this primer in somatic thinking with a few remarks about the policy of mutation.

From this point onward in the technological society of America (and those of Europe within a short period of time), the key word is *adaptation*, and the central human task will be to achieve a *somatic state of optimal adaptability*. During the first few generations of training ourselves in the art of adaptability, the emphasis will primarily be on the accommodative adaptation which takes place under the aegis of our sensual hungers. A technological society makes it invitingly easy to explore the uncharted labyrinth of our sensual hungers, but—far more significantly—this possibility is an invitation to human beings to discover the nature and extent of human wanting, so that men will at last live with their environment, knowing what they, as individual somas, *want* and *need* in their environmental intercourse. This is the only possible manner in which human beings will ever attain independence and, thus, personal freedom: by knowing that they, as somas, are the unique source and unique authority for determining what they want, what they need and what they shall do.

To attain this independence is to achieve the somatic state of optimal adaptability to one's constantly shifting environmental situation. And it is certain that, in order to attain this independent state of knowing one's own adaptational needs, the human being must learn to read his soma.

The educational goal of the traditional culture has been to learn to read the environment. The educational goal of the mutational culture is to learn to read oneself as soma.

Within our cultural tradition, the aim of educational

policies has increasingly become apparent as we have neared our goal of constructing a technological society: the educational goal was to train the human for effective aggression against the environment. Just as surely as the newborn Aztec infant of any rank had his umbilical cord symbolically buried with a shield and sheath of arrows while his elders pronounced that he had come into this world to fight, so have the children of the West been born to combat their environment. And they *have* combatted it. And they have conquered it.

The traditional educational policy is clear in its intention to train the human being for a role or vocation or profession which fits somewhere into the whole panorama of societal aggression against the earthly environment. The training method has, typically, been the transplanting of a pre-established program of serial, mechanical procedures which the trainee was then to apply methodically in his effective vocational attack on his environment. In this respect, traditional education is exactly like traditional Western morality in its ill-adaptive, mechanical approach to adaptation: morality has been a pre-packaged program of behavioral procedures implanted in the conscious behavior of young humans. Living and confident adaptation is immensely more efficient than a programmed set of rules. The new educational policy is the training of humans for optimal somatic adaptability; the old educational policy has become easy and will painlessly preserve our technological machinery.

Now that we have entered into the full technological period, this mechanical training becomes precise and matter-of-fact. The guesswork is largely a thing of the past: we need to train so many people for this industrial area, so many for that, this number of physicians, this number of electrical engineers, that number of teachers, and they will be deployed in this section of the country or that segment of the business world. With this situation the traditional culture has fulfilled itself: surviving and prevailing over the environment have now become child's play. The manipulations are simple and anyone can learn: like the army, the business and technological worlds require neither talent nor vision—but only the staple items of the Western world, a minimal intelligence and an acceptance of the work-mentality.

We have now entered into the extraordinary paradise where everything has become easy and where little is demanded. We have won the battle and the challenge has vanished. We could continue for a protracted period of time within this beehive paradise, except for the fact that there is less and less to do and fewer and fewer needed vocations and jobs to be trained for. Quite literally we have entered the epoch when we *don't know what to do*. We do not know *what* to do, because there is little left in the environment *to do*.

Put simply, the traditional culture has rested solidly on the ancient fact that *human need was supplied by the environment*. Formerly, men knew what to do because the environment required it of them if they were to survive. But, with the achievement of a technological environment, we have created an environment which no longer compels us to do anything; it does not create our needs for us, and we therefore discover that we live in a world where we don't *have to* do anything. And, consequently, there is nothing to do: we don't know *what* to do, because factually there is hardly anything left to do.

It is without question that the achievement of a technological environment is, simultaneously, the fulfillment and the destruction of the traditional culture of the West. By fulfilling the needs imposed by the environing earth, this culture destroyed the needs of the environment. In the most exact sense, *our present environment no longer needs our traditional culture.*

And when the salt has lost its savor, wherewith shall it be salted?—this describes the situation of our ancient culture: when we no longer discover our wants and needs from within our environment, where can we discover them? At this moment, what is a man needed for? What is his purpose and function? Does he any longer have a reason for being?

It is to just this extremity of human self-questioning which the traditional culture has led us, and it is totally incapable of grappling with or even comprehending the nature of the question which it has raised.

Let me say this as emphatically as possible: for anyone who has eyes to see, our traditional culture is dead. It is not "sick," it is not "in trouble," it is not suffering momentary "adjustment" problems: it is dead. It is adaptationally irrelevant and ludicrous. And those who remain embroiled within it are enmeshed in a somatic circumstance of sickness, blindness, madness and semi-humanity.

And with equal emphasis I must announce that the only option left open for the survival of mankind is the rapid development of a radically different relationship to our environing world—the development of a radically humanistic culture.

When we have, after so many centuries, so contrived it that the imperatives of the natural world no longer are the sources of our needs and wants, the only option remaining is simultaneously the most obvious option: namely, that we, as individuals, can be the absolute source of our wants and needs. It is not merely that we *can* be this source; rather, the beginning of this radically humanistic culture is the insight that we have *always* been the source of our wants, except that we have, through the centuries, strayed from the light and must learn again to adjust our eyes, blinkingly, to the unaccustomed immediacy and dazzle of our needing self.

If this primer in somatic thinking has shown nothing else, it has at least made clear that we human beings are the bearers of ancient and accomplished somas whose phylogenetic patterns of adaptational wisdom are already part of our very being. It is solely a question of allowing that somatic wisdom free play in expressing itself in adaptive response to our world.

Over three centuries ago, Sir Francis Bacon put the final trim on the sails to Western culture for its rush toward its fulfillment in technology. He enjoined humanity—if it were to understand and conquer the environment—to undergo a "humiliation of the spirit" before the natural world. Humanity responded to this injunction and surrendered to the imperatives of nature. Now that it has achieved this goal, a new and radically different surrender is required of mankind: a surrender to one's own somatic being.

Surrendering to one's own somatic being and learning the patterns of its own imperatives is the educational task as of this moment. The immediate achievement of optimally adaptive human beings is the only meaningful task before men in a technological society—any other tasks are not genuine and without issue. This is what the evolution-revolution is all about, and this is where the action is, as the proto-mutants resolutely or militantly challenge the rules of our society in favor of what must come.

Because our present educational institutions directly reflect the defunct and now ludicrous policies of the traditional culture, our schools and universities are both corrupt and corrupting. It is not that they are "in need of reform," or that the curricula and teaching techniques should be "thoroughly reviewed"; rather, the very concept of education must be revolutionized or there will simply not be any education taking place. Instead, there will be beehive activities which will merely mark time until the bees and the hive are destroyed. It is quite conceivable that, as of this very moment, *no* educational institutions of *any* kind would be better in the long run than our current futile pretense at education. Young Americans are *not* being guided in becoming strong, adaptable, independent human beings. They are being trained to be curtailed, functional semi-human beings who are presumably dependent upon a technological society for their motivation, their self-definition and their *raison d'être*.

The universities of the United States are whistling in the dark, naïvely trying to persuade themselves that these strange currents that seem to be flowing amongst the younger Americans will somehow go away—that all they need to do is ride out the storm and all will be well. But these educational traditionalists do not have the slightest conception of what the storm is all about, and as long as they continue to cajole themselves into *not* accepting the possibility that something radically new is afoot and into *not* seriously responding to this situation, they can mark down each day on their calendars as being a day of loss, of waste, of stupidity and of betrayal to the future of man.

Certainly there is a paucity of authentic teachers for the proto-mutants of America but, with our technological capacities, even a few are enough to begin the task of educating ourselves for our environment and of creating the mutant culture that must be created. Many of these teachers are young—very young. Many of them are completely outside of universities or have been forced out of universities. Many of them are older and are within universities, and you can spot them by the fact that their positive attraction of students is matched by their negative repulsion of administrators who finger their tenure papers and mutter that they just don't seem quite right for "our" university. They are correct.

But the teachers, the leaders are here, about us within our society, sharing the same fundamental understanding of what is transpiring and what is the educational goal before us. The first attempt is naturally that of trying to compel the schools, colleges and universities to become transformed into a vehicle of environmental relevance. There is perhaps only the slimmest of chances that this can happen. It is more than likely that absolutely unique and separate institutions will need to be created by deliberate action in order to implement the policies of an absolutely unique educational goal.

The specific manner in which mutational education will be conducted waits, in large part, upon the results of experimentations now taking place both informally, in the strategy planning of militant groups or the innovations within commune societies, and formally, in the scattered humanistic institutes and retreat centers which are burgeoning throughout the country. The general nature of these educational institutions is, however, obvious. The new schools and universities cannot be defined as *places* which are separate from the environing world, places where time is taken *out* of society while the "education" is being injected into the docile student. Rather than being places, the new schools and universities have no option but to be *ways of living* of an experimental nature. One cannot *stop* living and adapting to one's social and physical environment during education, but one must, instead, learn to live and adapt more intensely, more fluidly, more fully and efficiently.

In the same fashion that mutational education is not a *place apart*, it cannot conceivably be a *time apart;* that is, such an education cannot be limited artificially to a certain time of day or of night or to a certain age of life. It should fluidly begin and continue as long as its adaptational training is needed by some human being; when the human ceases to need it (and he may never cease to or he may never begin to) then he leaves off from the training and continues his own adaptive activities.

To speak of an educational institution as a way of life organically related to our immediate social-physical environment—and not as a place apart and a time apart—is a radically different conception of an educational institution. After all, say the traditionalists, it has to be some *place*—doesn't it?—and it has to take place at some *time.*

And of course, the answer is no. Education that has adapted to the nature and resources of a technological environment need not be *any* place or *any* time, inasmuch as it could be taking place *every*where and *all* the time within the society. I am not in the least invoking the tawdry vision of a world of teaching machines and "canned" televised lectures, which is the final educational achievement of the traditional culture in its stultified, mechanical response to its technology; mechanized training will continue as a necessary but minor aspect of the mutant culture, producing as many technically trained persons as wish to pursue vocations within the shrinking domain of the technological professions which support all of society through the activity of only a small segment of that society. There will always be those whose genius and greatest delight will be in the exploration of further fields of mathematics, computer science, electronics, automation, cybernetics and practical engineering. The continued presence of this technological segment of our society will be guaranteed not by what I call "education" but by the simpler, mechanical learning process of *vocational* training. In evoking the possibility of truly adaptational education, I am referring to the kind of education made possible by the living immediacy of our technological systems of communication and transportation. The "where" and the "when" of educational institutions is no longer a matter of importance; the single matter of importance is the "how" of education. And this "how" is the process of training in somatic adaptation—a training which cannot be given to the student but which can only be acquired by the student himself in the active process itself of adaptation.

Necessarily, training in perception is central to this mutant educational process. Human beings must finally learn what it is to really see and hear and touch without editing and monitoring these perceptions through the constrictions of conscious focusing or unconscious fear. Very few persons know *how* to relax and surrender to the entire inflooding panorama of the environing world. To do so, just once, is a revelatory and never-to-be-recovered-from experience—this is the profound effect of psychedelic drugs. But one does not need drugs in order to perceive; all that one needs is one's self and some guiding fellow human being or beings who can explain how they have learned to perceive in a sensual-accommodative manner and what this feels like to them. The whole literature of Indian Yoga is filled with similes and metaphors coined by gurus who were trying to describe "what it feels like" to experience certain somatic patterns: one is guided by being told to look for a certain "color" or a unique, soft-pitched "sound" or to feel a "snake uncoiling at the pit of one's abdomen." This is somatic talk. It doesn't refer to environmental events; it refers to very real and structured somatic patterns which cannot be "seen" or "heard" or "felt" in a consciously assimilative way but can only be perceived by surrender to the soma as it moves and fluidly restructures itself in subtle, immediate communication with its environment.

The gurus and teachers of adaptational education will devise their own methods for such perceptual training, as well as their own contemporary technological, metaphorical and somatic vocabulary for describing the experiences obtained.

In a fairly exact sense, this kind of training can be designated as "consciousness expanding," in that it is an expansion of perception beyond the limitations of traditional conscious perception. Somatic science and philosophy have made it obvious that human "consciousness" is a highly limited and inefficient form of perception; it is aggressively practical, rationally constricted and has a memory bank of auditory and visual atoms which are broken off pieces of reality. The goal of adaptational education is to train the human in the arts of trans-conscious perception, discovering the patterns of this kind of perception, the techniques of its deployment, the noting of the persistent forms of the environment and the consequent construction of a memory-bank of non-verbal, non-imagistic somatic and environmental memory patterns. In its simplest sense this is "somatic education."

But because such education is taking place within the context of this living world and this immediate task of adaptation, training of perception cannot be separated from expressive behavioral training. To behave is to move the soma. To behave adaptively is to move the soma in concert with all aspects of one's shifting environment, responding through assimilative as well as accommodative adaptations, as well as with combinations of both.

This is to say that, unlike traditional education, the educational experience of mutational education must involve real fear, real anger, real sensual acuteness and real sexuality. Otherwise it cannot be educational; it would not be training for environmental adaptability. Full behavioral expression as well as full perceptual experience are, in this instance, a common educational goal. And in recognizing this, we simultaneously recognize that future education is a positive, universalized fulfillment of what in the past has been vaguely designated as "therapy."

What will be the effects of educating human beings as optimally adaptive somas? An obvious effect will be that we will have produced incorrigibly healthy human beings. Another effect will be that such men and women will be totally autonomous units of moral responsibility: i.e., they immediately and intimately know their own somatic nature (this was traditionally referred to as knowing or discovering one's self: as knowing "who" one is) and have learned to give it free vent in adapting to any and every environmental event. Because they have learned to accept their whole soma as their all-sufficient adaptive source, they have no other thought nor option than to do "what is right." To behave "wrongly" has no meaning for them other than to be unhealthy, inefficient and inadaptable.

But the most explosive effect of somatic education for a mutational culture is that it is a releasor of human energy. Energy and power have always been the most profoundly fascinating and desired possessions of the human creature. The passion for energy, for fire and light, sent the mystics to the powerful godhead, it sent Prometheus to steal power from the gods, and it sent Icarus soaring upward toward the sun to merge with the source of that effulgence. And men have finally captured that power. Once they had ceased to seek it in the heavens, they began to find it within the earth; and during the last centuries we have focused all our effort upon discovering and opening up these energy conduits within the natural environment. And the ultimate and incredible expression of that power which we had finally traced to its lair was that within any quantity of matter there was as much energy as there was implied by squaring the speed of light and multiplying it by that given quantity of matter. The formula $E = MC^2$ was the ultimate and more-than-fulfilling discovery to be made by our traditional culture.

But this rational formula for grappling with the fantastic energy content of our environment was a discovery which was not an end in itself; rather than closing and completing a colossal pilgrimage of man toward controlling and wresting energy from the very bosom of his environment, this new discovery is, indeed, the yearning, beckoning vision that lay behind all the deeply felt myths of those men who had discovered and seized titanic power from legendary empyrean realms. Once men had fully and finally learned to open the conduits of energy in their natural environment, they had thereby freed man from the distracting tyranny of the earth and had made possible the pursuit of the only human goal that has ever finally mattered: the discovery of a way of releasing the energy which for aeons has been pent up within the soma of man.

I am being only moderately facetious when I ape Einstein's formula with a formula in a similar vein: $E = SA^2$ —the energy within a human being is equal to the square of the amount of adaptability achieved by any given soma. This formula cannot exactly fit the human situation, inasmuch as the speed of light is a known constant but the amount of human adaptability is unlimited and inconstant.

A somatically balanced and fluidly adaptive human individual is a controlled releasor of living energy whose upward limits are totally unknown. What is known is that, throughout history, man has never been able to release his energies; he has always been a restricted, crimped container of his energies, never giving full expression to his assimilative energies any more than he was able to express his accommodative drives. But even in this distracted, crimped somatic state, men have been able not merely to dominate their earthly environment but they have succeeded in the incomparable achievement of discovering and using the final energy secret of the entire physical cosmos. If a crippled human soma could achieve this, how much more will a balanced and fully adaptive human soma achieve? The energy which one single, balanced soma can now generate within a technological environment has no upward limits. And any attempt to estimate the effects of an entire society of balanced human mutants existing within a technological environment can only conjure up the vague, almost mythically explosive vision of a civilization where anything is possible.

Fully understood and fully learned, adaptation is a game: the gay science of existence. The only way in which the pent-up energies of the human soma can be fully released is through the explosive abandon of play. And this release is now possible: against the supporting background of our technological society, men can now play with their environment. It is too late, now, for work and for seriousness; we have destroyed it along with our ancient culture. It is no longer possible for us to be crimped, pent-up, suffering and serious: we are condemned—through our children—to be healthy, explosive and gay. The result of centuries of work has been the discovery that work is inefficient; it is a dismal waste of energies which remain unused as they either are blocked or are channeled through the narrow apertures of rational, serious effort.

If we are to further transform ourselves and further transform our human environment, we must play, we must be powerful, we must be balanced and adaptive to the least winds of challenge and change. And, already, we are becoming refreshed with keen noses and sharp eyes and agile movements for the adaptational dance that we call life. Eventually we shall be happily startled to realize that the evolution-revolution is not a transient event which will someday be over as we settle into a new cultural routine; rather, evolution-revolution describes our future state of constant, fluid, never-ending adaptation which is the playful manner in which a technologized race finally learns to live.

How amazing it is that, after so many aeons of groping and blundering, we have placed ourselves in the situation where we cannot help but become healthy, happy and powerful: it is our fate. And once that fate is fulfilled and a new human culture has become established, on that day there will be but one sadness: in achieving what we will have achieved, we will have lost all of our gods; which is a pity, because men are thus robbed of the ultimate human triumph of seeing their old gods look down upon them with envy.

So, then, nothing finally is perfect. That, after all, is why it's so much fun.